The Legitimacy of
Philanthropic Foundations

The Legitimacy of Philanthropic Foundations: United States and European Perspectives

Kenneth Prewitt, Mattei Dogan, Steven Heydemann, and Stefan Toepler, Editors

A Joint Project of The Mattei Dogan Foundation, Russell Sage Foundation, and Social Science Research Council

Russell Sage Foundation
New York

The Russell Sage Foundation

The Russell Sage Foundation, one of the oldest of America's general purpose foundations, was established in 1907 by Mrs. Margaret Olivia Sage for "the improvement of
social and living conditions in the United States." The Foundation seeks to fulfill this
mandate by fostering the development and dissemination of knowledge about the
country's political, social, and economic problems. While the Foundation endeavors
to assure the accuracy and objectivity of each book it publishes, the conclusions and
interpretations in Russell Sage Foundation publications are those of the authors and
not of the Foundation, its Trustees, or its staff. Publication by Russell Sage, therefore,
does not imply Foundation endorsement.

Library of Congress Cataloging-in-Publication Data

The legitimacy of philanthropic foundations : United States and European
perspectives / Kenneth Prewitt . . . [et al.], editors.
   p. cm.
"A joint project of the Mattei Dogan Foundation, Russell Sage Foundation, New
York, and Social Science Research Council."
Revisions of papers presented at a conference held in Paris, May 26–29, 2004.
ISBN 10: 0-87154-696-5
ISBN 13: 9780871546968
1. Endowments—United States—Congresses. 2. Endowments—Europe—
Congresses. 3. Charitable uses, trusts, and foundations—United States—Congresses.
4. Charitable uses, trusts, and foundations—Europe—Congresses. I. Prewitt, Kenneth.
II. Mattei Dogan Foundation. III. Russell Sage Foundation. IV. Social Science Research
Council (U.S.)

HV91.L363 2006
361.7'63094—dc22

         2006040875

Text design by Suzanne Nichols.

RUSSELL SAGE FOUNDATION
112 East 64th Street, New York, New York 10021
10 9 8 7 6 5 4 3 2 1

CONTENTS

Contributors   vii

Foreword   ix

Editors' Note   xi

Acknowledgments   xiii

PART I   INTRODUCTION

CHAPTER 1 Foundations and the Challenge
           of Legitimacy in Comparative Perspective   3
           Steven Heydemann and Stefan Toepler

CHAPTER 2 American Foundations: What Justifies
           Their Unique Privileges and Powers   27
           Kenneth Prewitt

PART II   AMERICAN PERSPECTIVES

CHAPTER 3 American Debates on the Legitimacy
           of Foundations   49
           David C. Hammack

CHAPTER 4 Accountability and Legitimacy
           in American Foundation Philanthropy   99
           Peter Frumkin

CHAPTER 5 Redistributional Effects of America's
           Private Foundations   123
           Julian Wolpert

CHAPTER 6 Foundation Legitimacy at the Community
           Level in the United States   150
           Kirsten A. Grønbjerg

PART III   EUROPEAN PERSPECTIVES

CHAPTER 7 Historical Changes in Foundation
           Functions and Legitimacy in Europe   177
           Giuliana Gemelli

CHAPTER 8   Roles of Foundations in Europe:
             A Comparison   192
             Helmut K. Anheier and Siobhan Daly

CHAPTER 9   Supporting Culture and Higher Education:
             A German Perspective   217
             Rupert Graf Strachwitz

CHAPTER 10   Industrial Foundations: Foundation
             Ownership of Business Companies   236
             Steen Thomsen

CHAPTER 11   Foundation Legitimacy at the Community
             Level in the United Kingdom   252
             Diana Leat

PART IV   CONCLUSION

             In Search of Legitimacy: Similarities
             and Differences Between the Continents   273
             Mattei Dogan

             Index   283

Contributors

Kenneth Prewitt is Carnegie Professor of Public Affairs in the School of International and Public Affairs at Columbia University.

Mattei Dogan is senior fellow at the National Center for Scientific Research in Paris, professor emeritus of political science at the University of California, Los Angeles, and chair of the Research Committee on Comparative Sociology of the International Sociological Association.

Steven Heydemann is director of the Center for Democracy and the Third Sector at Georgetown University.

Stefan Toepler is associate professor of nonprofit studies in the Department of Public and International Affairs at George Mason University.

Helmut K. Anheier is director of the Center for Civil Society and professor of social welfare in the School of Public Affairs at the University of California, Los Angeles.

Siobhan Daly is on the faculty in the Politics Division of the School of Arts and Social Sciences at Northumbria University, and research associate of the Centre for Civil Society at the London School of Economics.

Peter Frumkin is professor of public affairs and director of the RGK Center for Philanthropy and Community Service at the Lyndon B. Johnson School of Public Affairs at the University of Texas at Austin.

Giuliana Gemelli is director of the International Masters Program in Philanthropy and Social Entrepreneurship and professor of contemporary history at the University of Bologna.

Kirsten A. Grønbjerg is Efroymson Chair in Philanthropy at the Indiana University Center on Philanthropy and professor in the School of Public and Environmental Affairs at Indiana University.

David C. Hammack is Hiramm C. Hadyn Professor of History and member of the faculty council of the Mandel Center for Nonprofit Organizations at Case Western Reserve University.

Diana Leat is visiting professor at Cass Business School, London, and visiting research associate at the University of California, Los Angeles.

Rupert Graf Strachwitz is director of the Maecenata Institute for Philanthropy and Civil Society at Humboldt University in Berlin, Germany.

Steen Thomsen is director of the Center for Corporate Governance and professor in the Department of International Economics and Management at the Copenhagen Business School.

Julian Wolpert is Harry G. Bryant Professor of Geography, Public Affairs, and Urban Planning, Emeritus, at Princeton University.

FOREWORD

Privately established foundations were pioneered in medieval and early modern Europe. More recently, they have been distinctively prominent in the United States. Although there has been some learning from different experiences, there has been much less comparative research. This book seeks to encourage more mutual engagement between European and American researchers, and to make knowledge of the field of foundation philanthropy available to policy makers and a broader public.

The papers published here originated as presentations to a conference held in Paris in May 2004, but have since been revised. The conference was organized by the Fondation Mattei Dogan and the Social Science Research Council, New York, with the active support of the Russell Sage Foundation, New York. The meeting was hosted by the Ministry of Scientific Research and UNESCO. Twenty-two scholars, half of them European and half American, presented papers to an audience of more than two hundred.

The size of audience itself suggests the impressive level of interest that the topic aroused. As more new foundations are created, the models offered by established foundations in different countries increase in value. It is our hope that this book will stimulate further interest, new research, and the development of policies to facilitate the creation of philanthropic foundations and enhance the contributions they can make.

Of course, foundations are embedded in different local contexts and made possible by different legal structures. The term "foundation" refers to a range of different organizations and legal structures in different countries. Indeed, the extent to which foundations may be established by private contract or require an act of state is an important variable. These structures and national patterns are subject to change, however, as both individual and corporate philanthropists create new institutions.

The title of this book suggests a comparison between the two sides of the Atlantic. Comparing countries consists in weighing similarities against differences. From the outset, we knew, for several reasons, that comparing the role of foundations on the two continents would not be an easy task for the simple reason that in the domain of modern foundations, the "new" continent has a much richer experience than the "old" one. The historical, national, and social contexts are so different that, for specialists at least, differences often outweigh similarities. Another difficulty encountered was the extreme diversity of the European countries, each with its own heritages and legislations. Accordingly, most of the chapters in this book are also published in French in a volume entitled *Légitimité et fonctions des fondations en Europe et aux Etats-Unis,* which includes other papers not presented in this English edition.

Craig Calhoun
President of the Social Science Research Council
Mattei Dogan
Founder of the Fondation Mattei Dogan

Editors' Note

Authors represented in this volume were not presented with a pre-digested thesis or any definition of legitimacy as this concept is applied in studies of philanthropic foundations. Recognizing that scholarship is at a very early stage in theorizing about the legitimacy of foundations in advanced democracies, the editors turned to comparison of Europe and the United States to invite a diversity of formulations and emphases—and, even in their respective contributions, reach somewhat differing conclusions regarding the nature of the legitimacy challenge and the extent to which legitimacy rests on specific philanthropic achievements. We publish this volume confident that readers will extend the arguments and findings that they find persuasive, and equally vigorously critique those they find wanting.

Acknowledgments

This volume brings together selected papers given at an invitational conference on The Legitimacy of Philanthropic Foundations: U.S. and European Perspectives, which took place in Paris, May 26 through 29, 2004. Held at the French Ministry of Scientific Research, UNESCO and the École des Hautes Études en Sciences Sociales, the conference was graciously supported by the Russell Sage and Mattei Dogan foundations and co-organized by the Social Science Research Council. Mattei Dogan, directeur scientifique of the Fondation Mattei Dogan, Eric Wanner, president of the Russell Sage Foundation, and Craig Calhoun, president of the Social Science Research Council, were instrumental in making the conference a success, and we all owe deep gratitude to Kevin Moore, then program director at the Social Science Research Council, for carrying most of the organizational burdens on the American side, and Mattei Dogan for arranging the conference in Paris.

Part I

Introduction

Chapter 1

Foundations and the Challenge of Legitimacy in Comparative Perspective

Steven Heydemann and Stefan Toepler

"Foundations are dandy things, but the truth is few institutions are as complacent, and potentially unaccountable to the real world as private foundations. When I was a public official, my dealings with philanthropy often left me with the question—who do they think they are?"

—Douglas W. Nelson, President, the Annie E. Casey Foundation

"In the great jungle of American democracy and capitalism there is no more strange or improbable creature than the private foundation. Private foundations are virtually a denial of basic premise: aristocratic institutions living on the privileges and indulgence of an egalitarian society; aggregations of private wealth, which, contrary to the proclaimed instincts of Economic Man, have been conveyed to public purposes. Like the giraffe, they could not possibly exist, but they do."

—Waldemar A. Nielsen, *The Big Foundations* (1972, 3)

Who do foundations think they are? Why do they even exist? Why do democratic societies accept, even foster, the presence of "aristocratic institutions" that control large amounts of capital, in perpetuity, with few constraints on how their assets may be used? On what grounds are institutions that control vast wealth able to secure the consent of society and government? To whom are private foundations accountable? What, in other words, gives private foundations their legitimacy?

For foundations, the challenge of legitimacy is pervasive and enduring. It exists in every setting in which private assets receive privileged treatment by governments in exchange for an obligation—often very loosely defined—to use those assets for the public good. Today, the challenge of legitimacy occupies a central place in American debates about foundations and tends to manifest itself in political calls for increased regulation—most recently in the form of proposals for tightening payout rates, that is, the share of endowment values that foundations have to distribute annually, or further restrictions on executive compensation practices and self-dealing. Conversely, it is also at the heart of contrary European debates about whether and how to liberalize rules that govern the formation of private foundations (de Borms 2005).

In both cases, competing ideas about the sources of foundation legitimacy are at the core of these debates. For those who support higher payout rates and greater foundation accountability in the United States, for example, legitimacy depends on the willingness of foundations to maximize the current use of their resources for public purposes. For critics of higher payout rates, legitimacy hinges on the ability of foundations to preserve endowments to ensure their ability to address future needs.[1] Underlying both positions, however, is the question of how to balance autonomy versus regulation in the management of foundation assets—and perspectives are clearly shaped by differing views on the legitimacy question. Does legitimacy derive from the freedom of foundations to define their own priorities and procedures within the limits of donor intent, or from their responsiveness to the public service obligations they accept in exchange for their nonprofit, tax-exempt status? Both matter, and how the two are reconciled will have a powerful impact on the future of private philanthropy in the United States.

If legitimacy concerns are pervasive, however, the question of foundation legitimacy per se—the issue raised by both Douglas Nelson and Waldemar Nielsen—is often obscured in current debates, especially those taking place in the United States. The reasons for this are worth noting. If foundations in the United States confront real and serious legitimacy challenges, they do not face a legitimacy crisis. Debates about foundation management and grant making have become increasingly politicized, yet the idea that Congress might act to discourage or prevent the establishment of philanthropic foundations is implausible. Demands for foundation accountability from Congress and from watchdog organizations have intensified, but do not reflect public or official doubt about the need for and potential value of private philanthropy. Similarly, public concerns about corruption and mismanagement in the foundation sector have deepened in the face of highly visible scandals. Yet Americans' confidence in and their positive view of foundations, philanthropy, and charitable giving remain high, overall. The underlying legitimacy of the foundation form in the United States is not in question.

As a result, public debate in the U.S. case often focuses less on the normative questions of why foundations exist and whether they are a legitimate means for the accumulation and distribution of private wealth—matters that remain on the table in some European cases—than on questions of foundation governance, regulation, oversight, and, above all, accountability. Indeed, accountability has in many respects become the dominant language through which concerns about the legitimacy of foundation practices is expressed. It too, like notions of governance and oversight, has the effect of framing foundation debates in procedural and technocratic terms that often seem remote from the normative language of legitimacy.

However, it would be a mistake not to recognize the legitimacy challenges that such concerns evoke, or to overlook the tight links that connect the procedural and the normative in discussions of foundations and philanthropy in the United States. If the foundation form itself is not in question—benefiting as it does from deep public and official support for charitable giving, volunteering, and self-help—this core legitimacy does not mitigate normative concerns about what foundations do and how they do it—whether they in fact help the poor, promote innovation, cure disease, or otherwise provide the public benefit on which their privileged status rests. American foundations are not insulated by their core legitimacy from the need to reinforce and justify their privileged standing, and to ensure that both their procedures and their broader purposes are in keeping with public and official perceptions about the appropriate roles and limits of private philanthropy. And because these perceptions are never stable, foundations themselves can never take their "everyday legitimacy" for granted.

Thus, even when challenges to foundations are framed in procedural and technocratic terms, normative questions are never far from the surface. And once they break into plain view, such questions can rapidly redefine debates that had been framed in procedural terms. As one elected official asked recently in congressional hearings on the tax-exempt status of nonprofits, "are the tax breaks that propel our philanthropy justified? . . . The question . . . is, 'What is the taxpayer getting in return for the tens of billions of dollars per year in tax subsidy' offered to donors through tax write-offs or to nonprofits through their tax exemptions?" As reported in the *New York Times* in fall 2005, "The hearings have received little public notice but have terrified nonprofit leaders, more than a Senate Finance Committee threat to tighten regulation of charities. 'When you start to ask what is the fundamental underlying rationale for tax exemption and the charitable deduction for donors, it leads to questions that are far more difficult to answer than questions about greater disclosure and better governance,' said John D. Colombo, a tax-law professor at the University of Illinois who testified [at the hearings]. 'It gets you to questions like, why should an institution with billions in the bank get tax exemption?' " (Strom 2005).

The future of private philanthropy is likewise under debate in Europe. On the surface, the issues are very different. The question of whether foundations should—or could for that matter—be forced to pay out certain minimum amounts each year is among the American regulatory idiosyncrasies that remain largely foreign to European foundation debates and policies. Rather, Europe appears to be searching for ways, however tentatively, to improve foundation laws and tax incentives in hopes of marshaling more private philanthropic resources to help address a range of public needs. In this, the new-found policy interest also represents a call on foundations to be responsive to public obligations and has at least some observers worried about the future ability of foundations to serve as independent and autonomous actors in Europe's emerging civil society. As such, the basic premise of the autonomy versus obligation conflict that is evident in the United States is present in Europe as well.

Yet, with few exceptions, comparative efforts to explore foundations and their responses to the challenge of legitimacy have been few and far between. In the United States, the foundation policy debates of the past four decades have been largely insular, with few attempts to explore experiences elsewhere. Similarly, the knowledge of U.S. foundation practices and regulations mostly remain shrouded in myth in Europe. The purpose of this volume is to set the stage for a more coherent trans-Atlantic dialogue about the legitimate roles and functions as well as the capabilities and limitations of philanthropic foundations in modern society. In the following, we discuss the issue of legitimacy and how it was operationalized for the purposes of this book and provide an overview of some of the issues raised in various chapters. Before doing so, however, we begin with a few comparative notes on foundations in the United States and Europe to help ground and contextualize the later discussions.

Comparing Foundations

Among the most persistent obstacles to a comparative assessment of the respective roles and importance of foundations cross-nationally is the imbalance of empirical data. Due to a long-standing arrangement between the Internal Revenue Service and the New York–based Foundation Center, an independent information clearing house, data drawn from the annual tax returns of U.S. foundations are publicly available and lend themselves easily to evaluating the size and scope of the American foundation community. For example, U.S. grant-making foundations numbered approximately 66,000 in 2003, with a grants volume of $30 billion and assets of $477 billion (Foundation Center 2005). Similar data generally do not exist in Europe. Whether the accumulated assets and grants of European foundations compare favorably or not to their American counterparts remains a question without answer. However, given the frequent references to the United States in the European foundation literature and the growing interest in improving tax laws and liberalizing regulation to encourage future foundation growth, the underlying premise of the European debate is that the United States has a sizable philanthropic advantage over Europe that needs to be closed.

As notions about the economic and financial capacities and capabilities of foundations color at least implicitly the conceptions of what roles and functions foundations are expected to perform, it is worthwhile to revisit the issue briefly. Several American observers in the past have noted that the prominence accorded to foundations does not stand in relation to their relatively limited economic resources; there has also been some indication that the U.S. foundation community is not, in fact, much larger than in Europe, if measured in relation to broader economic parameters, such as GDP or public sector spending (Toepler 1998). This is borne out in table 1.1, which shows a range of size indicators and contrasts the United States with select European country data as presented by Anheier (2001). Anheier estimated the total number of foundations in nineteen western European countries and Turkey at 80,000 to 90,000, which means an average of seventeen to nineteen foundations per 100,000 inhabitants. Density varies significantly, with as few as one per 100,000 in France, two in Italy, three in Belgium, and as many as 111 in Switzerland and 200 in Sweden (table 1.1). The European average on this measure, however, is only somewhat below the U.S. ratio of twenty-two foundations per 100,000 inhabitants. Although there are fewer foundations in Europe in relation to total population, the question of whether there are significantly fewer remains open to debate.

Moreover, a similar picture emerges where Anheier (2001) and colleagues were able to derive estimates of other ratios from European data sources. As shown in table 1.1, U.S. foundation grants amount to the equivalent of one quarter of 1 percent of GDP—higher than the foundation expenditures to GDP ratio in Belgium and France, but lower than in Spain and Germany. The share of foundation grants of

Table 1.1   Comparative Measures, United States and Selected European Countries

	Foundations per 100,000	Expenditures as Percentage of GDP	Grants as Percentage of Nonprofit Sector Revenue	Assets per Capita
Belgium	3	0.07	—	
France	1	0.15	—	
Germany	10	1.50	1.80	€354
Italy	2	—	—	€1,340
Netherlands	5	—	2.11	
Spain	15	0.60	—	
Sweden	200	—	—	€1,500
Switzerland	111	—	—	€1,389
United Kingdom	16	—	2.81	€536
European countries average	17–19	—	—	
United States	22	0.24	1.49	$1,612

Sources: Authors' compilations. Anheier (2001); CIA (2006); Foundation Center (2005).

total nonprofit sector revenues appears to be actually lower in the United States than in the United Kingdom, Germany, or the Netherlands, whereas per capita assets of foundations are generally higher in the United States than in the five European countries where data were to be had (holding the euro-dollar conversion roughly at parity). However, only in the United Kingdom and Germany—where the real value of foundation assets is notoriously hard to gauge because many foundations either hold nonfinancial assets or stock in privately held companies—does the asset per capita ratio show a significant disparity. In relative terms, this rough cut at admittedly very unsatisfactory data suggests that the European foundation community may on balance not lag too far behind the United States. Notwithstanding those countries where foundation development has historically been stunted, such as Belgium, France, or Italy, any differences between the United States and Europe in the perceived roles and importance of foundations will more likely be grounded in factors other than economic weight and financial capacity.

Yet any attempt to draw comparative conclusions from the few hard data available on European foundations is hindered by their scarcity, and further complicated by a fundamental difference in the way Americans and Europeans tend to define foundations. In the continental European civil law tradition, there is a basic distinction between associations and foundations as the two main legal forms for nonprofit institutions. Associations are member-based, whereas foundations are asset-based organizations. Members may contribute assets to an association, but the foundation does not have members. Accordingly, the founding act and the donor's intention to transfer assets to an independent organization are integral parts of what constitutes a foundation in the European understanding. The nature of the required assets is generally not legally specified, and a foundation does not necessarily have to have a financial endowment or other revenue-generating assets. In fact, foundations can often be established with nonfinancial assets, such as art collections, or even institutions, such as a museum or a hospital. Where institutions form the core asset, European foundations may or may not hold an additional income-producing endowment to support the institution's operation.

In the United States, by contrast, the common law tradition does not proscribe a specific legal form for foundations. A donor may choose between a trust and a corporation, but at the level of establishment foundations are indistinguishable from all other types of nonprofit institutions. The Tax Reform Act (TRA) of 1969 first introduced a formal distinction, and legally the term "private foundation" is essentially a creation of the tax rather than the general law. For the purposes of tax regulation, foundations are donor-controlled (usually endowed) organizations that receive little if any external financial support on a regular basis. The defining characteristic, therefore, is the source of income rather than donor intent or the act of dedicating private assets to public purposes. However, the Internal Revenue Code grants a blanket exception from private foundation status to certain types of organizations, including hospitals and colleges and universities, independent of their revenue structure. Somewhat simplified, this regulatory slant has tilted the American foundation discourse (as well as foundation data which are based on tax designations) toward the endowed grant-making foundation.

All too easily masked by the apparent similarities, the small matter of the nature of foundation assets introduces a major conceptual challenge into the comparative discussion. If we follow the European tradition and argue that the nature of assets is irrelevant in defining what constitutes a foundation, then it follows that grant making is an incidental rather than a constitutive characteristic of the foundation as an institutional form per se. At issue, then, is the role and relative importance of operating foundations. In France, for example, it is not difficult to find hospital foundations, such as the Hôpital Rothschild, identified as significant parts of the foundation community, as Dogan points out in the foreword to this volume, and the same applies elsewhere. In the United States, hospital foundations exist as well, but they remain unaccounted for in the foundation discourse. Moreover, a good many of America's premier universities—such as Stanford, Chicago, and Johns Hopkins—are true foundations by European standards,[2] and rival the largest grant-making foundations in size, measured by financial endowments alone. The U.S. foundation literature also tends to exclude agencies funded by the government that act much like operating foundations—such as the National Science Foundation and the National Institutes of Health, as well as formal nonprofits which derive all of their funding from the government but act like grant-making foundations, such as the U.S. Institute for Peace. What the U.S. foundation sector would look like if such operating foundations were accounted for—as they currently are in Europe—

remains open to speculation, but in all likelihood, the dominance of the private grant-making foundation would not be as pronounced as it appears to be on the surface.

Following the American implicit assumption that a capital-based endowment (and hence the ability to make grants) is the defining characteristic of a foundation would, in turn, have severe consequences for our understanding of the European foundation field. Non-grant-making, operating foundations would drop from sight. Using rough data provided by Anheier (2001), this would mean that the foundation communities would shrink by at least 25 percent in Germany, by 30 percent in Finland, by 40 percent in Italy, and by 70 percent in Ireland. In Switzerland, Spain, Portugal, Greece, and France, the sector would essentially disappear. This unresolved comparative issue is reflected in the way in which the American and European contributors to the volume respectively approach the subject of foundation roles, legitimacy, and accountability, as these definitional and structural differences have some bearing on the nature of state-foundation relationships on both continents.

This relationship, in turn, reflects the balancing act between preserving foundation autonomy and ensuring the proper fulfillment of public obligations that we noted earlier, and finds its specific manifestation in the way foundations are regulated. Again generalizing somewhat, the regulatory concerns in Europe tend to center on the front end, that is the founding stage. This bias is apparent in the interest of policy makers in improving tax incentives to encourage new donors to form foundations, on the one hand, whereas on the other significant administrative burdens still complicate the process. In France, for example, establishing a foundation still requires a substantial initial endowment as well as approval at the highest levels of government. In other countries, such as Germany, the approval process remains lengthy and often involves intricate negotiations with the bureaucracy about the nature of activities to be funded and other administrative details. Once the approval is granted and the foundation established, European regulators seem less inclined to hold foundations to account for how well public obligations are performed.

The reverse is true in the U.S. case. Much to the envy of European observers, the very act of setting up a foundation requires no more than filing the requisite paperwork and paying a minimal incorporation fee. Once the foundation has legal personality and commences operations, however, tax regulation imposes a set of restrictions on foundation behavior that are largely unheard of in Europe. These restrictions originated with the Tax Reform Act of 1969. One of the key provisions of the act was an annual pay-out requirement for grant-making foundations of either all income or the equivalent of 6 percent of the asset value, whichever was greater. In the early 1980s, the pay-out requirement was changed to a flat 5 percent of asset value, but, as noted earlier, it has come up for debate again in the recent past. Other provisions prohibited self-dealing of any kind between foundation and donors, board members, and managers; prevented foundations from owning privately held businesses or controlling public corporations; and made it harder for foundations to make grants to individuals (rather than organizations).

Although the U.S. foundation community has learned to live with these provisions quite comfortably over the past three decades, they do nevertheless represent intrusions on the autonomy of foundations that are rarely found in Europe. Whatever functional equivalents there are for the payout requirement are at best lax and reflect a persistent disinterest in holding foundations to any particular efficiency or effectiveness standards (Toepler 2004). As Steen Thomsen's chapter suggests, foundation ownership of business corporations is not only uncontentious, but also regarded favorably in Europe; and even self-dealing is on occasion permissible. As but one, perhaps quaint, example, German law expressly allows foundations to set aside a portion of their annual income to pay a stipend to the donor or his or her immediate family or to maintain the donor's gravesite.

Foundations, Legitimacy, and Society

As these examples suggest, moreover, even if we acknowledge that foundations are here to stay, the nature of the legitimacy challenges they face extend well beyond immediate concerns about payouts and increased oversight in the United States or bureaucratic and regulatory reform in Europe. Different conceptions of how to balance autonomy and social accountability engage core questions about the appropriate uses of private wealth and the relationship between state, society, and capital. Like many other legitimacy questions, they thus reflect deep historical tensions around conceptions of national identity, social justice, economic inclusion, and the nature of the polity. For the authors in this volume, such links offer an important analytic opportunity. They permit us to use foundations as organizations that express deep—and often deeply contested—conceptions of how societies and polities should be organized, as lenses through which we can observe significant social processes play out, and as a useful basis for understanding patterns and variations in the trajectories of both the United States and European states.

In chapter 3, for example, David Hammack underscores these connections in the United States, recounting the social conflicts and deep political tensions that make up the contested history of foundations in the United States. In chapter 7, in her treatment on the emergence of distinctive foundation sectors in Italy and France, Giuliana Gemelli makes similar connections between historical contexts, social conditions, and the institutional structures that foundations adopt. She goes further, however, by noting that national contexts are not sharply circumscribed. Gemelli uses external interventions by U.S. foundations in the 1950s and 1960s in Germany, Italy, and France to trace the different trajectories that resulted from their efforts to build science infrastructure. Her findings point to significantly greater impact on local institutions in France than in Italy or Germany, and call into question the argument that Europe's extensive welfare states suppressed—whether intentionally or not—the development of a robust foundation presence. Instead, she argues, variation in the receptiveness of leading western European states to the work of foreign foundations requires that we treat this argument more skeptically, and subject it to case-by-case review grounded in careful assessment of the empirical evidence.

Kenneth Prewitt's chapter makes a different, and perhaps more provocative, claim about state-foundation relations in the United States. It links the legitimacy of foundations to their role as carriers of liberal values. Foundations "attach private wealth to public good without encroaching on political and economic freedoms." In his view, foundations thus represent a singularly American response to questions about the appropriate relationship between the state, the individual, and the community.

Thus legitimacy issues everywhere reflect broad social concerns about how private foundations are organized, how they operate, and how they interact with societies, governments, and markets. In this sense, we can look at the institutional forms that foundations take today, how they are governed and regulated, and the kinds of activities they support as expressions of the ways in which long-standing struggles over legitimacy have been resolved—if only for the moment. "For the moment" because no resolution of the legitimacy issue is ever permanent, universal, or fully secure. Although many of the legitimacy challenges that foundations face are entirely generic—and thus offer a basis for social scientists to generalize about the legitimacy challenge broadly defined—the particulars differ enormously across a wide range of variables. Macro-level legitimacy issues may look familiar from one setting to another (the need for foundations to appear fair and lawful in their dealings, for example), yet the precise form and content of specific legitimacy struggles are almost by definition the product of a given social, cultural, institutional, economic, and political context, even while they reflect distinctive historical experiences.

Today's legitimacy concerns are far removed from those that led to restrictions on the formation of private foundations in Europe during the era of modern state formation—notably the desire of new governments to curb the church's economic and political power. They differ profoundly, as well, from those of the late nineteenth-century United States, when a small group of former robber barons began the transformation of philanthropy from charitable giving as a way to alleviate individual suffering, to scientific philanthropy intended to address the root causes of social ills.

Indeed, variation in the nature of legitimacy challenges is almost endless. The issues faced by foundations in Europe differ from those confronting their counterparts in the United States, and within Europe we find considerable variation at the national level. If large banking foundations occupy the heights of the private foundation sector in Italy, their counterparts in Germany are the state-sponsored or initiated foundations such as the Volkswagen Foundation or the Federal Foundation for the Protection of the Environment, whereas some of the largest foundations in Scandinavia are the owners and managers of major global corporations, including Ikea and the Tuborg Brewing Company. In each case, the institutional form that private foundations take poses distinctive kinds of legitimacy challenges. In northern Europe, for instance, where foundations own a number of the region's largest corporations, these extend beyond the question of whether funds are used appropriately, or decisions are taken on an equitable basis, to include basic issues of economic performance. For these foundations, a central challenge is whether they can produce competitive rates of return. As Steen Thomsen shows, however, such foundations not only meet but also often exceed the profitability of their for-profit counterparts, projecting perhaps more of a socially responsible rather than strictly charitable image. From a comparative perspective, the northern European experience with industrial foundations is more than just a peculiar case study of a particular type of foundation. It is a salient example of how differences in political-economic environments lead to fundamentally different legitimacy outcomes. In fact, Thomsen's description of Danish and German assessments of these foundations stands in marked contrast to the United States, where foundation control of public corporations and privately held businesses was among the main reasons for the political backlash, increased tax regulation and general delegitimization of foundations that marked foundation-government relations in the late 1960s.

Similarly, in the United States, foundations created by firms that are accountable to shareholders face a different set of legitimacy challenges than do community foundations that depend on local citizens and businesses for support. For private corporations that engage in philanthropy, charitable activities must be integrated into the organizational culture and mission of a for-profit enterprise. They must be able to answer the basic question of why a firm should engage in philanthropic activity at all, and why the idea of corporate altruism isn't an oxymoron. In the case of community foundations, as Kirsten Grønbjerg's chapter points out, downward accountability, transparency, and responsiveness to constituencies are more important in securing the legitimacy of the communities in which they work—and from which they draw their revenues. As she argues, the demands of public accountability place a premium on procedural strategies for addressing legitimacy concerns among community foundations in the United States, including attention to issues such as inclusiveness, diversity, and equity in decision making. Yet these concerns are not shared to the same degree by community foundations in other settings. Diana Leat's chapter on community foundations in the United Kingdom underscores the extent to which their legitimacy context varies from that of their U.S. counterparts. Benefiting from the overall legitimacy extended to charitable organizations in the United Kingdom, community foundations have not felt pressed to justify themselves to the publics they serve. Nor have they experienced the intense, critical scrutiny of community foundations in the United States.

Alternately, for large, multipurpose foundations that operate globally, such as the Ford, Mott, MacArthur, and Rockefeller foundations, legitimacy challenges are transnational. The demands of securing the legitimacy of the Ford Foundation's work in both Israel and Palestine differ significantly from the demands it faces in Russia or in South Africa. No single resolution may be plausible or desirable, leading to highly complex strategies of legitimation within a single institution.

Thus, how foundations structure their work—whether grantmaking or operating—and how they secure their revenues matters for legitimacy. Sectoral differences—whether a foundation focuses on the arts, education, social services, human rights, the environment, and so on—will affect the kinds of legitimacy challenges they face. So do the legal and regulatory environments in which foundations operate. And, as indicated earlier, historical legacies shape legitimacy contexts in numerous ways.

Last, though in no sense least, the issue agendas that foundations adopt have a critical impact on the form and content of legitimacy challenges. Controversy about the role of private foundations for their support of voter registration drives in the 1960s or anti-apartheid movements in the 1970s has been superseded today by concerns about the possible use of foundation resources by terrorists. In the early twenty-first century, it is homeland security rather than civil rights that animates U.S. discussions about the legitimacy of foundations, their relationship to the state, and their role in a democratic society. Grant making to support research on HIV-AIDS, contraceptive practices, or abortion imposes different legitimacy demands on a foundation than does support for work on global poverty or diabetes, or sponsoring a local job training program, or building low-income housing. And, as is often the case, these variables can take on different values for different audiences at the same time, helping to ensure that legitimacy remains a hotly debated issue in its own right. For the Scaife Foundation in the United States, association with conservative political causes is a source of legitimacy for some, but a challenge to its legitimacy for others. Foundations identified as liberal face the identical dilemma, but in reverse.

Solutions to the challenge of legitimacy, however transient they might be, also exhibit a high degree of variation, and contribute to a highly differentiated and dynamic foundation landscape. In the United States, the rapid expansion of venture philanthropy, social enterprise philanthropy, and other new forms for the organization of private foundations reflects the increasing legitimacy of market-based and bottom-up strategies for addressing social problems. In Europe, the declining capacity of states to address demands for social services has reframed debates over the legitimate use of private resources for public ends. In this context, it is not surprising that efforts to liberalize rules governing the formation of private foundations are advancing in a number of states.

In both Europe and the United States, the rise of accountability as a major concern is changing foundation governance and reshaping patterns of grant making. Accountability, closely linked with the rise of market-based norms of nonprofit management, is often defined in terms of the measurable impact of foundation dollars. As the need to demonstrate short-term impact increases, funders may be less willing to support activities with longer time horizons, those where results are less easily measured, or where the risk of failure is high. This trend has significant implications for who will receive foundation grants and what kind of activities are most likely to secure support. It is also a source of potential conflicts within foundations as they struggle to reconcile the demands of competing institutional logics and modes of legitimacy. The pursuit of legitimacy via efficiency-based measures of accountability may not fit easily with mission-based sources of legitimacy, or with the view that foundations exist, in part, to provide an innovation function for societies—helping to launch new ideas, organizations, and services before they find support from either states or markets.

Advocates of increased accountability, on the other hand, find such concerns unpersuasive. As Frumkin notes, demands for accountability are justified not only by the privileged position foundations enjoy as a result of their tax-exempt status, but for two other reasons as well. First, he argues, the private assets held by foundations are used to bring about changes that affect the broader public. Second, the vast resources controlled by foundations place them in positions of power relative to their grantees: as in any such relationship, possibilities for exploitation and abuse are always present. Accountability is a means for addressing both these concerns, extending certain protections both to the communities affected by foundation programs and those who depend on foundation support. Yet, as Frumkin acknowledges, reconciling accountability demands with the autonomy of foundations will not be easy, even if the payoffs from accepting accountability procedures may well be to enhance their legitimacy.

For all these reasons, variation in the form and content of legitimacy struggles is a telling indicator. It sheds light on how states, societies, and the international system more broadly have changed over time. It also illuminates the tensions and conflicts that private foundations confront—internally as much as externally—as they navigate their interactions with society, state, and market. Moreover, foundations are not simply passive objects of the concerns directed at them by others. They are active participants in defining the conditions that generate, or undermine, their legitimacy. Through their programming, but also through public outreach, lobbying, support for grant makers' associations and interest groups, and other forms of intervention in the political arena, private foundations work assiduously to build public support for their work, shape the regulations that govern them, protect their autonomy, and otherwise contribute to an environment in which the legitimacy of foundations can be secured.

Location, sector, funding, institutional form and identity, the scope and priorities of programming—all of these contribute to the particular context in which legitimacy challenges play out, as does the broader social and political environment in which foundations work. Understanding the nature of this challenge in general thus requires keen attention to the many dimensions along which it varies. It also requires attention to the underlying conceptions of legitimacy around which such challenges play out.

Defining Legitimacy

Taken together, these issues suggest a level of complexity in approaching the subject of foundations in a comparative fashion that prohibits from the outset any attempt to impose a specific view of legitimacy or the nature of foundation accountability on the chapters in this volume—a caution reflected in the editors' comment. Nonetheless, the chapters that follow reflect shared features that permit us to establish the scope and importance of the legitimacy question as it relates to private foundations. In this limited sense, it is useful to distinguish between two broad levels or aspects of legitimacy and how they inform the chapters in this volume. At one level, legitimacy relates to the right to exercise power and the acceptance of that right by others. This combination of *procedural legitimacy,* in the sense of conforming to the requirements of law, and *normative legitimacy,* in the sense that the behavior of an institution is perceived as fair and just, are both part of the challenge that foundations face in securing the consent of society and the legal right from government to exist and operate that together constitute the base of their legitimacy. In adopting this perspective, we integrate conceptions of legitimacy that have often been treated as distinct—lexical and law-based definitions, on the one hand, and socially determined definitions, on the other. As Schaar has noted, the former are based on "the element of law or right," where "the force of a claim (whether it be a claim to political power or to the validity of a conclusion in an argument)" rests on "foundations external to and independent of the mere assertion or opinion of the claimant," whereas the latter "dissolve legitimacy into belief or opinion. If a people holds the belief that existing institutions are 'appropriate,' or 'morally proper,' then these institutions are legitimate" (Schaar 1984, 108).

Schaar and others have worked to differentiate these conceptions of legitimacy further. For our purposes, however, it is preferable to blur rather than to uphold this distinction. In part, this reflects our view of foundations as organizations that embody all three of Weber's sources of legitimate authority: tradition, charismatic leadership, and bureaucratic rationality, and thus—like many other social institutions—cannot be neatly categorized as reflecting one source of legitimacy in particular. The privilege accorded to foundation assets derives in part from law, yet legal frameworks themselves flow from deeply held and near-universal traditions that view charitable giving as an expression of individual and collective virtue. Further, foundations often rely on their standing as the organizational means through which the authority of a charismatic leader, the founding donor, acquires a bureaucratic-rational form of legitimacy—with important implications for the weight attached—socially if not legally—to a donor's original intent and a foundation's compliance with that intent as means for evaluating its legitimacy over time.

In addition, however, our hybrid conception of legitimacy reflects our sense of how best to capture the multidimensional quality of the challenges that foundations confront. It underscores the extent to which social and legal aspects of legitimacy have become interdependent in contemporary debates. In discussions of foundation accountability, for example, critics of foundations appeal to legal and social, as well as normative and procedural, conceptions of legitimacy in arguing for changes in the regulatory control of philanthropic assets. Those who argue that payout rates should be increased believe that the privileged treatment of private wealth requires a higher degree of responsiveness to social needs than is now demanded of foundations under the law. In their view, legal legitimacy and social legitimacy have diverged, and legal reform is needed to establish a socially more acceptable accommodation between them. Neither a legalistic nor a socialized conception of legitimacy could, on its own, capture the dynamic interplay between the two that is present in considerations of foundations and the challenge of legitimacy.

We see this blending of legitimacy concerns in other current debates, as well, notably as they touch on foundation governance and the perceived mandate of foundations to serve as representatives, whether of a broader public or an individual donor. Like many other institutions, foundations draw their legitimacy in part from their standing as agents, to which particular forms of autonomy and authority are delegated, whether by their founders or, via the state and law, by the public more broadly. Theoretically, individuals can delegate authority to the state (recalling contractual notions of legitimacy), thus legitimizing the exercise of power by government, including the authority to create rules that permit the accumulation, preservation, and distribution of private wealth by withdrawing it from the tax stream. Conversely, it can be argued that individuals have a derivative right to delegate authority to private institutions, even if these institutions pursue public purposes.

Although this proposition is contestable, a moral right to establish foundations thus rests on the notion of individual sovereignty. This view of legitimacy largely emphasizes the private aspects of foundations, and focuses mainly on donor intent, motivations, and control—issues that surface routinely in debates about whether, for instance, foundations should have the right to exist in perpetuity, or should have lifespans circumscribed by law as a guarantee against their deviation from the intent of their creators. In several notable instances, such as the Ford Foundation and the MacArthur Foundation, the decision by a founder's successors to use foundation assets for purposes either implicitly or explicitly at odds with the founder's intent is thought to undermine their legitimacy. Donor intent, as expressed in the vision of a sovereign individual, is accorded privileged standing in assessing the legitimacy of a foundation's grant making over its entire lifespan.

Thus, even when the answer to the question of the right to exercise power is affirmative (as it was not in the French Jacobinian tradition, for example), a second question arises as to whether power is exercised appropriately and responsibly, based on either pragmatic or normative assessments. Emphasizing the public aspects of foundations, the legitimacy issue then becomes a question of whether the (societal) performance of foundations justifies their preferential (tax) treatment and continued existence. In other words, the performance and effectiveness of foundations in pursuing their social roles and functions is a powerful determinant of foundation legitimacy. In the same sense, public debate and contention about what constitutes appropriate social roles, along with shifts in public culture and social norms, will help to define the kinds of challenges to which foundations must respond. One of the most visible of these shifts is the growing integration of market-based and philanthropic norms that is reshaping how philanthropy is organized and evaluated across the private, public, and nonprofit sectors. This change has altered perceptions about the centrality of the state-foundation relationship in determining foundation legitimacy, and elevated the importance of the market as a domain that is now crucial for the way citizens perceive of private foundations.

Social Roles and the Legitimacy of Foundations

The social nature of foundation legitimacy leads us back to our original question. Why do foundations exist? Their presence, after all, is intentional: they result from political decisions to extend special status, notably the exemption of income from taxes, to a particular class of institutions. First and foremost, therefore, foundations are a product of the belief that states may appropriately use the tax code to induce private actors to allocate their own resources in the public interest. But why? What social functions do foundations perform that justify this privileged treatment?

In part, foundations as institutions are the beneficiaries of deep normative commitments to charity, philanthropy, and volunteering that are so widespread as to be virtually universal. As Hammack stresses in chapter 3, foundations derive considerable legitimacy from their identity as nonprofit organizations. "Fundamentally," he indicates, "foundations derive their legitimacy from the nonprofit sector as a whole." It might also be said that in Europe, challenges to foundation legitimacy derive from enduring public and official skepticism about the legitimacy of a sector that is autonomous from the state. In this sense, the legal privileging of foundations in the United States, and increasingly in Europe, reflects the use of state power (and state legitimacy) to establish philanthropic values as central to a sense of identity that certainly goes beyond the national, but has nonetheless been appropriated as a core element of national citizenship. At a 1999 White House conference on philanthropy, for instance, William White, president of the Mott Foundation, called philanthropy "just as much a core value of our nation as freedom of speech or freedom of worship."

Thus, private foundations undoubtedly draw some measure of their legitimacy by virtue of their standing as formal, organized expressions of deeply held norms. Yet charitable giving and philanthropy do not require the presence of an organized foundation sector: governments can easily encourage volunteerism and giving by individuals without extending financial privileges to private institutions. To account for the presence of foundations, we must explain why the accumulation and persistence of endowments devoted to support for public purposes deserve legal protections above and beyond those that provide incentives for individual giving.

As the chapters in this volume suggest, one set of answers to the question of why foundations exist focuses on the social functions they are believed to perform. This argument is hardly new: indeed, it is the starting point for much of the small but growing literature on private foundations. And whether foundations are seen as complementing, supplementing, or ameliorating the role of states and markets, the range of functions assigned to them is exceptionally broad. Complementing Prewitt's U.S.-focused analysis of foundation functions in chapter 2, Anheier and Daly extend the discussion to Europe in chapter 8. Their comparative analysis underscores the exceptional breadth of possible functions as well as significant national differences in the way these functions are perceived, valued, and fit into conceptions, or visions, of what constitutes the good society and hence what are seen as appropriate and legitimate actions by foundations.

Frequently noted foundation roles include, prominently, a redistributive function, as Julian Wolpert discusses in chapter 5. Why is it reasonable to exclude the income and capital gains of foundation endowments from taxation? As Wolpert recounts, the privileges of nonprofit status are often justified on the grounds that foundation expenditures supplement the role of the state in the redistribution of resources from those who have to those who need. In this view, the short-term benefits of taxing large estates is outweighed, in theory, by the long-term social gains of foundation payouts for purposes that advance the public welfare. By exempting assets and the revenues they generate from taxation, individuals have an incentive to allocate resources in socially productive ways. However, Wolpert's data challenge the redistributive claims made about private foundations. In one of the few systematic assessments we have of the redistributive effects of foundation giving, he presents convincing evidence that their impact is more limited than advocates of this view might expect. With his work, we now have a new baseline for reassessing one of the most widely held views about the purposes and roles of private foundations.

Beyond their redistributive functions, the presence of private foundations is also justified on the grounds that they perform an innovation function, notably in the arts, sciences, research, and social policy. Absent the pressures and constraints faced by either for-profit organizations or public sector institutions, private foundations are seen as providing societies with a capacity for taking risk that goes beyond the limits of either states or markets.

While these two functions, redistribution and innovation, are compatible, other arguments about the sources of foundation legitimacy are more difficult to reconcile with this functional approach. If Prewitt's argument holds, for example—that the private foundation in the United States is an expression of the underlying liberalism of the American polity, its deeply rooted concern with the limits of state power, the virtue of markets, and the autonomy of the individual— then it matters little what foundations actually do. The more important point is what they represent. Their presence provides symbolic affirmation of America's commitment to economic liberalism. States provide incentives for individuals to use their wealth for public purposes, but intentionally leaves such purposes undefined. This ensures a limited role for the state in the oversight not only of foundation assets, but of their substantive activities as well. It explicitly avoids imposing on foundations a particular functional role.

Alternately, the presence of private foundations is sometimes justified not by their standing as an answer to the question of how a liberal society governs private wealth, but by their capacity to engage in what can be called positive discrimination. Unlike public institutions, which must treat citizens equally, private foundations can discriminate in the use of their resources, targeting funds toward particularistic purposes that benefit a social group or cause but "exclude" others (Smith 1999). Whether by allocating funds to support a particular region, religious affiliation, or social cause, foundations make it possible to accommodate plural identities within a given society. In one sense, this view is consistent with Prewitt's liberal polity argument: differing principles of inclusion and different criteria for access to funding permit private foundations to discriminate in their allocation of resources, and avoid conflicts that might otherwise result if public policies endorsed or permitted inequalities in the management of public funds. Diverse communities can ensure the presence of institutions and services that met their needs, without involving the state in divisive debates about whether and how public resources should serve particularistic ends.

Yet critics of private foundations might question whether these forms of discrimination have been positive in their effects, or served to reinforce distributive and other inequalities among social groups. In this view, what some describe as positive discrimination is seen by others in a different light: the capacity of private foundations to support negative forms of social exclusion. In Europe, where increasingly diverse societies exhibit growing tensions around issues of citizenship and religious identity, the capacity of private foundations for positive discrimination plays into debates about the nature of citizenship and how to accommodate egalitarian norms with increasing levels of social diversity.

In part, this proliferation of roles reflects the reality of a foundation sector populated, in both the United States and Europe, by highly diverse institutions engaged in a wide range of tasks. It also underscores the adaptive quality of private foundations as institutions, and their tractability as mechanisms for the pursuit of a wide range of ends. Yet the scope of arguments about the roles of foundations has an unresolved quality that is worth noting. It opens the door to an important debate, both theoretical and policy-related, about the social roles of private foundations and how these express a given set of legitimacy challenges. The key question is what we can learn from the proliferation of role-based arguments about the legitimacy of foundations, whether our focus is the underlying theories we use to explain foundations, or foundations themselves.

Structure of the Volume

Part I consists of this introductory chapter and Kenneth Prewitt's contribution—which in many ways throws down the gauntlet from a distinctively American perspective. Part II takes up the challenge by highlighting salient functionalist arguments and analyzing deep-running legitimacy concerns as they have played out in the United States, both historically and in contemporary debates. Part III provides a counterpoint by opening the debate to European perspectives. Although there are similarities in the way arguments for or against foundations are shaped, the chapters in this section make a striking case for how different the premises of the European foundation debate are, and hence how the legitimation needs of European foundations vary from their U.S. counterparts. If nothing else, this section clearly outlines how the often insular and self-referential American debate could profit from more serious engagement with European perspectives in efforts to rethink our fundamental understanding of the roles and legitimacy of foundations. Although this volume and its chapters are not intended as a decisive answer to the legitimacy of foundations question, they offer the basis for broader, more truly comparative approach to the issue, and provide many new starting points for how we think about it in the years ahead.

Notes

1. See Billiterri (2005) for an overview of the American payout debate.
2. Yale and Harvard were originally public institutions founded by the seventeenth-century colonial administration.

References

Anheier, Helmut. 2001. "Foundations in Europe: A Comparative Perspective." In *Foundations in Europe: Society, Management and Law*, edited by

Andreas Schlüter, Volker Then, and Peter Walkenhorst. London: Directory of Social Change.

Billiterri, Thomas. 2005. *Money, Mission, and the Payout Rule: In Search of a Strategic Approach to Foundation Spending.* Washington, D.C.: Aspen Institute.

Central Intelligence Agency. 2006. *The World Factbook.* Washington: Central Intelligence Agency.

de Borms, Luc Tayart. 2005. *Foundations: Creating Impact in a Globalised World.* West Sussex, UK: John Wiley & Sons.

Foundation Center. 2005. *Foundation Yearbook 2005.* New York: Foundation Center.

Nielsen, Waldemar A. 1972. *The Big Foundations.* New York: Columbia University Press.

Schaar, John H. 1984. "Legitimacy in the Modern State." In *Legitimacy and the State,* edited by William Connoly. New York: New York University Press.

Smith, James A. 1999. "The Evolving Role of American Foundations." In *Philanthropy and the Nonprofit Sector,* edited by Charles Clotfelter and Thomas Erlich. Bloomington: Indiana University Press.

Strom, Stephanie. 2005. "Aftermaths," *New York Times,* November 14, 2005.

Toepler, Stefan. 1998. "Foundations and their Institutional Context: Cross-Evaluating Evidence from Germany and the United States." *Voluntas* 9(2): 153–70.

———. 2004. "Ending Pay-out As We Know It: A Conceptual and Comparative Perspective on the Pay-Out Requirement for Foundations." *Nonprofit and Voluntary Sector Quarterly* 33(4): 729–38.

Chapter 2

American Foundations: What Justifies Their Unique Privileges and Powers

Kenneth Prewitt

Should nations that do not have a modern philanthropic foundation sector bother to establish one? If so, on what grounds? What is it they do or represent that cannot be provided by the government, the market, or the nonprofit sector more generally? To address the principles of legitimacy and accountability that underlie these questions I draw on the U.S. case. This is not to suggest that American practices should be adopted elsewhere, but simply to pose a theoretical question: what is the source of foundation legitimacy, of the widespread acceptance and public endorsement of the privileged status of foundations as appropriate institutions for fulfilling basic societal functions?

A Question Posed

Much confusion in the discussion of legitimacy derives from the failure to distinguish the comparatively small foundation sector from the larger charitable and philanthropic giving and that, in turn, from the much more substantial nonprofit sector. Although these three levels interact and are lumped together under that loose term civil society, their dissimilarities matter in any discussion of legitimacy.

The nonprofit sector meets an obvious performance test. Colleges, hospitals, relief agencies, art institutions, advocacy organizations, and think tanks provide what others are willing to pay for—80 percent of the nonprofit sector's revenues derive from membership dues, tuition payments, fees for services, and government contracts. Nonprofits survive only if what they provide is wanted.

The remaining one-fifth of the sector's revenues are charitable in origin—tax-deductible gifts by individuals, in small as well as large amounts, to hospitals, universities, museums, and relief agencies. These tax-deductible gifts meet a simple legal test. Is the donation directed to what, in the tax code, is defined as a charitable purpose? Although foundations also meet this test, and provide about 2 percent of the funds that sustain the nonprofit sector, the private foundation differs from charitable giving along a key dimension.

The prototypical foundation is uniquely privileged. Once established, it never again needs to raise funds. Its in-perpetuity endowment allows it to design grant-making programs that reach to hundreds, even thousands, of other nonprofit institutions. It has an extraordinary license to spend tax-protected wealth on projects and purposes of its choosing, with only minimal accountability. Trustees and officers change guidelines, start new program lines, and otherwise reallocate grant dollars on their own authority—as long as grant making serves the public interest. And there is wide latitude in how the public interest is defined—from housing the homeless to space exploration, from policy briefs to art collections.

Approximately 65,000 private grant-making foundations are licensed to operate in the United States, though as many as a quarter of these are in name only (that is, make no grants) and many thousands more give less than a million dollars a year in grants. These small-scale operations do not raise the legitimacy question in the same way that the foundations with assets large enough to have a professional staff engaged in systematic grant making do. It is these larger foundations that aspire to eliminate diseases, reform education, advance civil rights, alter public policy, change public opinion, and otherwise operate at the scale of the market and the government. Restricting attention to these staffed, larger-asset organizations leaves us with fewer than 200, and only half that number have enough of an asset base to give more than $12 million a year in grants. One could narrow the subset even more. The twenty-five largest foundations (.00004 percent of the foundation universe) account for more than 25 percent of the sector's asset base (Foundation Center, 2004). The names are familiar: Gates, Pew, Ford, Rockefeller, MacArthur, Lilly, Carnegie, Hewlett.

The agendas pursued by the large, independent grant-making foundations self-consciously differ from charity or service delivery. They are about social change, in the spirit of what John D. Rockefeller, Sr.

argued a century ago. In establishing his philanthropies, Rockefeller remarked: "I do not believe in giving money to street beggars, but this is not reason why one should be exempt from doing something to help the situation represented by the street beggar" (1984, 110). "Scientific giving," in Rockefeller's term, is changing the conditions that give rise to begging. Charity can feed the hungry or shelter the homeless, but because it does not change what causes hunger or homelessness, it cannot interrupt the endless flow of those in need. "The best philanthropy," Rockefeller wrote, "involves the search for cause, an attempt to cure evils at their source" (cited in Fosdick 1952, 22).

The American foundation tradition owes much to this formulation—though the term strategic grant making has now displaced Rockefeller's more charming nineteenth-century term—scientific giving. The ambition of the American foundation is to improve the world: less poverty, war, sickness, illiteracy, violence, parochialism, hunger; and, conversely, more freedom, art, peace, understanding, opportunity, security, education, and health.

These ambitions can be very grand indeed. Francis X. Sutton, for many years a senior Ford Foundation officer, wrote to the author on February 13, 2004, that he and his colleagues thought that they might, "in some way or scope, change the course of history, usually overseas, and thus had to envisage a course of events other than that which otherwise lay ahead." He offered that this ambition "was not so unnatural in the Ford Foundation when it was far and away the biggest foundation in the world, had a bigger budget than the [United Nations] and an endowment about three-fourths as large as all the endowed private universities and colleges of the [United States]." Grand ambitions were not limited to the Ford Foundation, however. Sutton continues:

> "There was a time when American foundations, and not only Ford, thought that they were already 'at scale' to change whole societies or important parts of them," Sutton continued. "I think of the General Education Board's aim to change the whole landscape of American higher education by endowments, or Carnegie's effort to pension the whole profession of American college teachers, or Rockefeller's aim to lift China out of 'medieval' conditions." (Personal correspondence 2004)

To realize such ambitions, foundations operate with an open-ended time frame. The much celebrated Green Revolution initiated by the Ford and Rockefeller Foundations involved grants that spanned decades, and in important respects (genetic modification of developing country food staples) continues today, more than a half a century later. Another half-century project is the Ford Foundation's commitment to bringing area studies to American universities. Though much modified to reflect changing international conditions, the Ford Foundation is still active on behalf of this cause. The Gates Foundation took up the cause of a vaccine for HIV-AIDS more than a decade ago, and has not wavered despite early disappointments when candidate vaccines were field tested. The Packard Foundation has since its founding in 1964 given an annual grant of approximately $30 million to the same grantee, and intends to continue doing so indefinitely. There are many such examples.

The American foundation, endowed with untaxed private wealth, designs grant strategies not governed by election cycles, annual reports to stockholders, or short-term bottom line considerations. More generally, the foundation stands outside the controls of the state or the market, and yet is granted the right to intervene in the workings of both.

Though neither state nor market, the foundation shares traits with each. With the state it is expected to provide public services or goods that do not occur through the normal functioning of the market. Although it has no coercive powers and cannot legislate or regulate to bring about desired social conditions, foundation responsibility for the public good is often discharged by substituting for the state or by persuading the state to do what it might otherwise not take up. The foundation has enormous powers to try to set a public agenda and to manipulate incentives on behalf of its policy preferences.

Incentive manipulation is, of course, what market actors do, and in this sense the foundation is quasi-market even as it is quasi-state. But because it earns no profit and offers no return to the investment of its donor or donors, and because its endowment frees it from having to meet any marketplace test, it is not fully a market actor. In fact, the foundation finds much of its purpose in correcting for market failures.

These observations that place the foundation outside the state and the market frame a question that, though simple to ask, is difficult to answer. What, specifically, do foundations accomplish or represent that would otherwise be missing in society? Do they serve the public interest in some way that is superior to the combined efforts of the government, market actors, and other institutions in the nonprofit sector?

The common answer emphasizes that foundations compensate for state inadequacies and market failures. That is, they "do good" in ways otherwise missing. In this line of reasoning, society encourages and the state permits foundations because of their beneficent consequences, a point of view elaborated by various contributors to this volume.

An alternative answer, which I favor in this chapter, emphasizes less what foundations do and more what they represent in a nation guided by liberal political doctrine.

What Foundations Do

I start with the more common answer—that is, the impact or consequences that foundations have.

The Poor and the Powerless

One explanation for the privileged status of American foundations, and for the nonprofit sector more generally, is that they serve population groups too poor to purchase from the market and too politically weak to matter to the state (DiMaggio and Anheier 1990). If private foundations want to provide, say, college tuition for students of poor families, they are welcomed to do because it relieves what would otherwise be demands on the government or reveal a failure of the market.

The argument that the market is indifferent when foundations serve groups too poor to purchase services or products has merit because market indifference evaporates when profit-making opportunities appear, even opportunities initiated by private foundations. The hybrid seeds of the famed Green Revolution emerged from research institutions funded by foundations but were quickly commercialized. A sector of the higher education system—low-end career preparation— is suddenly viewed as a profit-making enterprise, and today millions of students purchase education from for-profit providers. When market actors discover new profit opportunities, they are quick to oppose competition from taxpayer-subsidized enterprises (the university bookstore is often cited in this regard). In fact, the foundation takes pride if the outcome of a grant investment is "taken to scale" by commercial enterprises.

However, the proposition that foundation privileges derive from providing what market actors can safely ignore overlooks the extent to which foundations have, time and again, declared the market a failure not on a piecemeal basis, but because, by definition, it cannot protect the society against inevitable negative externalities of market transactions.

There is a similar partial truth if we shift attention to the state. Certainly governments throughout history have welcomed poverty relief or health provision by charitable organizations. But these same governments are less welcoming when the private foundation threatens to empower the disenfranchised or alter the balance of political forces. Congressional committees in the United States have periodically investigated foundations viewed as too political in their grant making, giving rise to limits on what foundations can do in the legislative and electoral arenas.

These examples suggest that only up to a point is the foundation granted a privileged status because it takes up tasks neither government nor market actors want to worry about. This point is quickly reached if the root cause metaphor is taken seriously. In specifically rejecting charity as the philanthropic project and focusing instead on changing underlying conditions, the American foundation has been in continuous search of market and policy failures. In fact, the foundation can be successful in its progressive mission only by identifying and correcting such failures. Market actors pollute? Fund studies of regulatory reforms or support advocacy groups organizing consumer boycotts. Market actors ignore diseases of the poor? Subsidize R&D on tuberculosis or malaria and then create pressure for products to be made available at subsidized costs. Public schools are failing? Fund policy analysis, voucher experiments, or local reform efforts designed to change how the government is managing public schools. Government is pursuing a short-sighted foreign policy? Use the universities to create a new cadre of policy experts, or support advocacy organizations with more "visionary" views (for example, arms control starting in the 1950s, or the more muscular foreign policy endorsed by conservative foundations starting in the 1970s).

A rationale for the private foundation premised on the assumption that its privileged position results from doing what the state and market allow it to do does not explain what happens when the foundation intrudes into their respective spheres. The American foundation is deliberately and even forcefully intrusive in this regard. Taken as a whole, the foundation sector is an independent power center in America's political economy and has steadily expanded in numbers, assets, and program reach. This cannot logically be explained by emphasizing that foundations provide what the government and the market are only too happy to shift to charitable organizations.

Redistribution

A variation of the poor and the powerless explanation is that foundations earn their privileges because they are redistributive. Foundation grants, in this argument, redirect money from the wealthy to the poor—what is generally described as vertical redistribution. This answer is especially important where the tax code exempts from taxation the private funds that establish foundations. Because these funds do in fact come from the wealthy, and because foundation programs do often disproportionately benefit the less well-off, redistribution presents itself as a plausible explanation for the public encouragement of foundations. It also has the merit of continuing the very long tradition—dating from Elizabethan England's 1601 Statute of Charitable Uses—that allowed donors to entrust property for eleemosynary purposes.

Julian Wolpert, in chapter 5 of this volume, summarizes the empirical evidence on redistribution, noting that although unresolved measurement issues make a definitive answer elusive, on balance the benefits of foundation grants flow downward, though probably less dramatically than foundation claims imply. Charles Clotfelter (1992, 22), investigating the nonprofit sector more generally, reaches a similar conclusion: "There is great diversity within the nonprofit sector, and no overarching conclusions about distributional impact can be made." But there is no "evidence that benefits are dramatically skewed away from the poor and toward the affluent."

Even if the net flow is redistributive, the question remains as to whether the foundation asset is more redistributive than had it been taxed in the first place. On this issue, however, Wolpert is persuasive in arguing that, for the United States, the wealth placed in foundations might not otherwise have found its way into the tax stream.

There is a second reason to doubt the depth of the redistribution explanation: the irony in the fact that American foundations result from the accumulation of substantial private wealth and yet in instance after instance declare that their mission is to improve the less well-off. They go about that mission by helping to lower the barriers to upward mobility, by working to ensure basic civil and political rights or by contributing to education and health for the poor.

Foundations have not, however, gone about that mission by calling into question the political-economic arrangements that allow for great inequalities in wealth acquisition in the first place, this despite their promise to eliminate root causes of poverty and deprivation. Private capital accumulation in very large amounts and the substantial economic inequality that results is simply not viewed by wealthy philanthropists and the successor trustees as a root cause of the social maladies to be ameliorated.

Neither empirical evidence nor philanthropic logic leads easily to the conclusion that redistribution can serve as the primary rationale for the ubiquity of the American private foundation.

COST-EFFECTIVENESS   A quite different approach is the oft-heard argument that foundations and the nonprofit organizations they fund have a better ratio of accomplishment to funds spent than the public sector does (Weisbrod 1988). The flexibility and imaginativeness of foundations, at least compared to cumbersome, risk-adverse government agencies, is given as the reason.

This is a difficult hypothesis to test, and in one important respect is counterintuitive. Efficient use of resources presumes a bottom line, a way to hold those who allocate funds accountable for their performance. Market inefficiency is rapidly followed by ruthless punishment in shrinking markets and falling share prices. For government, the softer but still meaningful bottom line is found in the electoral theory of democracy and its premise that there are always office-seekers eager to show that they can more effectively discharge public responsibilities than those currently holding power.

Nonprofit institutions not blessed with a permanent endowment also have a bottom line—there are competitors trying to attract the membership base, user fees, tuition payments, government contracts, or public acclaim. At times, the competitors are for-profits, as indicated in the example of commercialization in the higher education market.

We endlessly repeat that foundations are uniquely protected from bottom-line preoccupations—no shareholders, no customers, no voters, no campaign contributors, no dues-paying members, and no clients who can withhold financial or moral support. Although it is easy to understand why foundation officers claim to be excellent stewards of funds in their trust, the conditions that make foundations what they are—latitude of choice and absence of external accountability—make this claim difficult to assess.

The argument from efficiency and effectiveness also falters when we recall that foundations say that they take risks, even welcome failure. A foundation that does not fail is, presumably, not living up to its promise to explore what the market and the government shy away from. If a foundation were to take this promise seriously, it would announce what it believes to be the optimal ratio of program failure to program success and self-correct if it became too risk adverse. It is hard to know what mixture of program failure and success would constitute cost-effectiveness, and to my knowledge no American foundation justifies itself by calling attention to its program failures.

SOCIAL CHANGE   American foundations generally operate on the assumption that philanthropic dollars can change the underlying conditions that lead to bad things in human history. They are in constant search of the point of intervention that increases the odds that grants will change some condition or policy. Do ideas drive change, or technologies or social movements, market incentives, government interventions, or moral exhortation? If ideas drive change, invest in research and intellectual efforts; if government interventions are more important, invest in policy analysis and advocacy; if exhortation matters, invest in media campaigns or public education; if it is markets that count, practice entrepreneurial philanthropy. Grant making seeks the point of leverage judged to be most productive of the social change favored by the foundation.

The popularity of a social change rhetoric is simultaneously a way for the foundation to talk to itself about its aspirations and a way to justify itself to others. Bringing about desirable social change is probably the most common rationale advanced on behalf of foundations. There is no doubt that the American private foundations can claim credit for a long and still growing list of serious achievements, starting with Carnegie's libraries and Rockefeller's public health campaigns. More recent additions to the list include the Ford Foundation's long investment in area and international studies, the Open Society of George Soros, the Annenberg Foundation's school reform efforts, W. W. Kellog's support of the community college movement, early research on AIDS funded by the Aaron Diamond and the Robert Wood Johnson Foundation, the MacArthur Foundation's transformation of the field of security studies, and the Lilly Endowment's long and productive relationship with religion and theological education. Also appearing on many lists is the concerted effort by a handful of conservative foundations to change the basic premises of the welfare society and to justify privatization of what earlier were considered public responsibilities.

Although not wishing to subtract from the worthiness and social significance of these achievements, skeptics might ask, "how can we assess what would have been achieved in these domains in the absence of private foundations?"—for in practically none of the cited examples were foundation funds the sole source of support. They might also ask how we can assess the magnitude of social change in relation to the funds spent. There is no metric of foundation impact; there is not even a theory of social change that might point to a measurement strategy.

For the sake of argument, however, we set aside the skeptic's question and concur that significant, specific achievements can be attributed to foundation grant making.

With few exceptions, what cannot be claimed is foundation credit for social change—if we take that term to mean change at serious scale, which benefits large numbers of people, which is consequential over an extended period. I grant that this "if" sets a high standard, but it is one that foundation rhetoric has adopted, as can be easily seen in the glossy annual reports and promotional material of many large American foundations.

Consider the second half of the twentieth century. This is period in which the philanthropic foundation sector came to maturity in America. Foundations accumulated substantial resources, had strong and self-confident leadership, enjoyed widespread public support, and had ample opportunity to engage the standard repertoire of foundation causes. We ask of this period, what the significant social changes were and what the role was of foundations in shaping them.

It was certainly a half-century of enormous cultural change: the civil rights movement, the university-based antiwar movement that opened up government to more participatory democracy and greater transparency, the transforming feminist movement, gay and lesbian rights, the mainstreaming of environmental causes.

Across this political-cultural agenda, American foundations played catch up with forces far more powerful than any they could have launched. Consider environmental issues: it was government funded science (European as well as American) that shaped the late twentieth century issues of climate change, ozone depletion, energy inefficiencies, air and water quality, and sustainable development. Membership-based organizations, funded by dues and private contributions, forced policy changes. Public opinion changed in response to media coverage. Civic leaders and politicians adopted environmental causes, often in response to electoral pressures. Foundation funds figured in this mix, significantly so and in some instances catalytic (environmental law, for instance), but were only a small fraction of the research, advocacy, and public education resources garnered by the environmental movement.

The latter half of the twentieth century also witnessed a seismic shift in assumptions about the respective merits of the public and private sectors. The Reagan-Thatcher years put wealth redistribution on the back burner and challenged the assumption that a regulated economy is a just economy. The political left adopted a "third way" in which the public good is, apparently, better served under privatization and liberal market assumptions. Foundation money was everywhere present as these policies were debated, with the mainstream foundations no less ideological in their defense of the regulatory and welfare state than the more conservative foundations who mounted a challenge. In the United States, a vast policy industry emerged—think tanks, public policy schools, university centers, dedicated publishing programs—with important support from America's foundations (Rich 2004).

It is difficult to measure the impact of foundation funds in this enormous shift in public policy. It is suggestive, however, that the revolution in thinking took place in Thatcher's Great Britain, with minimal help from a foundation sector, no less successfully than it did in Reagan's America, where foundations were hyperactive. To the extent that credit is assigned to the conservative foundations, we would have to conclude that the liberal foundations were largely ineffective in protecting policies they had earlier championed. On balance, a political transformation of this magnitude required electoral energy and well-funded interest group activity beyond anything foundations could offer.

And, of course, the second half of the twentieth century was defined by the most sweeping technological change since fossil fuels were harnessed. The computer revolution came from government-funded research and the market, leaving to nonprofits worries about the digital divide, the promise of distance learning, or the hope that poor countries might propel themselves into the modern era on the back of IT. These are not small matters, and are fitting as foundation programs. But, again, it is foundations doing what they can to minimize harm and maximize good of large transformations well beyond their control.

Large-scale social change—whether from social-political movements, shifts in political ideology endorsed by mass electorates, or technology-driven market forces—can be affected at the margins by foundations. Their grants can selectively and partially prevent unfortunate side-effects, and can bring causes to public attention. These achievements are properly celebrated in foundation circles. But to tie the rationale for the private foundation to its capacity to bring about social change is, I suggest, a claim not confirmed by recent history, at least if we have in mind change at serious scale. If there are exceptions at present, it is restricted to a handful of super-sized foundations with highly focused agendas—as could be said of the Soros Open Society Institute's effort in Central Europe or the Gates Foundation's ambitious vaccine initiative in the developing world. In these rare instances, resources do scale to the changes desired, as did Carnegie's public library philanthropy and or the Rockefeller program of medical research and public health earlier in the century.

The four themes reviewed—foundation funds as a substitute for or complement to the market and state, as redistributive, as particularly cost-effective, as a generator of social change—each contribute to an explanation for the steady growth and social acceptance of America's foundation sector. But they are not fully convincing. The substitution argument falters because in their grant making foundations are not simply complementary but intrusive and challenging to market and state. Redistribution is clearly part of an explanation, especially in that it echoes the long association of philanthropy with charity for the poor. But if redistribution were the central justification, we would expect a much clearer empirical trace than systematic investigation has uncovered. The warrant for cost-effectiveness has logical inconsistencies that reduce its persuasiveness, and is in any case an argument not advanced through systematic social science but instead anecdotally asserted.

Social change—that is, the litany of specific foundation achievements—is no doubt the strongest candidate to justify the special privileges of private foundations. To move forward on behalf of this argument requires an answer to a simple question. Given the level of foundation investment, how much social change should we observe and how much do we observe? Until that question is addressed, we are left with anecdotes, case studies, and the self-promotional rhetoric of foundations themselves.

A serious answer has to break free of the internalist methodology that has characterized studies of foundation impact—the methodology that uses foundation documents to trace the line between the goals they announce and the accomplishments they report. A richer methodology would systematically investigate failed or inefficient lines of foundation work (there are many) and compare those to successful efforts. A more ambitious research design would take broad areas in which foundations have been active—such as the environmental cause indicated above or America's public health system—and measure the foundation contribution in comparison to the many other forces from government, the market, and civil society organizations that were also active.

On balance, the thesis that foundation legitimacy is earned by the good works that foundations do is unpersuasive. A more convincing explanation comes into view if we shift attention from what they do to what they represent.

What Do Foundations Represent?

The starting point is America's preference for a weak state. American constitutional doctrine limited the power of the state by establishing a weak executive, separation of powers, extensive checks and balances, frequent elections, and strong state's rights. A minimal government implied that collective action would be organized outside the state—in part through the normal workings of the market but also by a vast array of nonprofit institutions providing what in other nations is taken to be government responsibility. Over time America produced regulatory and tax policies hospitable to a robust nonprofit sector in education, social welfare, health, and arts and culture. A corollary was and continues to be a strong tradition of charitable giving and organized philanthropy.

It was in this setting that the American foundation sector emerged. In the latter decades of the nineteenth century, political and economic doctrine allowed those who controlled oil, steel, banking, and transport to amass huge private fortunes. Conspicuous consumption could rid its owners and heirs of part of this wealth, but for some it was too great to spend or too much to leave to children, and for others ostentatious spending was limited by religious scruples. Charitable giving was the option available. And if wealth free of taxes accumulates in amounts too substantial to be given away in one's lifetime, as Rockefeller and Carnegie were quick to learn, the obvious solution is to create trust funds that would link private wealth to public purposes into perpetuity.

This was a tidy solution to an old problem for liberal doctrine. Public goods are underproduced by free market transactions. A social demand for public goods, and for their corollary, a public sector, thus arises. The state produces public goods by regulating market actors and by exercising such powers as taxation, conscription, and eminent domain. Liberal doctrine, however, warns that an interventionist government tends to coerciveness, hampers market flexibility, and encroaches on private property and personal freedoms.

Is there a way for the liberal society to provide public goods with minimum infringement on economic choice and political freedoms? Perhaps by turning to the nonprofit sector that does not have to return a profit and that has no coercive power and thus produces public goods at minimal risk to personal freedoms. This is what the liberal society wants, and what religious charity, private patronage, and philanthropy provide.

From this perspective, the legitimacy of the nonprofit sector arises out of its insistence that it provide public goods but retains its right to push back if the state encroaches too far into the sphere of personal freedom—that is, its right to be an independent power center. An offshoot of this argument leads to America's vaunted pluralism, an inevitable result of organizing collective action in the private, nonprofit sector.

If this helps to account for a nonprofit sector, how does the privileged private foundation fit in? Recall that our focus is on the endowed foundation, one not beholden to clients or customers. Its mission is, on the whole, more permissive and open ended than other endowed institutions, such as museums or universities, which have only institution-specific purposes. The foundation, in its focus on underlying social conditions, is free to choose (and change) its priorities and the manner in which it will serve the public good.

The foundation is the preeminent exemplar of the noncoercive, nonextractive funder of public goods. The foundation need not do its job well. It may not be redistributive or cost effective or capable of bringing about important social changes. These are matters for empirical determination, and have gone unanswered during a century of spectacular expansion of America's foundation sector. They have gone unanswered because they don't much matter, at least from the perspective of legitimacy.

Legitimacy is unproblematic because foundations emblemize a central quest of the liberal society—a way to attach private wealth to public goods without encroaching on political and economic freedoms. The public see foundations much the same way they do the nonprofit sector more generally—not always efficient, maybe elitist, sometimes tempted by self-dealing, but solidly in the American tradition of using private resources for public benefit—and solidly in the pluralistic tradition of encouraging multiple, contending versions of the public interest (Prewitt 1999).

This perspective on the source of foundation legitimacy explains a seeming puzzle. Why are these highly privileged institutions—endowed into perpetuity—subjected to such light accountability regimes?

Accountability of Foundations

Peter Frumkin reminds us in chapter 4 of this volume that foundations are subject to accountability claims for three reasons: they are publicly subsidized; they project their private vision of the public good into the public arena; and they create a state-protected power asymmetry between those with money and those who want it. The foundation sector is, by definition and in law, largely undemocratic, for how else to characterize a wealthy elite who apply tax-protected dollars to enact their vision of the public good. Activities that are undemocratic, we presume, should meet an accountability test.

If the justification of foundations rested on what they do, we should expect that accountability to focus on what foundations say they intend to do and then on how well they live up to their promises. But holding foundations accountable for their missions and their accomplishments moves toward substantive accountability, and that is nowhere to be seen in American law or practice. American politics is not designed to judge that one "good cause" is better than another—that it is fine to make a tax-protected gift to the soup kitchen but not to donate one's art collection to the Metropolitan Museum. Congress has periodically tried. The evils of concentrated industrial wealth (Walsh Commission in the 1920s), the soft on communism charge (the Cox Committee in the 1950s), and the liberal social agenda that had to be checked (Reece Committee in the 1960s) were instances of trying to impose substantive accountability. None of these efforts did more than nibble at the edges of grant portfolios or foundation mission statements.

The congressional action that did, in the late 1960s, make a difference focused on financial abuses more than the substance of grant making. More recently, politicians have made speeches about foundation giving being insufficiently charitable, but these turned out to be about foundation salaries or payout rates, not about the choice of grantees, let alone the right of the foundation to define the public interest as it sees fit.

There is a reason that foundation mission statements and program goals are couched in highly permissive terms—"the well-being of mankind around the world"—and why the government accepts this. An institution endowed into the indefinite future requires the flexibility to reinvent its programs as conditions change, new challenges appear, and so on. The government is neither politically nor legally equipped to do more than ask if the mission is in the public good and then hope that that mission is more or less realized.

Certainly by their own testimony, foundations are hugely successful. The Council on Foundations circulates to its members a list of ten achievements that can be used to convince the public that foundations are worthy institutions. It is an interestingly eclectic list: the 911 system for emergency calls, the hospice movement, the pap smear in cancer treatment, public libraries, the polio vaccine, rocket sciences, PBS's *Sesame Street* series, white lines on highways, the Green Revolution, and yellow fever vaccine. It is no accident that the list tilts toward public health, a generally safe area, and ignores achievements with more political content—such as civil rights funding, environmental causes, voter registration, or pro-life advocacy. It is the latter type of grant making that calls forth demands for more accountability, though for reasons just cited the government is not inclined to impose limits on the agendas pursued by foundations.

Neither is the government likely to ask the efficiency question. There is simply no conceptual or empirical base on which to do so. If political agreement on what constitutes good works is elusive, even more so would be the metric for measuring its realization. The government is not even able to measure its own performance, though in recent years it has begun to try.

It is to be expected, then, that accountability is framed not around mission statements, grant-making portfolios or actual foundation performance but around issues of transparency, administrative efficiency, and fiscal responsibility (including officer compensation). This recurring attention to procedural accountability focuses not just on foundations but also on the entire nonprofit sector (Fleishman 1999; Bradley, Jansen, and Silverman 2003).

Accountability arrangements for the nonprofit sector stress legal and regulatory mechanisms that mandate particular practices or establish conditions that must be met before funds can be made available. These arrangements can be effective for those nonprofits that do not have the luxury of an endowment that offers protection against, especially, funding conditionalities. But accountability arrangements that work for the fee or contract dependent nonprofits have limited impact on foundations, whose endowments leave the government few regulatory options.

The American foundation sector has been successful in deflecting demands for substantive accountability by expanding in such procedural areas as transparency and professionalism, which, as Frumkin (1999) notes, are less threatening to foundations than substantive accountability. Foundations have become adept at generating information about their grant-making criteria and program priorities—often in glossy annual reports and expensive Web sites easily the equal of commercial firms. Foundations have also turned to self-evaluation. Grants and sometimes entire programs are subjected to extensive retroactive evaluations, using a mixture of in-house staff and outside consultants. Although these evaluations often improve foundation practice, they are also used to deflect external assessments of foundation priorities and accomplishments.

There has been some interest in peer review to strengthen the accountability of foundations, modeled on the accreditation systems used by higher education in the United States. Depending on its design, such a system could move closer to substantive accountability—and perhaps for that reason has remained an issue for discussion in scholarly journals more than an active topic among foundation trustees and officers.

It is likely that the foundation sector will continue to improve its procedural accountability—its treatment of grantees, its financial management, its public reporting, its overall professionalism, its ability to detect and maybe punish corrupt practices. It is certain that foundations will strongly resist accountability of a more substantive type—a review of their program priorities or of the effectiveness with which they accomplish their self-defined missions.

Society grants unique privileges to foundations and in return requires that philanthropic wealth promote the public good. But there is circularity in this formulation. What emerges as the public good is itself the result of private deliberation. There is no mechanism through which interests in society can voice preferences about foundation agendas—can argue for more support of health research and less attention to civil rights or can punish foundations for spending too much (or too little) overseas. This would require substantive accountability of a sort that foundations resist and that the government has shown no appetite to impose.

Conclusions

Viewing the American foundations less from the perspective of what they do than what they represent offers fresh insight into issues of legitimacy and accountability. Legitimacy itself is not problematic. Foundations are widely accepted as appropriate institutions for linking private wealth to public good, and there is every reason to expect the American foundation sector to continue to flourish.

A half dozen times over the last century, foundations have come under sharp public criticism for activities thought to transgress accepted boundaries—including charges that they have been un-American. Never, however, has public criticism led to an effort to curtail the growth of the foundation sector or, except very marginally, to any attempt at restricting what a foundation selects as its mission and how it pursues that mission.

If public criticism has never led to serious questioning of the legitimacy of foundations, it has led to reforms—sometimes mandated by regulatory or tax law but more often self-generated by the foundation sector in an effort to forestall more onerous restrictions. The reforms, whether imposed or self-generated, have been procedural rather than substantive—about payout rates but not about choice of grantees, about issuing annual reports but not about the mission statements introducing those reports, about detecting abuse but not about detecting poor performance.

The argument I have presented indicates why this is so, and why it cannot be otherwise. American foundations exist because of what they represent—a perch beyond the reach of the market and the state, a perch from which to articulate and implement a private vision of the public good. At issue is not the coherence of that vision or even the success with which it is implemented. It can be, and often has been, ideological—from the political left as well as the political right. That finally does not matter, because any attempt by the government to control foundation mission and grant-making strategy undermines the very essence of what the autonomous foundation represents in American politics. To seriously restrict its substantive autonomy would be to call its legitimacy into question, and that is not on America's political agenda.

References

Bradley, Bill, Paul Jansen, and Les Silverman. 2003. "The Nonprofit Sector's $100 Billion Opportunity." *Harvard Business Review* 81(5)(May): 94–103.

Clotfelter, Charles T. 1992. "The Distributional Consequences of Nonprofit Activities." In *Who Benefits from the Nonprofit Sector?* edited by Charles T. Clotfelter. Chicago: University of Chicago Press.

DiMaggio, Paul J., and Helmut K. Anheier. 1990. "The Sociology of Nonprofit Organizations and Sectors." *Annual Review of Sociology* 16(1): 137–59.

Fleishman, Joel L. 1999. "Public Trust in Not-for-Profit Organizations and the Need for Regulatory Reform." In *Philanthropy and the Nonprofit Sector in a Changing America,* edited by Charles T. Clotfelter and Thomas Ehrlich. Bloomington: Indiana University Press.

Fosdick, Raymond B. 1952. *The Story of the Rockefeller Foundation: Nineteen Thirteen to Nineteen Fifty.* New York: Harper and Brothers.

The Foundation Center. 2004. *Foundation Growth and Giving Estimates.* Foundations Today Series, 2004 ed. New York: The Foundation Center.

Frumkin, Peter. 1999. "Private Foundations as Public Institutions: Regulation, Professionalization, and the Redefinition of Organized Philanthropy." In *Philanthropic Foundations: New Scholarship, New Possibilities,* edited by Ellen Condliffe Lagemann. Bloomington: Indiana University Press.

Prewitt, Kenneth. 1999. "The Importance of Foundations in an Open Society." In *The Future of Foundations in an Open Society.* Gutersloh, Germany: Bertelsmann Foundation Publishers.

Rich, Andrew. 2004. *Think Tanks, Public Policy, and the Politics of Expertise.* New York: Cambridge University Press.

Rockefeller, John D. 1984. *Random Reminiscences of Men and Events.* New York: Sleepy Hollow Press and Rockefeller Archive Center

Weisbrod, Burton A. 1988. *The Nonprofit Economy.* Cambridge, Mass.: Harvard University Press.

Part II

American Perspectives

Chapter 3

American Debates on the Legitimacy of Foundations

David C. Hammack

Defined as large stocks of wealth controlled by independent, self-perpetuating boards of trustees and devoted to the support through grants of charitable purposes—or to no specific purpose except "the general good"—philanthropic foundations first attracted notice in the United States only at the beginning of the twentieth century. By the time of World War I, such foundations had won attention as distinctively American phenomena. Since then, though they have often attracted critical scrutiny, their diversity and their close integration with the American nonprofit sector as a whole—together with the commitment of America's political culture to the rights of individuals and of private property—have enabled them to defend their legitimacy to this day.

American foundations support a wide array of causes, religious as well as secular. They have sought to call attention to particular problems and to shape public opinion. They have worked to identify or devise and to popularize "best practices" for nonprofit and government agencies and to promote specific government policies. They have also sought to reorient and reorganize existing service providers and to create new ones, whether nonprofit or government. Most often, of course, American foundations have simply supported nonprofit organizations, or have purchased services from or subsidized the supply of services by nonprofit and governmental agencies that provide health care, social welfare, educational, cultural, or religious services. Many foundation subsidies are intended to make such services available to specified, often disadvantaged or specially defined populations.[1] But very often, foundations support advanced intellectual work: scientific or scholarly research, creative work in literature and the arts, studies in public policy, reframing of public discussions, as well as religious study and reflection.

Observers have held American foundations responsible for many things. Foundation advocates credit them with remarkable innovations. They have won most praise for their key roles in developing world-class scientific research universities and medical centers, and more generally in helping Americans respond to the challenges posed by industrialization and urbanization in the first half of the twentieth century. Foundations, it is said, have introduced vital qualities of flexibility, responsiveness, and diversity into American institutions, public as well as private. And American foundations have often "invested in people," or even sought to support "genius" (Hollis 1938; Weaver 1967; Cuninggim 1972; Karl and Katz 1981; Ettling 1981; Lagemann 1983; 1999; Bulmer 1984; Lagemann 1989; Geiger 1986; Wheatley 1988; Kohler 1991).

Yet American foundations have often attracted harsh criticism as being fundamentally undemocratic. Conservatives object that foundations promote collectivism (Wormser 1958; DiLorenzo, Oliver, and Winters 1990; Olasky 1992), secularism, or internationalism (Quigley 1981; Josephson 1952). Recently, conservatives have added that in pursuing such goals unelected foundation leaders who did not earn the money they spend have refused to honor—have in fact subverted—the charitable intent of the donors who did earn the money (Wooster 1994; Holcombe 2000). Some traditionalists have objected that foundations have promoted racial integration (Goulden 1971, chap. 8). Individualists complain that government-granted foundation status confers unfair competitive advantage on certain individuals, families (Lundberg 1937, 320–73; Wormser 1958; Lundberg 1969, chap. 10; Allen 1989), or business firms (Troyer 2000, 52–53; Goulden 1971; Lundberg 1969, chap. 10)—and on managers who gain control of foundation assets. Labor leaders and liberals have complained that foundations perpetuate economic (U.S. Senate 1916; Wormser 1958; Goulden 1971; Odendahl 1990; Colwell 1993) and racial inequality (Harlan 1958; Stanfield 1985; Anderson 1988; Anderson and Moss 1999) and the dominance of white Protestant men (Lindeman 1939). Critics on the left insist that foundations restrain or suppress movements for social reform (Arnove 1980; Roelofs 1987, 2003; Fisher 1993; Colwell 1993), exert reactionary influence on certain academic disciplines and professions (Noble 1977; Brown 1979; Berliner 1985), or more generally exert "hegemonic" influence on academic disciplines or on public opinion (Arnove 1980; Fisher 1993; Roelofs 2003). More than one recent critic has insisted that certain foundations are currently attempting to dismantle the welfare state (Covington 1997; Stefancic and Delgado 1996; Diamond 1995). Liberal internationalists and others argue that certain foundations promote capitalist expansion (Ransom 1975; Arnove 1980; Berman 1983) in U.S. foreign policy and provide illegitimate cover for CIA and other U.S. interventions in the affairs of other nations (Andrews 1973; Arnove 1980; Weissman 1975; Saunders 2000; Coleman 1989). Critics left and right have denounced foundations for lack of imagination (Barzun 1959; Freund 1996), ineffectiveness (Nielsen 1972, 1985; National Commission on Philanthropy and Civic Renewal 1997; Dowie 2001; O'Connor 2001), maintaining outdated activities (Hobhouse 1880; Goff 1919; Young 1926, Rosenwald 1929), and for merely hoarding wealth (Gaul and Borowski 1993). Some critics object to specific foundation actions or policies, but a good number attack the legitimacy of the foundation as an institution.

Charitable foundations exist, of course, in many societies. Foundations supported many churches and charities in medieval and early modern Europe; waqif supported mosques, schools, and other charities in Ottoman society. In the first decades of the twentieth century, American writers sometimes quoted Jacques Turgot's article on foundations in the eighteenth-century *Encyclopédie* as a classic criticism of perpetual foundations: "how easy it is to do harm in wishing to do good!" and how difficult it is for a donor to "communicate his own zeal from age to age" (Keppel 1930; Hollis 1938; Harrison and Andrews 1946).[2] But some writers have seen U.S. foundations as characteristically American, different—for good or ill—from anything to be found in Europe or other parts of the world. Other writers insist that wealthy, autonomous foundations are quasi-aristocratic institutions that can play no legitimate role in any democratic republic. General purpose foundations simply could not exist in the United States before 1900; severe critics won a hearing in the early teens, in the 1930s, in the 1950s, and again in the 1960s. On several occasions they succeeded in limiting foundation options. Yet American foundations have defended themselves, and since the beginning of the twentieth century their legitimacy has never been under serious threat.

How have American foundations made themselves legitimate in the face of such diverse criticism? Perhaps the most fundamental answer is that, in the United States, foundations are an integral part of the nonprofit, nongovernment sector. Nonprofit organizations have played key roles in American life since the adoption of the Constitution and the rise of the corporation. We can date their prominent role to the period between 1787 and 1833 when the Constitution, the Bill of Rights, the Marshall Court, and other actions affirmed the rights of private property, separated church and state at the national and state levels, and fragmented national power over domestic affairs. From the 1830s, Americans have used nonprofit organizations for an increasing variety of purposes. Most notably, Americans use nonprofits to put their individual and group preferences into action, to provide assistance and to open opportunities to individuals who appear to deserve assistance, to celebrate their wealth, and perhaps most distinctively to handle many conflicts, especially conflicts over matters of religious and cultural belief, practice, and social action (Hammack 1998, 2002).[3]

In the U.S. context, religious organizations are nonprofits. So are a wide variety of other entities: civic organizations; a majority of the leading medical centers; most of the social service organizations that provide counseling, job training, and other active services to those who do not find their way to employment through the public schools and community colleges; nearly all liberal arts colleges, many of the research universities, and the largest share of the professional schools; and all the great museums (with the sole exception of the National Gallery and other Smithsonian museums, which have always depended on private donors for their collections), orchestras, operas, and dance companies. By practice and under the influence of the law, foundations direct most of their giving to nonprofits. Nearly all other foundation giving goes to provide opportunities to individuals deemed willing and able to advance themselves and contribute to society. Fundamentally, then, American foundations derive their legitimacy from the nonprofit sector as a whole.

Nonprofit organizations won legitimacy early in the nineteenth century. By the 1830s, many (though not all) American courts and legislatures had accepted the view that nongovernment, nonprofit organizations provided essential services, reinforced religious education in ways important to civil peace, reduced the need for tax-supported government action, permitted variety and flexibility in the provision of services. They accepted the fact that nonprofits serve a very wide array of religious and cultural views, allowing minorities to put their views into practice—though many state legislatures sought, through the nineteenth century and beyond, to favor Protestants and their organizations. Collectively, as legislators and judges came to recognize, nonprofits help the United States manage dangerous conflict over religion and identity. Forced to the question, American legislators (except in the South) decided to leave nongovernment organizations a wide scope of freedom in which to act. After a period of hesitation in the mid-nineteenth century, legislators also agreed to allow nonprofit organizations to hold as private the property they needed for their operations. Operating nonprofits hold property for their particular charitable purposes. Foundations, by contrast, hold property for any charitable purpose, or for all.[4]

Working within the context of the American nonprofit sector, foundations first won legitimacy at the end of the nineteenth century. Whenever a challenge to their legitimacy has arisen, American commitments to private property, corporate autonomy, separation of church and state, and the values of the First Amendment have allowed foundation leaders to head them off by taking steps to tie foundations more closely to the nonprofit organizations and by making concessions to transparency. Foundations have sometimes sought to lead public opinion, but foundation leaders have always deferred to legislative and judicial opinion, and have accepted the need to work through established nonprofits. Foundation donors have preferred to operate behind closed doors, but in response to the suspicions of their critics foundations have provided more and more information to the public. Relatively small groups of very large foundations have always held the great majority of foundation wealth, but the foundation form has also served numbers of people of modest means, and this has also helped foundations maintain their status as legitimate institutions. Overall, defenders of American foundations have successfully appealed to widely accepted notions of property, citizenship, and nongovernment action.

One last point should be made here. Although a number of American foundations have held very large fortunes indeed (especially the Carnegie and Rockefeller charities in the early twentieth century, the Ford Foundation in the early 1960s, and the Gates Foundation today), foundations have never held decisive resources in relation to the fields they have addressed. And even as foundations have grown in recent years, the nonprofit sector as a whole has grown even faster, so that philanthropic giving of all kinds, including foundation giving, has declined sharply as a source of nonprofit support. Together, these factors have made the United States a very hospitable environment for foundations since the early years of the twentieth century.

What Is To Be Explained?

Impressive reported growth of foundations in numbers, assets, and regional distribution provides a prima facie case that they have indeed achieved legal, political, and social legitimacy in the United States. American law and legislation greatly expanded the scope for foundations after 1890. Critics combined to challenge their legitimacy in the 1910s, the 1930s, and the 1950s and 1960s. They succeeded, with the Tax Reform Act of 1969, in limiting the powers that U.S. foundations enjoy. This act may well have slowed foundation growth during the 1970s and 1980s, but the growth resumed in the 1990s.

The Growth of Foundations in the United States

Only a few foundations existed in 1900; tens of thousands do today. Judging from the incomplete data for periods before the late 1950s, their numbers increased rapidly until the Great Depression, then a little less rapidly until 1969. Foundation numbers increased little through the 1970s, and resumed growth at a somewhat slower pace in the 1980s and 1990s. A log table makes visual the leveling-off in the rate of new foundation creation in the 1930s and again in the 1970s and 1980s clear (see figure 3.1).

The history of foundation assets tells a similar story. Foundations assets have grown, though not nearly as much as many suppose if taken as a share of all financial assets in the United States. Measured in relation to the total U.S. gross domestic product, foundations grew strongly in three spurts that coincided with strong run-ups in the stock market: during the 1920s (again judging from incomplete data), the 1950s and 1960s, and the 1990s. In relation to the total market value of all U.S. stocks, foundation assets grew more rapidly than the market until the late 1960s, more slowly until the 1990s, then more rapidly again. Very rapid growth after World War II attracted critical attention, and ultimately federal intervention. The recently renewed

Table 3.1   Reported Charitable Foundations in the United States, 1915 to 2000

1915	27
1926	179
1938	188
1944	505
1955	1,488
1964	6,007
1975	21,877
1985	25,639
1995	40,140
2001	61,810

Sources: Andrews (1973, 82–86, 220); The Foundation Center (2003a). Before the late 1950s, all counts of foundations were incomplete.

Note: The Foundation Center's 1960 *Directory* reported (p. ix) that it had the names of about 12,000 foundations, but listed only the 5202 whose 1959 assets exceeded $50,000 or grants had exceeded $10,000, did not make annual appeals for public funds, were not limited by charter to supporting one or several named institutions, and did not function as endowments for such institutions.

growth of American foundations has brought increasing criticism of specific abuses.[5] By 2005, however, as in the 1910s and the 1930s, criticism has not led to new federal restrictions. Criticism of U.S. foundations has always targeted abuses, but has never seriously undermined the legitimacy of their position.

Figure 3.1   Reported Foundations in the United States, 1915 to 2001 (Log Scale)

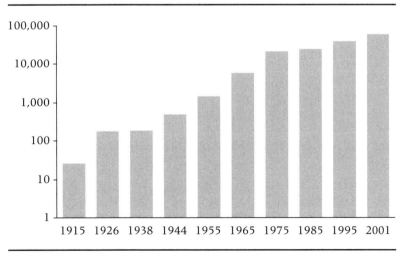

Source: Author's compilation.

Note: For the incompleteness of the data used for this chart, see notes to table 3.1 and figure 3.2.

Figure 3.2   Ratio, Reported U.S. Foundation Assets to U.S. GDP, 1930 to 2001

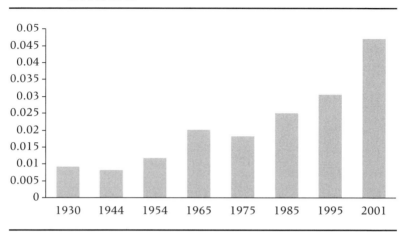

Source: Author's compilation.

The total assets of U.S. foundations exceeded 4.5 percent of gross domestic product in 2001, a substantial number and probably the highest in U.S. history. But the U.S. stock market also reached its highest valuation in history at that point. As figure 3.3 shows, the ratio of foundation assets to the total value of all U.S. common stocks was higher in the mid-1960s, just before the Tax Reform Act of 1969 curtailed some of the legal advantages a foundation charter provided to donors.

The concentration of foundation assets has been very marked; data does not allow a rigorous test of the possibility that concentration has declined over time. In 1959, ten very large foundations held 51 percent of all assets identified by the new Foundation Center. The same year, 129 "large" foundations—those whose assets exceeded $10 million—accounted for over three-quarters of the assets of all 5,202 foundations. The 1959 report was much more complete than previous reports, but certainly omitted many foundations and reported unaudited numbers (Foundation Library Center 1960). In 1979, the 231 foundations whose assets exceeded $25 million (the CPI equivalent of $10 million in 1959) accounted for two-thirds of a fuller inventory of foundation assets (Foundation Center 1981). In 2001,

Figure 3.3   Ratio, Reported Assets of U.S. Foundations to Total Value
of U.S. Common Stocks, 1930 to 2001

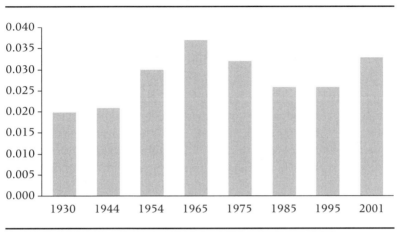

Source: Author's compilation.

the hundred largest U.S. foundations, each with assets greater than
$475 million, held almost 40 percent of all foundation assets
(Chronicle of Philanthropy 2002). The 2001 equivalent of $10 mil-
lion in 1959 was about $60 million, meaning that the share of foun-
dation assets held by foundations as large as that had probably not
changed much.

In 2003, the most current data available, 900 grant-making foundations had assets of at least $60 million. Their combined assets totaled
65.5 percent of the $476.7 billion in total assets of all 66,000+ (66,398,
to be precise) grant-making foundations in the United States. The
majority held only a few hundred thousand dollars each. Donors manage most foundations with the occasional assistance of their attorneys
and investment advisers; in 2001 just 3,000 foundations reported that
they employed their own staff (Foundation Center 2003b).

Clearly, by the 1940s the foundation had become an established
institutional form in the United States. Equally clearly, it did not dominate American nonprofit finance. Observers often exaggerate the
financial significance of foundations. Foundation spending runs at
about 5 percent of assets. In 2001, total foundation spending averaged
under $192 per capita in the Northeast, $109 in the Midwest, $66 in

the South, $99 in the West. Nationally in 2001, foundations gave $30.5 billion, just 0.3 percent of the U.S. gross domestic product (Foundation Center 2003a).

The Growth of U.S. Foundations: Definition and Distribution

Nearly all discussions of American foundations emphasize the large nonsectarian grant-making foundations that first appeared in the economically developed northeastern and Great Lakes states between 1900 and World War I. But religious and other charitable foundations have a longer history, and by 1950 were distributed more evenly across the nation. They continue to be very important—and their existence has always reinforced the claim to legitimacy made by foundations of all kinds.

Regional and substantive bias shaped the collection of information about foundations before the 1960s—and biased information has in turn shaped almost all work by historians and policy analysts. Until the late 1950s, students of foundations had to rely on information provided by foundations themselves, because the U.S. Internal Revenue Service refused to share data it collected about individual foundations.[6] Early students also relied heavily on the *New York Times* (Andrews 1973, 85, 182; Hollis 1938, 310 n. 15). The foundations at the center of the early accounts—those founded by Andrew Carnegie, John D. Rockefeller, Margaret Olivia Sage, Elizabeth Milbank Anderson, Anna Harkness, Julius Rosenwald, Lincoln Filene, and the Guggenheims—promoted secular, research-based, cooperative, often nongovernmental solutions to problems in health, education, and welfare. On a number of occasions these foundations also sought to demonstrate the value of certain activities in public health, education, and scientific research. Some of the demonstrations persuaded American governments to undertake new activities, including public libraries, public schools in the South, kindergartens, more systematic approaches to poverty, unemployment, and juvenile justice, campaigns against hookworm and tuberculosis, scientific research at state universities, and federal funding for scientific research. The Rockefeller and especially the Carnegie foundation also sought explicitly to supplement, transform, and sometimes to replace the efforts of Protestant denominations. All of these early foundations, with the single exception of Rosenwald, worked from offices in New York

City. The Ford Foundation joined this group after 1960. As part of its effort to promote change, each of these foundations published extensive information about its activities; each also encouraged its leaders to publish personal accounts (for example, Commonwealth Fund 1963; Embree and Waxman 1949, Flexner 1915; Fosdick 1952, 1962; Gates 1977; General Education Board 1964; Glenn, Brandt, and Andrews 1947; Harvey and Abrams 1986; Keppel 1930; Kiser 1975; Rockefeller Foundation 1972; Lomask 1964; Weaver et al. 1967). In writing about foundations in general, historians have relied heavily on this material—and on the Rockefeller Archive Center and the availability of archives of the Carnegie, Harkness, Russell Sage, and other foundations in this group. The result has been a history skewed by its sources of data.

A number of mid-sized foundations outside the Northeast did sometimes cooperate with the Carnegie-Rockefeller-Rosenwald group as they pursued more local civic and educational causes. Well-documented among these were the Castle Foundation in Honolulu, the Rosenberg and Haynes foundations in California, Woodruff in Georgia, Hill and Wilder in Minnesota, the Children's Fund of Michigan, the Chicago Community Trust, the Cleveland Foundation, the Maurice and Laura Falk and the Buhl foundations (and later the Howard Heinz Endowment and the Pittsburgh Foundation) in Pittsburgh, the Z. Smith Reynolds and Winston-Salem foundations in North Carolina (Richards and Norton 1957; Starrett 1966; Jarchow 1981; Tittle 1992; Sitton 1999; Castle 2004). El Pomar in Colorado, Samuel Roberts Noble in Oklahoma, and M. D. Anderson in Texas might be included, and no doubt others, too, that have not been favored with good histories (but see Noel 2000). In 1960 the first *Foundation Directory* also noted that the University of Wisconsin Alumni Foundation already had assets of $40 million—largely derived from research patents, and devoted to purposes shared by the several Carnegie and Rockefeller foundations.

But the foundation form served many purposes from the beginning, and by the 1930s numbers of foundations had appeared outside the Northeast; some of these already reported substantial assets in the 1950s. The Duke Endowment for the Carolinas, the Lilly Endowment (Indianapolis), the W. K. Kellogg (Grand Rapids, Michigan) and the Danforth (St. Louis) foundations reported assets that ranked among the ten largest in 1959, with the Kresge Foundation (Detroit) ranking just behind. Several others—including California's James Irvine, Hearst, Weingart, and perhaps Norton Simon, and Texas's Brown and Moody foundations and Houston Endowment—would almost certainly have ranked in or near that top group if they had reported their assets at full value, something the law did not require until the mid-1970s.[7] These were the largest foundations outside the Northeast, and they were joined by a score or more that were relatively large.

These foundations—like several in the Northeast—served purposes quite distinct from those of the Carnegie-Rockefeller group. Many supported local causes. Several favored not research and the building of central institutions but the application of what they took to be best current practices in public health, education, recreation, or economic development.[8] A number were devoted more or less exclusively to religious aims. A major purpose of the Irvine and Moody foundations, the Houston Endowment, and a number of others including Duke, John Hartford, Kellogg, Kresge, Lilly, and Pew, was to help an individual, a family, or a core group control a substantial business enterprise. In many more cases, donors hoped that their foundations would encourage specific philanthropic and family values among their children and grandchildren. Most of these foundations did not seek much publicity in their own states, let alone fame in Manhattan. Yet all would have insisted that they sought, through grant making, to advance the general good.

Thus though the Carnegie, Rockefeller, Rosenwald, and Ford foundations and those that worked with them have dominated scholarly discussion of American foundations,[9] the foundation world itself was always much wider and much more diverse. The fullest early effort to compile a really comprehensive list is *American Foundations* (Harrison and Andrews 1946) which took 1944 as its research year, identified just fourteen foundations in California and only three in Texas. But the first edition of the *Foundation Directory* (1960), produced with previously unavailable Internal Revenue Service data, identified thirty-five California foundations and twenty-four Texas foundations as having existed before 1944. Several of these had substantial resources.

Since the 1960s, foundation numbers and assets have grown more rapidly in the Southwest, the Pacific Coast, and the South than in the Northeast and the Great Lakes states, so that foundations are now fairly evenly distributed across the United States. Financial information reported to the IRS did not become reliable until the late 1970s.

Figure 3.4 Regional Distribution of U.S. Foundation Assets, 1979 to 2001

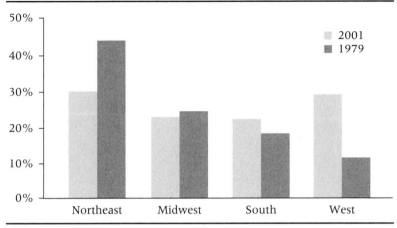

Source: The Foundation Center (1981).

Figures 3.4, 3.5, and 3.6 show both that assets have become more evenly distributed, and that foundations are still disproportionately prominent in the Northeast.

The broad history of assets and locations suggests that a discussion of foundation legitimacy in the United States must address several

Figure 3.5 Ratio, Share of Foundations to Share of Population, U.S. Regions, 2001

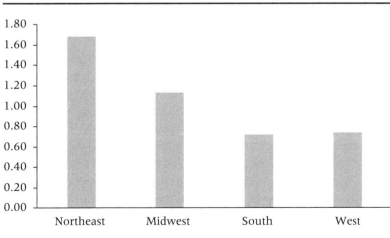

Source: U.S. Census (2001); Foundation Center (2001).

Figure 3.6   Ratio, Share of Foundation Assets to Share of
U.S. Population, 2001

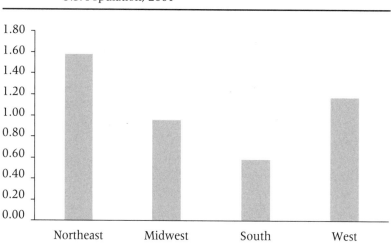

Source: U.S. Census (2001); Foundation Center (2001).

questions. Why did they appear only at the beginning of the twentieth century? How have regional variation and change affected foundation efforts to gain legitimacy? How have foundations defended their claims to legitimacy against attacks that slowed or reversed their growth in the 1930s and again in the 1960s?

Making Foundations Legitimate by the Beginning of the Twentieth Century

Dramatic legal, intellectual, and material transformations converged in the last years of the nineteenth century to create an environment that favored foundations. State legislatures began to lift traditional legal proscriptions against general purpose charities. Northeastern intellectual elites moved away from the religious commitments that had long shaped nearly all charities and charitable regulations. The new universities replaced religious denominations as the largest and most comprehensive of charities, and a small number of railroad and industrial leaders had to consider what do with fortunes of unprecedented size.

Until the end of the nineteenth century, varied statutory and legal restrictions combined to make modern general purpose foundations impossible. The nineteenth-century funds that are sometimes cited as the earliest American foundations all supported specific purposes that were quite narrowly defined. Usually these purposes were religious: the interdenominational Magdalen Society (1800)—later the White-Williams Foundation—for the care and moral education of girls in Philadelphia, and the Swedenborg Foundation (1850) for the "sole purpose" of printing and distributing "the theological writings of Emanuel Swedenborg."[10] The Peabody Education Fund (1867), sometimes listed as the first true foundation, supported efforts— usually seen by donors as religious or moral—to improve education in the South, especially for African Americans.[11]

Indeed, until the end of the nineteenth century, old rules that made it difficult in many states to bequeath assets to an undefined or prospective charity continued in force. In the late 1880s, these rules allowed distant relatives of Samuel J. Tilden to break his will, diverting to themselves more than half of the $6 million bequest he had intended for the creation of a great New York public library. At about the same time, New York State officials successfully prevented Cornell University from accepting a gift of more than $1 million, on the ground that the university's charter limited its assets to $3 million, a figure already reached (*New York Tribune,* November 28, 1888, 1, cited in Hall 1992).[12]

Most American voters approved the legal traditions that enabled potential heirs to prevent an aged paterfamilias from alienating the family farm or disbursing the assets of a respectable career to a vaguely defined charity. But such traditions seemed out of place when they enabled the distant relatives of a very rich man to deny a great fortune to a university or a library intended to provide wide public benefit. In 1893, New York State changed its laws regulating the creation of charitable trusts, making it possible to create foundations (Katz, Sullivan, and Beach 1985). One new law allowed the creation of a general foundation and exempted from tax

the real property of a corporation or association organized exclusively for the moral and mental improvement of men and women or for religious, charitable, missionary, hospital, educational, patriotic, historical or cemetery purposes, or for two or more of such purposes, and used exclusively for carrying out thereupon one or more of such purposes.

[A second new law laid it down as state policy that] no gift, grant, bequest or devise to religious, educational, charitable, or benevolent uses, which shall in other respects be valid under the laws of this state, shall be deemed invalid by reason of the indefiniteness or uncertainty or the persons designated as the beneficiaries thereunder in the instrument creating the same. (State of New York 1893, I:1077–78, II:1748)

The next year, the United States Congress passed a federal income tax act that specifically exempted "corporations, companies, or associations organized and conducted solely for charitable, religious, or educational purposes . . . the stocks, shares, funds, or securities held by any fiduciary or trustee for charitable, religious, or educational purposes" (Diamond 2002, 134–35).[13]

The U.S. Supreme Court struck down this income tax law on the ground that it violated a constitutional prohibition against direct taxes. Once the Sixteenth Amendment allowing an income tax was adopted in 1913, Congress did pass an income tax act—and it contained the same broad exemption for charitable organizations.

A new intellectual and institutional climate provided the context for these changes in tax law. All through the nineteenth century, Protestant denominations and the Catholic Church dominated what is now called the nonprofit field. Religious organizations sponsored most nonpublic schools and colleges; religious organizations ran nearly all orphanages and homes for abandoned and wayward children and homes for the aged; most clinics and hospitals operated under the auspices of a religious group.[14] Denominational and interdenominational funds supported students in colleges and divinity schools.[15] Men educated in denominational colleges and often then in theological schools headed most private organizations of these kinds, and public schools, county hospitals and poorhouses, and state asylums for the mentally ill drew their leaders largely from this source (Haskell 1977). These patterns suggest how Princeton, which lacked professional schools apart from divinity, could serve as a national center for the education of Presbyterians for such public service; Yale, for Congregationalists; Columbia, for Episcopalians; Harvard for Unitarians; Brown for northern Baptists. John D. Rockefeller initially intended that the University of Chicago would educate Baptist leaders for the West, as Sewanee was doing for Southern Episcopalians, Baylor for Southern Baptists, Emory for Southern Methodists (Rudolph 1962).

But the rise of new science-based research universities—pioneered by the Johns Hopkins University, Clark, and Stanford as well as by new initiatives at Harvard, Yale, and Columbia—challenged this pattern. By the end of the nineteenth century, the institutions sponsored by religious bodies had already fallen behind research universities in the size of their assets. With their laboratories, museums, libraries, theaters, and expanding facilities for student life, the new research universities had also become far more general and comprehensive than the traditional charities in their purposes and activities. To the teaching of undergraduates they added expanding programs of graduate and professional study; to the study of classic books their faculties added scientific research in a limitless array of fields and topics. As America's leading private universities built up substantial endowments to support their expanding activities, they became, in effect, the prototype for the general purpose foundation.

A critical shift in the intellectual environment reinforced these shifts. In the last two or three decades of the nineteenth century, influential intellectuals—especially in the cities of the Northeast, the Great Lakes states, and the Pacific Coast—turned away from the explicit belief in revealed religion and the immanent presence of God that had previously dominated institutional life in the United States. As historian Thomas Haskell has demonstrated, authority for social knowledge and social practice increasingly came via peer review by "communities of the competent" rather than from the study of the revealed truths of religious texts (1977; compare Turner 1985). Especially in the Northeast, the Midwest, and the far West, university-trained professionals—doctors, engineers, lawyers, and economists more than professors—were rapidly replacing Unitarian, Episcopalian, Presbyterian, and Congregationalist ministers as arbiters of social belief and as institutional leaders.[16]

It was in this context that Andrew Carnegie published his famous thoughts on the proper uses of wealth for charitable purposes, and that John D. Rockefeller began to make his great donations. Persuaded that donations could easily do more harm than good, Carnegie gave careful thought to his giving. He struck a remarkable balance among some of the most influential values and rhetorical themes of his day: he favored individual self-reliance, self-improvement, and social mobility, as well as stable community institutions designed to promote self-help. The "rich man," Carnegie concluded, should "know that the best means of benefiting the community is to place within its reach the ladders upon which the aspiring can rise—free libraries, parks, and means of recreation, by which men are helped in body and mind; works of art, certain to give pleasure and improve the public taste; and public institutions of various kinds, which will improve the general condition of the people" (1889/1990).

Carnegie ultimately gave away over $300 million (almost $6 billion in 2005 dollars) for such objects. To help with this task, he placed funds for various purposes under the control of boards "dominated by men of affairs, who have within reach the expert element with which they can confer," and included on his boards individuals "directly from the people . . . in touch with the masses" and therefore capable of adding a "popular" perspective.[17] The Carnegie Institution of Pittsburgh (1895) followed this model, as did the Carnegie Institution of Washington, D.C. (1902), and the Carnegie Endowment for International Peace and the Carnegie Foundation for the Advancement of Teaching for purposes indicated by their names (1910). Carnegie's proto-foundations put large endowments to the service of nonsectarian, nonreligious activities. But each of them was devoted to a specific purpose. The same was true of the early funds set up by Rockefeller and others.[18]

Given the legal context of their times, Carnegie and Rockefeller's vast fortunes were leading them toward the general purpose foundation. But it was Margaret Olivia Slocum Sage who took the final decisive step. In 1902 she had inherited a fortune of more than $70 million from her husband, Russell Sage. Five years later she devoted the largest portion of that fortune to a general purpose foundation. Its 1907 New York State charter, developed for Mrs. Sage by her attorney, Robert W. deForest, committed the Russell Sage Foundation simply (and grandly) to working for "the improvement of social and living conditions in the United States of America" (Glenn, Brandt, and Andrews 1947; Hammack and Wheeler 1994). This act won widespread praise, and several very large general purpose foundations quickly followed the Russell Sage example: the Carnegie Corporation of New York (1911); the Rockefeller Foundation (1913); the Julius Rosenwald Fund and the Surdna Foundation (1917); the Commonwealth Fund (1918) (for brief sketches, see Keele and Kiger 1984). Avoidance of federal taxes was not a motive in most of these cases; the

Russell Sage Foundation, the Carnegie Corporation, and the Rocke-feller Foundation all predated the U.S. income tax. For Sage, Carnegie, Rockefeller, and Rosenwald, the attraction of the foundation form lay in the fact that if cleverly employed a foundation could influence a large number of institutions.

Through the 1950s: Big Eastern Foundations

No sooner did they appear on the American scene than the big east-ern foundations found themselves under attack. Even as they took strong action to promote a new set of secular, research-based organi-zations, the Carnegie, Rockefeller, and related foundations deflected criticism by aligning themselves with well-established and more broadly based institutions and practices. They built on the American commitments both to the right of free expression and to private prop-erty, arguing that those who build large fortunes have a right to direct them to charitable purposes largely of their own choosing. But the big eastern foundations did defer to public opinion, limiting or ending studies of labor and race. And with few exceptions, they quickly decided not to act on their own, but through grants to other institu-tions, especially America's already well-established nonprofit organi-zations. In addition, key foundation leaders took steps to enable people of quite limited means to give through community foundations, build-ing on long-standing religious-based fundraising traditions to extend more widely the possibility of involvement in foundation activity. And, over the years, foundations gradually made themselves more transparent. Together, these steps enabled American foundations to defend their autonomy and their claims to legitimacy.

The enormous fortunes of some late nineteenth-century business leaders had, of course, attracted strong criticism.[19] Some of the wealth-iest responded by contributing to foundations and endowed insti-tutions; in addition to foundations, major gifts went to the Johns Hopkins, Stanford, Duke, and Rice universities as well as to Columbia, Pennsylvania, Yale, and Harvard, and to a number of more narrowly focused hospitals, museums, and orchestras. Many large fortunes, it should be added, did not go to such charities.

Perhaps the best way to deflect criticism for excessive wealth was to create a new institution under the authority of the federal govern-ment, and for a time political leaders encouraged such acts. In 1902

President Theodore Roosevelt agreed to sit on the board of the Carnegie Institution in Washington. John D. Rockefeller obtained a special congressional charter for the General Education Board in 1903, and in 1906 Andrew Carnegie obtained a congressional charter for the Carnegie Foundation for the Advancement of Teaching. At the beginning of the twentieth century, others also sought the prestige of a federal charter for private enterprises that aspired to national leadership: the Red Cross received a congressional charter in 1900, the Boy Scouts, in 1916 (Wall 1970, 860, 873; Chernow 1998, 484).[20]

But many continued to disapprove of great wealth, and when John D. Rockefeller sought a charter for the Rockefeller Foundation in 1910, Congress refused. At the time, the U.S. Department of Justice was seeking to break up the Standard Oil Company on antitrust grounds, and political leaders were not willing to honor Rockefeller with a federal charter. Then in 1913 Congress authorized a special body, the U.S. Commission on Industrial Relations, to investigate the causes of violent conflict between capital and labor. Frank Walsh, who became the leader of this commission, used its hearings to attack John D. Rockefeller, Jr., who had been in charge of affairs during a mining conflict that had led to the deaths of coal miners and more than a dozen of their wives and children in what was known as the Ludlow Massacre in Colorado. Walsh made a special point of criticizing Rockefeller, Jr.'s use of foundation funds to employ a specialist—University of Chicago graduate William Lyon MacKenzie King, who would go on to a long career as prime minister of Canada—to advise him on labor relations.

Walsh concluded that "foundations appear to be a menace to the welfare of society." The Rockefeller Foundation in particular, he insisted, took "money . . . from the toil of thousands of poorly nourished, socially submerged men, women, and children," then dispersed it "thru a board of personal employees" in such a way as to "exact a tribute of loyalty from the whole profession of scientists, social workers, and economists" (Walsh 1915, 262–64; on Rockefeller, Jr., and William Lyon MacKenzie King, see Chernow 1998, chaps. 28, 29). American Federation of Labor leaders added that through its salaries to experts, the Rockefeller Foundation and the General Education Board were covertly seeking to "Rockefellerize" federal studies of agriculture and education. "Information," Samuel Gompers concluded in 1917, "is of value only when salient facts associated with its development are known. Research, inspired by Standard Oil funds, should bear the Standard Oil trade-mark—research that bears the imprint of government sanction should be made by bona fide government agencies" (207).

Walsh and the American Federation of Labor criticized Rockefeller's philanthropies from the viewpoint of labor. Conservative Christians also criticized them. When Andrew Carnegie created a large fund to provide pensions to college professors, the fund's administrators operated under requirements that forced several church-related colleges to abandon denominational ties. Affected colleges included Wesleyan (Connecticut), Drury (Missouri), Drake and Coe (Iowa), and Central University of Kentucky (Hollis 1938). In 1909 Baptist leader Warren A. Candler denounced Carnegie's "Vast Scheme for Capturing and Controlling the Colleges." Two years later Presbyterian Princeton complained that the Carnegie Foundation was separating the church from "her colleges" (Candler 1909; Bryan 1911). The influential conservative publicist Marvin Olasky recently reminded his readers that the small initial group of eastern general purpose foundations encountered criticism for hostility to religion and support for federal power. By 1920, Olasky asserts, the president of the National Conference of Social Work (whose offices were in the Russell Sage Foundation's New York building) was stating that his professional colleagues "did not wish to 'defend' the Bible, the Church, the flag or the Constitution" (1992, 144).[21] The charge, advanced by some critics, that early foundations failed to take bold action—like the parallel claim of some early foundation leaders that they took pains to avoid controversy—simply ignores the Carnegie demand that colleges sever denominational ties and John D. Rockefeller's refusal to support Baptist missions.

These criticisms prevented Rockefeller from obtaining a federal charter for the Rockefeller Foundation, though they did not lead to general antifoundation legislation.[22] Rockefeller and his advisers rethought their approach to philanthropy. Raymond B. Fosdick, a close associate of Rockefeller charities from 1913 and president of the Rockefeller Foundation between 1936 and 1948, wrote somewhat disingenuously that the foundation's leaders concluded that

> except for a narrow range of noncontroversial subjects, notably public health, medicine, and agriculture, the foundation's participation in the areas it wished to assist must be limited to grants to outside agencies

competently organized and staffed to carry on the work in question. In other words, the foundation must become primarily not an operating agency but a fund-dispensing agency. This new policy obviously did not imply that the foundation would avoid controversial questions. It meant that its approach to such questions would take the form of grants to agencies independent of foundation control. In no other way could the objectivity of research be established beyond cavil and the projects freed from suspicion of ulterior motive. (1952, quoted in Goulden 1971, 96)

The Carnegie Institution expressed similar conclusions: "It appears to be the part of wisdom to pursue chiefly those researches which meet with approval, rather than opposition, from contemporary society" (Hollis 1938, 246).

The largest general purpose foundations sought to avoid criticism through two tactics. They worked through a few prominent existing nonprofit organizations (and some new ones), focusing their gifts on universities and other "agencies independent of foundation control" that nonetheless shared their determination to raise American standards in nonsectarian, science-based higher education and research. And they developed what Ellen Condliffe Lagemann (1983) has usefully called "technologies of influence" for their efforts to shape private action and public policy.

Grants to nonprofit institutions fit seamlessly into existing American patterns of philanthropic behavior, and no doubt helped the big foundations gain legitimacy. Initially, the Carnegie and Rockefeller foundations emphasized grants for buildings and endowment. Andrew Carnegie set the stage through his personal gifts for public library buildings and for the support of a selected group of institutions that helped young men gain technical education: Hampton Institute, the Franklin Fund in Boston, the Cooper Union in New York, the Stevens Institute in Hoboken, New Jersey, the Carnegie Institute in Pittsburgh (Wall 1970, 816–19, 823, 826,1043). Carnegie's foundations, like Rockefeller's, went on to make large grants for endowment and buildings to several colleges and universities, then to emphasize "special endowments, such as medical education [and] teachers' salaries" and the great professors' retirement fund that evolved into the remarkable Teachers' Insurance and Annuity Association (Hollis 1938, 32).[23]

These gifts came with strings, requiring colleges to eliminate debt, maintain a significant endowment, find matching grants, standardize basic admissions policies.[24] Most controversially, the Carnegie Endowment for the Advancement of Teaching required that a college board of trustees demonstrate independence from a religious denomination; initially, Vanderbilt was the sole southern college to accept this condition.[25] To win support for its medical school, a university had to introduce specific organizational reforms and win approval as a national leader (Wheatley 1988). The big eastern foundations concentrated their gifts on an elite group of institutions; in the 1920s and 1930s, according to a well-informed estimate, just twenty universities received almost three-quarters of their funds.[26] University, denominational, and community leaders objected to the conditions attached to many grants, and to the emphasis on a short list of institutions.[27] In effect, we might well conclude, the big eastern foundations held assets for the support of specific initiatives at a select group of universities and colleges.

Although early foundations did support an approach to southern education that southern legislatures accepted, many African American leaders found it far from uncontroversial. The Peabody Fund, the Southern Education Board, and the other early proto-foundation endowments for southern education insisted that they did as much for African American education as possible in the context of brutally harsh southern white suppression of African American aspirations. Southern states provided little education to white or blacks, so the northern funds undertook to advance education for all. The northern funds did provide monies for the education of African Americans that were not otherwise available in the South. But they could do so only on terms acceptable to white southerners, and many statements of foundation leaders read as though their policies reflected a shared racism. Louis Harlan, Eric Anderson, John Stansfield, and other historians have argued that the result was, at least in some ways, to increase the relative disadvantage of southern blacks (Harlan 1958; Stanfield 1985; Anderson 1988; Anderson and Moss 1999).

Lagemann (1983) described as "technologies of influence" the second approach taken by the Carnegie, Rockefeller, Russell Sage, Twentieth Century Fund, and a few other foundations. Responding to allegations that the Rockefellers intended to control of knowledge—and eager to exert influence beyond the value of their grants—the leading foundations arranged their studies with great care. With many studies they sought the sort of influence attributed to the White Papers sometimes commissioned by British governments; in the cases of medical education, the definition of an undergraduate college, and perhaps race relations, they came close to success. The Russell Sage Foundation introduced another protective device when, in response to unhappiness with the pro-labor stance of Mary Van Kleeck, one of its chief investigators, it began to add to each book it published a disclaimer stating that

> In formulating the problem for study, in mapping out a plan of work on it, in collecting facts, in drawing conclusions, and in the presentation of findings, authors of Foundation studies, who are always either members of the staff or specially commissioned research workers, have the benefit of the criticism and advice of their colleagues in the organization. Full freedom is given research workers for the final decision on all of these steps, and in presenting and interpreting both factual material and conclusions in their own way. While the general responsibility for management of the Foundation is vested in the Board of Trustees, the responsibility for facts, conclusions, and interpretations rests with the research workers alone and not upon the Foundation, its trustees, or other members of its staff. Publication under its imprint does not imply agreement by the organization or its members with opinions or interpretations of authors. It does imply that care has been taken that the research on which a book is based has been thoroughly done.[28]

The Milbank Memorial Fund, the Russell Sage Foundation, and the Twentieth Century Fund established themselves through their own publications, but the biggest northeastern foundations worked, again as Fosdick put it, through "agencies independent of foundation control." In this way, they hoped to establish "the objectivity of research . . . beyond cavil" and free their projects "from suspicion of ulterior motive" (1952, 28). The Rockefeller and Carnegie foundations set up and contributed to creditable research institutes and scientific and scholarly associations in many fields (examples include the Social Science Research Council, the National Bureau of Economic Research, the American Council of Learned Societies, and several scientific societies). They provided fellowships for advanced study in the fields they favored, enabling capable people to develop expertise and also to gain impressive credentials.[29] They found study directors whose qualities and credentials would impress target audiences; Abraham Flexner was one of the first, Gunnar Myrdal one of the best known. In such fields as public health, mental health, social work, education, and city planning, the Milbank Memorial, Commonwealth Fund, Russell Sage, and Carnegie foundations found ways to engage civic and governmental leaders from across the United States (Eaton and Harrison 1930; Hammack and Wheeler 1994).

Community foundations also helped establish the legitimacy of the foundation form. Composed of a group (or community) of funds, a community foundation serves a limited geographic region (or occasionally an otherwise specified community) of donors and potential beneficiaries (Hammack 2005). Frederick H. Goff, one of John D. Rockefeller's Cleveland attorneys, organized the first community foundation in 1914. As a witness before Frank Walsh and the Commission on Industrial Relations, Goff won praise for the community foundation. Goff's Cleveland Trust Company sponsored the Cleveland Foundation, but arranged for civic leaders as well as public officials—the mayor and two senior judges—to appoint members of the "distribution committee" that approved grants. Goff added, "our trust, lacking the resources of the Rockefellers, is especially open to poor people with enough idealism about small amounts of philanthropy to want these to be kept always useful as the years go by" (Howard 1963, 21). Walsh could only agree that such a foundation was an excellent idea. Newspapers across the nation praised the community foundation idea as Goff presented it. Within months, bankers in several other cities established community foundations: Chicago, Minneapolis, Boston, and Los Angeles in 1915, Philadelphia in 1918, Winston-Salem in 1919, New York City in 1923. Community foundations enjoyed considerable support from local chambers of commerce. In their devotion to generalized notions of doing good, in their deference to local leaders whose virtue was widely recognized, and in their reliance on gifts, small as well as large, from many donors, community foundations resembled denominational education and mission funds, and that resemblance, too, must have helped make community foundations, and perhaps foundations in general, seem more legitimate (Hammack 1989; Hall 1989).[30]

For several decades, many foundations fought to remain out of the public eye. But a small group began early to publicize information about foundations and their work. As early as 1915, the Russell Sage Foundation, the Twentieth Century Fund, and the fundraising firm Raymond Rich and Associates assembled and published lists of foundations; they counted twenty-seven in 1915, 179 in 1929, and 243 in

1939.[31] The early lists emphasized substantial funders of efforts to improve "social welfare," as the Russell Sage Foundation understood it, including health, education, social services, poor relief, job training, and housing, as well as higher education and research. Although they were not among the very biggest, Russell Sage and the Twentieth Century Fund maintained close relations with the Carnegie, Rockefeller, Rosenwald, and associated foundations in the Northeast and the Great Lakes states, and their lists emphasized these fields and regions.[32]

F. Emerson Andrews's 1943 effort to prepare the first really comprehensive list of all United States foundations demonstrated some of the divisions among American foundations. Andrews and his Russell Sage associates identified 505 active, independent, nonreligious foundations in the field of social welfare whose assets exceeded $50,000 as of 1944. They gathered evidence that as many as 400 other foundations met these criteria, but despite persistent effort failed to win enough cooperation from them to include them in the final book (Harrison and Andrews 1946). Three-fifths of the 505 Andrews did include were in New York, Massachusetts, and Pennsylvania. Andrews had taken on a difficult task. In the 1940s the Internal Revenue Service "did not open its records to public inspection," and of the 505 funds Andrews was able to include in his 1946 directory, "141 (28 percent) would not cooperate, 49 refusing information and 92 never replying to repeated requests" (1973, 85, 86).[33] A Raymond Rich and Associates 1948 study asserted that foundations "which refuse or fail to reveal their purposes and the main outlines of their operations endanger their own status and the privileges enjoyed by all other foundations." To emphasize "the quasi-public character of these endowments" and to press for "full cooperation" in the future, it listed the name and address of more than 400 foundations that had provided "little or no information" (Rich and Deardorff 1948, 244–65).

With funds from other foundations as well as from its own resources, the Russell Sage Foundation undertook other efforts to obtain and publish information on foundations through the 1950s and 1960s. Together, these efforts produced much of the first round of reliable reports[34] and also the first scholarly work on philanthropy in the fields of history and economics.[35]

Andrews undertook a much more ambitious survey in 1956 when he launched the Foundation Center. The task had become only a little easier, though he enjoyed substantial financial support from the Carnegie Corporation and Russell Sage, as well as promised access to reports that foundations filed with the Internal Revenue Service. The Ford and Rockefeller foundations soon provided substantial additional funding, making it possible for the center to create a much more definitive *Foundation Directory* (1960), which in its first edition of 1960 provided information on 5,202 foundations with assets of at least $50,000. But Andrews soon learned that although his assistants could look at foundation reports to the IRS, an order of President Eisenhower forbade them to photograph them. (Eisenhower was responding to the embarrassment of one of his business friends and supporters at the publication of a photograph of part of his tax return.) Continuing hard work and increasing congressional and public demand for information enabled the Foundation Center to break through these limitations.[36] His consistent efforts to obtain information won a place for Andrews as a spokesman for legitimate foundations at several congressional hearings (Andrews 1973).

Through the 1950s: Regional Diversity

If nearly all American foundations had pursued a single national, nonsectarian, moderately progressive agenda from a base in New York City, their effort to establish themselves as legitimate American institutions might very well have provoked stiffer opposition, and perhaps failed altogether. A neglected key to the persistence of the American foundation is the fact that foundations existed across the entire United States, serving many purposes. It is true that the Carnegie, Rockefeller, and associated foundations—including, from the 1960s, the Ford Foundation—did hold the bulk of the money—at least, of the acknowledged money. But those pursuing other agendas were numerous, and held much more money than outsiders knew. Often at odds with the big eastern foundations and with "The East" in general, many southern and western foundations refused to participate in the early listings that have shaped our understanding of foundation history.[37]

Foundations are almost always chartered by state governments, almost never by Congress, making states the most important foundation regulators. States make and enforce their own rules. A donor who does not like the rules in one state can go to another. New York State liberalized its rules regulating the creation of charitable trusts in the 1890s after the Tilden will—New York Public Library case. Thenceforth, New York's hospitality to foundations accounted for a good deal of its early prominence in the field. New York City's position at the center of North America's investment and publishing markets reinforced this advantage. If other states wished to encourage wealthy people to establish foundations within their own borders, they had to consider New York as a formidable competitor. Andrew Carnegie made much of his fortune in Pittsburgh, John D. Rockefeller in Cleveland, Henry Ford in Detroit, James B. Duke in the Carolinas, William Randolph Hearst in California: all based their foundations in Manhattan.

Competition for charitable funds, as well as competition for some of the business of managing them, led other states not to restrict foundations, but to encourage them. A 1925 Texas law, to take a striking example, imposed an inheritance tax of up to 20 percent on property left to charities outside the state, but exempted from tax property left for "any religious, educational, or charitable organization, when such bequests were to be used within the state of Texas" (Nielsen 1972, 152). This law remained on the books for forty years, and it helps explain why Texas became home to so many foundations, including a goodly number of large ones.

And in Texas many foundations supported religious, especially Protestant, purposes quite distinct from those favored by the Carnegie-Rockefeller-Rosenwald group. Among the lone star state's notable foundations were the Oldham Little Church Fund, the LeTourneau Foundation "for the gospel of Jesus Christ," and the Baptist Foundation of Texas. Of the thirty-seven Texas foundations listed in the *Foundation Directory* for 1979 (the first to reflect the fuller reporting requirements of the Tax Reform Act of 1969) as founded before 1950, twenty funded Protestant causes specifically, four funded Jewish causes.[38]

Throughout the South and West, many foundations supported Protestant and local institutions. Among the largest southeastern foundations (after the Duke Endowment, which supported Southern Methodist Duke and Southern Baptist Furman) were Georgia's J. Bulow Campbell Foundation for Southern Presbyterians and Lettie Pate Evans Foundation for "poor Christian girls." Kentucky was home to the Christian Education and Ministerial Relief of the Presbyterian Church in the United States (southern) of Louisville, and the Student Loan Fund of the Board of Education of the Methodist Church, based in Nashville. State Baptist foundations appeared in North Carolina in

1919 and in Virginia in 1923 (Smart 1970, 17). Oklahoma's large J. E. and L. E. Mabee Foundation also aided Protestant organizations. California's George Pepperdine Foundation, Colorado's El Pomar, and others in the far West supported Protestant causes. Of sixty-six California foundations listed in the 1979 *Foundation Directory* as predating 1950, fifteen specifically funded Protestant, six Jewish, and three Catholic causes.

In the Midwest, Lilly, Danforth, and Kresge all provided direct support to Protestant theological schools, denominational education, and churches (Pattillo and Mackenzie 1965; Chitty 1979). So did many other substantial foundations, including the Carrie J. Loose Fund of Kansas City, the Siebert Lutheran Fund of Wisconsin, and the Christian Foundation of Indianapolis.

Indeed, despite a general commitment to nonsectarian and scientific efforts, the Rockefeller (Schenkel 1995) and several of the other very large early American foundations provided substantial support to religious, and specifically to Protestant causes. Given the scale of religious activity in the United States, it would have been surprising if this had not been so. The 1940 edition of the *Christian Education Handbook* listed more than 500 church-related colleges in the United States, not including schools of theology, junior colleges, and bible colleges. Catholics sponsored 154. Methodists and Baptists (divided among northern and southern, white and African American branches) each sponsored more than sixty. Presbyterians (also divided north from south) and Congregationalists together sponsored another sixty. Various Lutheran denominations sponsored more than twenty-five. Twenty or more smaller denominations sponsored one college—or a dozen. The *Christian Education Handbook* included "a selected list" of fifty-three "educational and religious foundations" relevant to church colleges (Wickey and Anderson 1940, 306–09).[39]

The Baptist Foundation of Texas served, in effect, as a community foundation for the state's Southern Baptists and institutions. In the late 1920s, Baptist business leaders found that the several Baptist colleges of Texas "had no money; that they had no assets, or if they did, no one knew how to handle them" (Smart 1970, 5). Even the largest, Baylor University, "did not have anything except some old buildings . . . [its only assembly hall was] an old frame shack" (5). To manage existing resources and persuade donors to provide more, the committee concluded, it would be essential "to create a foundation, under the supervision, ownership, and control of the Baptist General Convention, to be managed by competent, experienced laymen, who will be given the responsibility of handling and investing and re-investing" the funds of all Baptist institutions (5). The Baptist Foundation of Texas managed the endowment funds of more than a dozen colleges, hospitals, and orphanages, and raised new funds for these institutions or for donor-designated Baptist causes from hundreds of individuals. A few donors had made substantial fortunes in oil, cattle, or real estate, but many had placed their modest retirement assets with the foundation in return for a life income. By 1948 this foundation claimed assets of nearly $14 million (the CPI equivalent of $110 million in 2004), enough to put it in the top twenty-five nationally. In view of the size of its assets and the large number of its donors—and in view of the size of the Texas delegation in Congress, it was not surprising that A. B. Culbertson, one of its most active directors, testified before a congressional committee that was considering revisions to the laws regulating foundations in 1950 (66, 81–82).

Protestants did not monopolize early foundation effort. Wisconsin's de Rance, Oklahoma's Warren, California's Doheny, and several others focused on Catholic efforts. Quite a number of smaller foundations, located in New York City and also in many other places, have always supported Jewish causes.[40]

Other relatively well-funded early foundations supported the institutions—including the religious institutions—of their own regions. The Mary A. Crocker Trust in San Francisco dated from 1889. The Dallas Foundation, a community foundation launched in 1929, and the Houston Endowment, created by businessman Jesse H. Jones in 1937, put considerable resources into local nonprofits in many fields. Pew in Pennsylvania, Callaway in Georgia, the W. K. Kellogg, and Charles Stuart Mott foundations in Michigan, and many others all devoted substantial resources to local causes before 1960.[41]

The W. K. Kellogg Foundation applied principles typical of midwestern foundations devoted to local causes. Kellogg trustees early concluded that though several "foundations were supporting basic research in the health and educational fields . . . the gap was too great between this research and what was known concerning many of the health and education problems at the community level." Kellogg therefore focused on "the application of existing knowledge." Kellogg also decided to support only responsible government and private agencies that had identified important problems, had "a good plan for accomplishing results," and were "willing to contribute some of their own time and resources to a solution" (Savage 1956, 9–10; see also Fugate 1997). In practice Kellogg encouraged local communities and state colleges to improve small hospitals, clinics, and schools, and to develop short practical courses to improve the skills of those who worked in them. After World War II, Kellogg emphasized county extension services and state college continuing education efforts.

Conclusion: Ties to Nonprofit Sector Provide Legitimacy

The key turns in American debates on the legitimacy of foundations occurred at the end of the nineteenth century and in the second and seventh decades of the twentieth. Those debates concerned a basic question. Can a donor or group of donors create a permanent fund for a general and unspecified charitable purpose? Before the 1890s, the answer was always "no." By the second decade of the twentieth century, it was generally "yes." The question had to be answered at the state level, but Congress also took it up, first when Carnegie and Rockefeller sought federal charters for their foundations, then in the context of early debates about exemptions from the income tax. As early as the 1920s, critics of foundations had lost the argument both on Capitol Hill and in most states, which quickly began to compete with one another in efforts to keep charitable funds within their borders. The much-studied group of big eastern foundations—Carnegie, Rockefeller, Rosenwald, and several others that shared their goals— long focused their donations on efforts to build nonsectarian scientific and medical research institutes and universities. During World War II and the Cold War these foundations also supported the commitment of private as well as state universities and institutes to American military and diplomatic campaigns in ways that enhanced foundation legitimacy in the eyes of some and but not others.[42] But the big foundations also followed Andrew Carnegie's public library campaign with support for public education and public health. And many early foundations always favored more traditional religious and community purposes. Foundations of all kinds did most of their work through grants to nonprofit organizations. As the nonprofit sector grew, foundations grew—in size and numbers as well as in legitimacy—with the sector as a whole.

American foundations came under renewed attack in the early 1950s and the late 1960s. Their critics mounted extensive congressional hearings, intrusive investigations, and sustained efforts to arouse public opinion (Lankford 1964; Andrews 1968; Shulman et al. 1972; Andrews 1973; Hall 1992; Diamond 1992, 299–301; Kelley 2004, 67–68). In the mid-1950s the Rockefeller Foundation, for example, "checked the names of BAAS officers and committee members against 7 anticommunist indices, including the 'Cumulative index to publications of the Committee on un-American Activities,' 'Cox-Reece committee index,' and the 'McCarthy Committee composite index'" (Parmar 2004, 22). Yet Congress took no substantial action on the basis of these attacks. Although they did not fully balance the timidity of some foundations, others, ranging from the Ford and Cleveland foundations to the Stern Family Fund, the Field Foundation of New York, and the Taconic Foundation, became bolder. By 1960 these foundations were providing grants—mostly quite small—for assertive social justice causes ranging from "civil liberties, economic well-being, minority rights (including citizenship and voter registration)" to "health and environmental safety" (Rabinowitz 1990, 6–8, quoted in Bothwell 2005). And foundations continued to grow strongly in numbers and assets.

The attacks that culminated in the Patman hearings did result in significant legislation. The Tax Reform Act of 1969 was followed by an extended period in which foundation assets grew less rapidly than the American economy. Congressional criticism and new regulations may well account for the slowdown, though it may also have been due to the combination of inflation and slow economic growth in these years. And, after an extensive struggle, the foundations emerged with their powers largely intact (see, for example, Brilliant 2000; Edie 1987). In the 1980s foundation growth did revive.

How did they defend their legitimacy, their right to exist and to expand, against the successive postwar attacks? Foundation leaders did not strongly defend the use of foundations to control businesses, let alone to enrich donors and their families. Although they objected to government regulation on principle, foundation leaders accepted new rules that imposed such limits under the Tax Reform Act of 1969. They also accepted the requirement—already anticipated by many of the leading foundations—that they limit their grants to tax-exempt public charities, to government agencies, and to individuals only for the acquisition of new knowledge or skills, or as prizes recognizing achievement.

American foundations also reorganized and professionalized to improve their ability to interact with the public and with government. More and more individual foundations added professional staff. Through extensive consultations that focused in part on the Peterson Commission and the Filer Commission, both organized by John D. Rockefeller 3rd, they created a new set of national umbrella organizations. They expanded the Foundation Center and turned an association of community foundations into the comprehensive Council on Foundations. They supported establishing Independent Sector, Incorporated, to represent the interests of all American nonprofits. They created the National Center for Charitable Statistics, long hosted by Independent Sector, now at the Urban Institute.[43] The struggles of these organizations to persuade foundations to join and support them provide a continuing illustration of the cultural and regional diversity of foundations in the United States.

Foundations did object to congressional proposals to require a 6 percent payout rate and to pay a 4 percent annual federal tax. By the mid-1970s Congress had agreed to reduce the payout rate to 5 percent and cut the annual tax to 2 percent; in 1986 the tax was further reduced to 1 percent. Continuing a very old trend, American foundation leaders also accepted the new legislation's demand that they reveal more information. After 1969 foundations filed more complete and accurate reports with the Internal Revenue Service, the Foundation Center greatly expanded its provision of information, and as digital technology improved foundations created and supported the GuideStar Web site through which the reports that foundations and other nonprofits file with the Internal Revenue Service are made available to anyone who has access to the web.

Most important, American foundations emerged out of an American nonprofit sector that was already well established at the end of the nineteenth century, and they have always worked largely through nonprofit organizations. Many westerners and southerners continued to criticize the Rockefeller, Carnegie, and other big eastern foundations for godlessness, statism, and arrogance. But outside the labor and liberal movements, few critics have argued that the wealthy should not have the right to dispose of wealth as they pleased, especially if they directed their gifts through nonprofits. Influential public officials, in the South and West as well as in the Northeast and Midwest, have always been well aware of the religious and community-oriented foundations in their own states. As early as the 1920s, leaders in most states were much more interested in increasing local foundation resources than in curbing the activities of the most famous northeastern foundations. They understood that national regulation would affect foundations they liked, as well as foundations they did not like. The result has been a political culture that accepts the legitimacy of foundations across the United States.[44] When Congress did move to tighten the regulation of American foundations in the 1970s, it acted only to bind them more tightly than ever to the nonprofit sector as a whole.

Notes

1. A classic statement appeared in the 1938 report of the Baptist Foundation of Texas: "It is endowment or death! . . . . faculties cannot live from tuition alone, lest the tuition be raised to a point where boys and girls of ordinary means cannot pay" (Smart 1970, 56). The list of foundation purposes in this paragraph is expanded from the one I included in an earlier study (Hammack 1999, 43–68).
2. Hollis further quotes Turgot as writing, "To forsee with certainty that an establishment will produce only the effect desired from it, and no effect at variance with its object; to discern, beyond the illusion of a near and apparent good, the real evils which a long series of unseen causes may bring about—this would need the effort of the most profound genius."
3. Peter Dobkin Hall (1992) has argued that the nonprofit sector has been a recognized sphere of American life only since the 1970s. Much evidence suggests otherwise. The term nonprofit sector was not widely used before the 1960s, but the concept, under the term "eleemosynary," was clearly stated in the John Marshall's Decision and Joseph Story's concurring opinion in the *Dartmouth College Case* of 1819. It was involved in debates over the boards of the Protestant denominations in the antebellum decades. It was restated in national debates over tax exemption for charitable organizations in the 1870s, the 1890s (the income tax act of 1893 exempted "corporations, companies, or associations organized and conducted solely for charitable, religious, or educational purposes"), and the 1910s. Discussions of "endowments" by money managers in the early 1930s and of "philanthropy" in a Carnegie-subsidized, YMCA-published overview of the 1940s explicitly grouped religious, educational, medical, and social service organizations in a single category (see following discussions as well as Wood, Struthers & Co. 1932, chap. 1; Jenkins 1950).
4. Economists have argued that nonprofits provide goods that cannot win government support because they lack support from the "median voter," and that profit-seeking businesses cannot provide due to the "free rider,"

"contract failure," and other problems. All this is true, but of course voters operate within the framework of specific constitutions and political cultures, and consumers can use only the institutional forms available to them.

5. The U.S. Senate has recently increased its attention to foundations (see, for example, Strom 2004; Wolverton 2004; and the Finance Committee of the United States Senate website).

6. The earliest efforts to list American foundations seem to have been carried out by the Russell Sage Foundation and the Twentieth Century Fund. The relevant publications include:
   - Russell Sage Foundation (1915), 27 foundations
   - Russell Sage Foundation (1920), 54 foundations
   - Russell Sage Foundation (1924), 127 foundations
   - Russell Sage Foundation (1926), 179 foundations
   - Twentieth Century Fund (1928)
   - National Association of Social Workers (1929–1960)
   - Russell Sage Foundation (1930), 185 foundations including 33 community trusts
   - Clark (1931), 122 foundations
   - Clark (1932), 129 foundations
   - Clark (1935), 123 foundations
   - Russell Sage Foundation (1938), 188 foundations
   - Raymond Rich Associates. (1939, 1942)
   - Harrison and Andrews (1946)
   - Raymond Rich Associates (1948)
   - American Foundations Information Service (1955), 4,164 foundations

7. Six of these seven foundations are listed with assets that exceeded $175 million in the eighth edition of the *Foundation Directory* (1979 data), yet though each existed at the time of the first edition in 1959, only the Houston Endowment acknowledged substantial assets at that time (for a discussion of reasons to think that these foundations sharply underreported their assets, see Nielsen 1972, 126–134, 151–69; 1985, 214–18, 222–24, 390–93).

8. The big eastern foundations also paid serious attention to the implementation of "best practices" in public health (Ettling 1981), and in education (Lagemann 1983).

9. This is true of my own earlier article on foundations; its footnotes list most of the studies of these foundations that had appeared by the late 1990s (Hammack 1999).

10. http://www.swedenborg.com.

11. Like the similar John F. Slater Fund (1882), the Peabody Fund directed most of its grants to religious schools (Schaff 1879, 245; McPherson 1975).

12. In 1891, the New York Supreme Court also invalidated a bequest from the estate of William B. Ogden to a university, on the ground that beneficiary was not specified with sufficient precision (Miller 1970, 154–56). Hall notes that political associates of David B. Hill seem to have played

roles in denying the bequests to both the New York Public Library and Cornell: as Democratic governor of New York, Hill was a contender for the Democratic presidential nomination and if he did have a hand in these cases, it may have been part of his effort to demonstrate loyalty to antimonopoly values held by Democratic voters across the United States and especially, perhaps, in the South. Hill may also have been motivated by rivalry with the influential group of wealthy Democrats who associated with Tilden; Tilden's protégé, Andrew H. Green, was executor of both the Ogden and the Tilden wills.

13. Some states used similar language for similar purposes at the time; an 1895 Minnesota law, for example, imposed a 3 percent gross receipts tax on railroad property in the state, but exempted from this tax railroad property held by "certain enumerated classes of property, such as universities, schools, churches, burying grounds, etc." Justice White, "Separate Opinion" in Stearns v. Minnesota, 1900.

14. Religious bodies sponsored nearly all of these colleges and hospitals. In the early 1890s, about seventy-five colleges had endowment income greater than $10,000 (implying endowment assets greater than $200,000); a thorough study published in 1897 put the total endowment of all U.S. colleges and universities at $100 million (Ely 1894; Thwing 1897). The Congregationalist American Education Society, and others raised and held funds for the support both of college student scholarships and for colleges themselves; other denominations had similar funds (for the very small size of nineteenth-century endowments in support of scientific research in the United States, see Miller 1970; for general accounts of the roles of denominational sponsorship, see Baird 1844/1998; Oates 1995).

15. Shelby Harrison and Emerson Andrews included the Northern Baptist Education Society (1791), the American Missionary Association (1846), and the Board of Education of the Methodist Church Student Loan Fund (1872) in their list of foundations active in 1944 (1946, 18, 106, 112, 159, 175); see also American College and Education Society (1875) and Society for the Promotion of Collegiate and Theological Education at the West (1867), which reported a wide variety of gifts through its offices as well as directly to many colleges and theological schools; for the Presbyterian boards of home and foreign missions see, for example, the Princeton Review (1860/2002).

16. These intellectual currents had considerably less influence in the South, the border states, and the Great Plains and mountain West. Historians have neglected the intellectual history of these regions, and of the Southern Baptists, Southern Methodists, Stone Campbell, and other Protestant churches that dominate them. Historians have also neglected intellectual currents within Catholicism, currents that exerted substantial influence in the Northeast and Great Lakes states.

17. Letter, Andrew Carnegie to W. M. Frew, Secretary of the Carnegie Institute at Pittsburgh, December 2, 1895 (quoted in Wall 1970, 833–34).

18. Rockefeller's Institute for Medical Research (1900) and Sanitary Commission (1909, after 1913, International Health Board), and his General

Education Board (1903) which, like the Anna Jeanes Fund (1907) and the Phelps-Stokes Fund of New York (1911), supported education for African Americans in the South. Another notable early special-purpose fund was the Milbank Memorial Fund for Public Health (1905).

19. By one calculation, almost half of the 100 largest fortunes in U.S. history, measured in relation to the size of the entire U.S. economy, appeared in the last twenty-five years of the nineteenth century (Klepper and Gunther 1996). Those ranked in the top thirty include, in addition to Sage, Carnegie, and Rockefeller, Cornelius Vanderbilt, A. T. Stewart, Frederick Weyerhauser, Jay Gould, Marshall Field, James G. Fair, William Weightman, Moses Taylor, John I. Blair, E. H. Harriman, Henry H. Rogers, J. P. Morgan, Oliver Payne, Henry Clay Frick, Collis P. Huntington, Peter A. Widener, and Philip Armour. Economic historians have calculated that the proportion of American wealth held by richest 1 percent of the U.S. population reached its highest point—more than 50 percent—in 1900 (DeLong 2003, 49).

20. Associations rather than individually endowed institutions had received federal charters in the nineteenth century; one example is the American Academy for the Advancement of Science, which received a federal charter in 1863 (Miller 1970, 126). The anti–birth control, anti-abortion New York Society for the Suppression of Vice, led by Anthony Comstock and heavily funded by industrialist and YMCA promoter Morris K. Jesup, secured federal legislation banning the use of the mails for "obscene" purposes and assigning to the society the power to enforce that law; see Beisel (1998). Several leaders of big business, including some who advised Carnegie and Rockefeller, favored federal incorporation of business firms at this time (see Urofsky 1982/1994, 160–83).

21. Olasky quotes J. Gresham Machen, a Christian conservative, as appropriately objecting in 1924 that "modern theological liberalism" (funded by the Rockefellers) had forgotten that "according to the Bible, man is a sinner under the just condemnation of God" (1992, 145). All this led, in Olasky's view, to Rockefeller Foundation reports that supported the provision of government aid to "families without fathers" and to Russell Sage Foundation staffer Mary Van Kleeck's activities in support of "industrial democracy" and "a socialized, planned economy" (144–46, 156). By 1943 another Russell Sage Foundation product, Donald Howard's study of the WPA and other federal welfare programs, "seemed" to support efforts "to extend [public] relief in every direction at once," without regard to the recipients' personal behavior or beliefs.

22. Depression-era critiques of foundations as bastions of privilege and power for super-wealthy white Protestant families (see especially, Lundberg 1937; Lindeman 1939), similarly failed to lead to restrictive legislation. From 1913 until 1954, foundations were treated the same way as other charitable organizations: they were exempt from federal taxation, and donors could deduct from their "gross income" subject to federal tax the value of charitable gifts up to 20 percent of such income (Hopkins 1979, 354).

23. Foundation funds have always been limited, but by one serious estimate they added up, in 1932, to more than a third of all college and university endowment funds (Wood, Struthers & Company 1932, 6; for accounts of TIAA and related developments, see Curti and Nash 1965; Lagemann 1983).

24. Carnegie had set this approach with his libraries. To win funds for a Carnegie library, a community had to agree to pay for the books and subject itself to a permanent library tax.

25. Vanderbilt's decision to cut its ties to the Southern Methodists met strong resistance. In 1910, Methodist leaders prevented Randolph-Macon College from doing the same (Hohner 1987). Centre College of Kentucky, connected to the Southern Presbyterians, cut its ties with that denomination to qualify for Carnegie pensions, but later rejoined the denomination (Hollis 1938, 54). Tulane did follow Vanderbilt's example; in Missouri, Washington University easily qualified for Carnegie support, but Drury College separated from the Congregationalists only with difficulty.

26. Hollis (1938, 274) lists these institutions with their percentages of total grant share, in four groups: first, Chicago, 13.64; Carnegie Tech, 7.23; Johns Hopkins, 6.72; Columbia, 6.58; Vanderbilt, 6.30; second, Yale, 4.64; Harvard, 3.58; Cornell, 3.43; Duke, 3.28; Cal Tech, 3.26; third, Washington U. St. Louis, 2.44; University of Rochester, 2.31; Princeton, 1.91; Peabody College, 1.57; Tulane, 1.49; and, fourth, University of Iowa, 1.42; Stanford, 1.23; University of Pennsylvania, .82; Swarthmore, .69; New York University, .67.

27. In addition to the common effort to promote scientific medicine and scientific research at several institutions across the United States, several foundations concentrated their donations on particular institutions: Carnegie on Carnegie Tech, Rockefeller on the University of Chicago, the Duke Endowment on Duke University, the Peabody Fund on Vanderbilt and Peabody College. Elsewhere, to take just a few examples, the M. D. Anderson Foundation led the creation of the Texas Medical Center, the Horace Rackham fund supported the University of Michigan, the Elizabeth Severance Prentiss Fund supported medicine at Western Reserve University, the Thomas H. White Charitable Trust supported Case Institute of Technology.

28. This statement is worth quoting in full: "Russell Sage Foundation was established in 1907 by Mrs. Russell Sage 'for the improvement of social and living conditions in the Unites States of America.' In carrying out its purpose the Foundation maintains a staff which, among other duties, conducts studies of social conditions, authorized by the General Director, where new information, its analysis and interpretation seem necessary in order to formulate and advance practicable measures aimed at improvements. From time to time the Foundation publishes the results of these studies in book or pamphlet form.

   "In formulating the problem for study, in mapping out a plan of work on it, in collecting facts, in drawing conclusions, and in the presentation of findings, authors of Foundation studies, who are always either members of the staff or specially commissioned research workers, have the benefit of the criticism and advice of their colleagues in the organization. Full freedom is given research workers for the final decision on all of these steps, and in presenting and interpreting both factual material and conclusions in their own way. While the general responsibility for management of the Foundation is vested in the Board of Trustees, the responsibility for facts, conclusions, and interpretations rests with the research workers alone and not upon the Foundation, its trustees, or other members of its staff. Publication under its imprint does not imply agreement by the organization or its members with opinions or interpretations of authors. It does imply that care has been taken that the research on which a book is based has been thoroughly done." For the dispute that prompted this statement—a dispute between Russell Sage researchers and John D. Rockefeller, Jr., regarding a study of labor relations at the Colorado Fuel and Iron Company in the wake of the 1913 strike, see Glenn, Brandt, and Andrews (1947, vol. 2, 379–81).

29. The Rhodes Scholarships set one model; those funded by U.S. foundations include the Guggenheim Fellowships, the fellowships of the Commonwealth Fund and the Danforth Foundation, as well as more recently the awards of the MacArthur Foundation (Lomask 1964; Commonwealth Fund, 1963; Harvey and Abrams 1986). The best general accounts of these foundation strategies include Ogg (1928), Hollis (1938), Lagemann (1983, 1989), and Wheatley (1988).

30. Newton D. Baker, the attorney, former mayor of Cleveland, and secretary of war under Woodrow Wilson, did much to promote the community foundation idea during the 1920s and 30s; he was also a trustee of the Religious Education Foundation (Clark 1935, 39).

31. Andrews (1973, 82–83). Ironically, the Russell Sage Foundation did not publish regular annual reports on its own activities. Hollis criticized it for this failure(1938, 69). At the end of its first era, it did issue a comprehensive report (Glenn, Brandt, and Andrews 1947). See note 6 for a list of relevant publications.

32. On the role of the Russell Sage Foundation, which often worked closely with the Rockefeller and Carnegie foundations and with the Julius Rosenberg Fund, see Hammack and Wheeler (1994). The Russell Sage Foundation undertook the famous Pittsburgh Survey, helped consolidate newsletters of the Boston, New York, and Chicago charity organization societies into *Survey* magazine, and provided the entire staff for the Cleveland Foundation's influential survey of elementary and secondary education in Cleveland (Tittle 1992). F. Emerson Andrews (1973, 180) noted that leaders of the Ford, Rockefeller, and Carnegie foundations, of the New York Community Trust, and of Chicago's Field Foundation attended the opening reception for the Foundation Center in 1956. For a West Coast foundation that connected with Russell Sage and others in New York and Chicago, see Sitton (1999).

33. Indeed, until the Tax Reform Act of 1969 went into effect in the mid-1970s, American nonprofit organizations, including foundations, were not required to file statements of the value of their current assets, but could report assets in a variety of ways. Many foundations preferred to minimize their wealth (personal conversation with Frederick Bartenstein III, former director of the Dayton Foundation, in 1989).

34. The relevant books include: Andrews (1950, 1952, 1956, 1958, 1974), Taylor (1953), Kiger (1954), Freemont-Smith (1965), Zurcher and Dustan. (1972).

35. Among the works supported at least in part through the Russell Sage Foundation, several of which began in Merle Curti's seminars at the University of Wisconsin, include the Russell Sage Foundation (1956), Wyllie (1959), Jordan (1960, 1961), Miller (1961), Fox (1963), Dickinson (1962), Owen (1964), Curti (1965), Curti and Nash (1965), Cutlip (1965), and Miller (1970).

36. Eventually, Andrews succeeded in arranging for the Foundation Center to make copies of foundation tax reports. By the early 2000s, the IRS had agreed to allow the GuideStar Web site to make available the tax form submitted by every nonprofit organization in the United States, and had approved plans that would require each nonprofit, including foundations, to file the form in the electronic format (pdf) that would allow it to be posted on the GuideStar site almost immediately.

37. Two of the thirteen Texas foundations that did not announce support for religious activity were corporate foundations; two were community foundations. Only one of these foundations was listed in Harrison and Andrews' 1946 *American Foundations for Social Welfare*—and at that time the LeTorneau foundation "for the gospel of Jesus Christ" was located in Peoria, Illinois (146). Many western foundations continue to hold themselves aloof from northeastern institutions; the Communities Foundation of Texas did not join the Foundation Center. More recently, new leaders of the Daniels Foundation in Denver adopted policies that led to the resignation of a top official who had come from the Rockefeller Foundation (*Rocky Mountain News*, January 31, 2004).

38. Kelley lists 178 foundations established in the state before 1950; she concludes that nearly one-sixth of these were chiefly concerned with religious causes (2004, 98).

39. This handbook also listed scores of "educational and religious associations" and about sixty denominational boards of education, several of which held substantial funds. The 1942 edition of *American Foundations and Their Fields* listed thirty-six college student loan funds, several of them sponsored by these boards.

40. Joseph (1935); Goldin (1976); Hirschmann (1981); Brandeis University (1994); Joselit (1996).

41. As noted, more than one northeastern foundation also directed its attention to local community interests (see, for example, Spencer 1972; Weaver 1975).

42. An extensive review of the record with many references is Cumings (2002).
43. Peter Frumkin (1998) has argued that federal regulation has forced foundations to divert charitable funds into bloated bureaucracies, but we should note that foundations have also had to deal with a much larger nonprofit sector, and with nonprofit organizations that themselves must deal both with greatly increased federal regulation, and with many more purchasers of their services.
44. In effect, this essay offers an explanation for the legitimacy that Americans accord the legal arrangements that American foundations enjoy. For a similar argument focused more particularly on the law, see Katz (1998).

References

Allen, Michael Patrick. 1989. *The Founding Fortunes: A New Anatomy of the Super-Rich Families in America.* New York: E. P. Dutton.

American College and Education Society. 1875. "49 Annual Report." Boston, Mass.: American College and Education Society.

American Education Society. 1825. *First Annual Report.* In *American College and Education Society, 49 annual report.* Boston, Mass.: American Education Society.

American Foundations Information Service. 1955. *American Foundations and Their Fields,* vol. 7. New York: American Foundations Information Service.

Anderson, Eric A., and Alfred A. Moss, Jr. 1999. *Dangerous Donations: Northern Philanthropy and Southern Black Education, 1902–1930.* Columbia: University of Missouri Press.

Anderson, James. 1988. *The Education of Blacks in the South, 1860–1935.* Chapel Hill: University of North Carolina Press.

Andrews, F. Emerson. 1950. *Philanthropic Giving.* New York: Russell Sage Foundation.

———. 1952. *Corporation Giving.* New York: Russell Sage Foundation.

———. 1956. *Philanthropic Foundations.* New York: Russell Sage Foundation.

———. 1958. *Legal Instruments of Foundations.* New York: Russell Sage Foundation.

———. 1968. *Patman and Foundations: Review and Assessment.* New York: The Foundation Center.

———. 1973. *Foundation Watcher.* Lancaster, Pa.: Franklin and Marshall College.

———. 1974. *Philanthropy in the United States: History and Structure.* New York: Foundation Center.

Arnove, Robert F., ed. 1980. *Philanthropy and Cultural Imperialism: The Foundations at Home and Abroad.* Bloomington: Indiana University Press.

Baird, Robert. 1844/1998. *Religion In America, Or, An Account of The Origin, Progress, Relation to the State, And Present Condition of the Evangelical Churches in the United States: With Notices of the Unevangelical Denominations,* reprint. New York: Harper, Blackie and Son.

Barzun, Jacques. 1959. "The Folklore of Philanthropy." In *The House of Intellect.* New York: Harper and Row.

Berliner, Howard S. 1985. *A System of Scientific Medicine: Philanthropic Foundations in the Flexner Era.* New York: Tavistock.

Berman, Edward H. 1983. *The Ideology of Philanthropy: The Influence of the Carnegie, Ford, and Rockefeller Foundations on American Foreign Policy.* Albany: State University of New York Press.

Bothwell, Robert. 2005. "The Decline of Progressive Policy and the New Philanthropy." Available at: http://comm-org.utoledo.edu/papers2003/bothwell/theorigins.htm#N_125_ and http://comm-org.wisc.edu/papers2003/bothwell/bothwell.htm#progressive (August).

Brandeis University. 1994. *The Impact of Foundations with Jewish Interests of the North American Jewish Community.* The 1993 Alexander Brin Forum sponsored by the Benjamin S. Hornstein Program in Jewish Communal Service. Waltham, Mass.: Brandeis University, Center for Modern Jewish Studies.

Brilliant, Eleanor L. 2000. *Private Charity and Public Inquiry: A History of the Filer and Peterson Commissions.* Bloomington: Indiana University Press.

Brown, E. Richard. 1979. *Rockefeller Medicine Men: Medicine and Capitalism in the Progressive Era.* Berkeley: University of California Press.

Bryan, W. S. Plummer. 1911. *The Church, Her Colleges, and the Carnegie Foundation.* Princeton, N.J.: Princeton University Press.

Bulmer, Martin. 1984. *The Chicago School of Sociology: Institutionalization, Diversity, and the Rise of Sociological Research.* Chicago: University of Chicago Press.

Candler, Warren A. 1909. *Dangerous Donations and Degrading Doles or a Vast Scheme for Capturing and Controlling the Colleges and Universities of the Country.* Atlanta: Privately printed.

Carnegie, Andrew. 1889/1990. *The Gospel of Wealth and Other Timely Essays.* New York: The Century Company.

Castle, Alfred L. 2004. *A Century of Philanthropy: A History of the Samuel N. and Mary Castle Foundation,* rev. ed. Honolulu: University of Hawai'i Press for the Hawaiian Historical Society.

Chernow, Ron. 1998. *Titan: The Life of John D. Rockefeller, Sr.* New York: Random House.

Chitty, Arthur Ben. 1979. *Ability, Power and Humility: Eli and Ruth Lilly and their Church.* New York: Seabury Professional Services.

Chronicle of Philanthropy. 2006. "100 Largest Foundations by Assets." *The Chronicle of Philanthropy.* Available at: http://philanthropy.com/premium/articles/v14/i13/13001602.htm (accessed May 9, 2006).

Clark, Evans, ed. 1931. *American Foundations and Their Fields.* New York: Twentieth Century Fund.

———. 1932. *American Foundations and Their Fields. Covering Activities of the Year 1931.* New York: Twentieth Century Fund.

———. 1935. *American Foundations and Their Fields. Covering Activities of the Year 1934.* New York: Twentieth Century Fund.

Coleman, Peter. 1989. *The Liberal Conspiracy: The Congress for Cultural Freedom and the Struggle for the Mind of Postwar Europe.* New York: The Free Press.

Colwell, Mary Anna Culleton. 1993. *Private Foundations and Public Policy: The Political Role of Philanthropy.* New York: Garland Publishing.

Commonwealth Fund. 1963. *The Commonwealth Fund: Historical Sketch, 1918–1962* New York: Harkness House.

Covington, Sally. 1997. *Moving A Public Policy Agenda: The Strategic Philanthropy of Conservative Foundations* Washington, D.C.: National Committee for Responsive Philanthropy.

Cumings, Bruce. 2002. "Boundary Displacement: Area Studies and International Studies During and After the Cold War." In *Learning Places: The Afterlives of Area Studies,* edited by Masao Miyoshi and H. D. Harootunian. Durham: Duke University Press.

Cuninggim, Merrimon. 1972. *Private Money and Public Service: The Role of Foundations in American Society.* New York: McGraw-Hill.

Curti, Merle. 1965. *American Philanthropy Abroad.* New Brunswick, N.J.: Rutgers University Press.

Curti, Merle, and Roderick Nash. 1965 *Philanthropy in the Shaping of American Higher Education.* New Brunswick, N.J.: Rutgers University Press.

Cutlip, Scott M. 1965. *Fund Raising in the United States: Its Role in America's Philanthropy.* New Brunswick, N.J.: Rutgers University Press.

DeLong, J. Bradford. 2003. "A History of Bequests in the United States." In *Death and Dollars: The Role of Gifts and Bequests in America,* edited by Alicia H. Munnell and Annika Sundén. Washington, D.C.: Brookings Institution Press.

Diamond, Sara. 1995. *Roads to Dominion: Right-Wing Movements and Political Power in the United States.* New York: Guilford Press.

Diamond, Stephen. 1992. *Compromised Campus: The Collaboration of Universities with the Intelligence Community, 1945–1955.* New York: Oxford University Press.

———. 2002. "Efficiency and Benevolence: Philanthropic Tax Exemptions in 19th-Century America." In *Property-Tax Exemption for Charities: Mapping the Battlefield,* edited by Evelyn Brody. Washington, D.C.: Urban Institute Press.

Dickinson, Frank G., ed. 1962. *Philanthropy and Public Policy.* New York: National Bureau of Economic Research.

DiLorenzo, Thomas J., Daniel T. Oliver, and Robert E. Winters. 1990. *Patterns of Corporate Philanthropy: the "Suicidal Impulse."* Washington, D.C.: Capital Research Center.

Dowie, Mark. 2001. *American Foundations: An Investigative History.* Cambridge, Mass.: MIT Press.

Eaton, Allen, and Shelby M. Harrison. 1930. *A Bibliography of Social Surveys.* New York: Russell Sage Foundation.

Edie, John A. 1987. "Congress and Foundations: Historical Summary." In *America's Wealthy and the Future of Foundations,* edited by Teresa Odendahl. New York: The Foundation Center.

Ely, Richard T. 1894. "The Universities and the Churches." In *University of the State of New York—107th Annual Report of the Regents 1893.* Reprinted in Peter Dobkin Hall, *Documentary History of Philanthropy and Voluntarism in the United States, 1600–1900.* Cambridge, Mass.: Harvard University Press. http://ksghome.harvard.edu/~.phall.hauser.ksg/dochistcontents.html.

Embree, Edwin R., and Julia Waxman, 1949. *Investment In People; The Story of the Julius Rosenwald Fund.* New York: Harper and Row.

Ettling, John. 1981. *The Germ of Laziness: Rockefeller Philanthropy and Public Health in the New South.* Cambridge, Mass.: Harvard University Press.

Fisher, Donald. 1993. *Fundamental Development of the Social Sciences: Rockefeller Philanthropy and the United States Social Science Research Council.* Ann Arbor: University of Michigan Press.

Flexner, Abraham. 1915. *The General Education Board: An Account of Its Activities, 1902–1914.* New York: The General Education Board

Fosdick, Raymond B. 1952. *The Story of the Rockefeller Foundation* New York: Harper and Row.

———. 1962. *Adventure in Giving: The Story of the General Education Board, A Foundation Established by John D. Rockefeller.* New York: Harper and Row.

The Foundation Center. 1960. *Foundation Directory.* New York: Russell Sage Foundation.

———. 1981. *Foundation Directory,* 8th ed. New York: The Foundation Center.

———. 2001. "Aggregate Foundation Fiscal Data by Region and State, 2001." Available at: http://fdncenter.org/findfunders/statistics/pdf/01_found_fin_data/2001/01_01.pdf (accessed May 11, 2006).

———. 2003a. *Foundation Yearbook, 2003.* New York: The Foundation Center.

———. 2003b. "Highlights of the Foundation Center's *Foundation Staffing.*" Foundations Today Series 2003. New York: The Foundation Center.

Fox, Daniel M. 1963. *Engines of Culture: Philanthropy and Art Museums.* Madison: The State Historical Society of Wisconsin.

Freemont-Smith, Marion R. 1965. *Foundations and Government: State and Federal law and Supervision.* New York: Russell Sage Foundation.

Freund, Gerald. 1996. *Narcissism and Philanthropy: Ideas and Talent Denied.* New York: Viking.

Frumkin, Peter. 1998. "The Long Recoil From Regulation: Private Philanthropic Foundations and the Tax Reform Act of 1969." *American Review of Public Administration* 28(3): 266–86.

Fugate, Sandy. 1997. *For the Benefit of All: A History of Philanthropy in Michigan: An Engaging Look at the Philanthropic Traditions of the Great Lakes State and Its People.* Battle Creek, Mich.: W. K. Kellogg Foundation, and Grand Haven, Mich.: Council of Michigan Foundations (distributor).

Gates, Frederick Taylor. 1977. *Chapters in My Life; with the Frederick Taylor Gates lectures by Robert Swain Morison.* New York: Free Press.

Gaul, Gilbert M., and Neill A. Borowski. 1993. *Free Ride: The Tax-Exempt Economy.* Kansas City, Mo.: Andrews and McMeel.

Geiger, Roger L. 1986. *To Advance Knowledge: The Growth of American Research Universities, 1900–1940.* New York: Oxford University Press.

General Education Board. 1964. *Review and Final Report, 1902–1964.* New York: General Education Board.

Glenn, John M., Lilian Brandt, and F. Emerson Andrews. 1947. *The Russell Sage Foundation, 1907–1946.* New York: Russell Sage Foundation.

Goff, Frederick Harris. 1919. "Community Trusts." An Address Delivered September 30th, 1919, before the Trust company section of the American Bankers' Association at its national convention in St. Louis. Cleveland: The Cleveland Trust Company.

Goldin, Milton. 1976. *Why They Give: American Jews and Their Philanthropies.* New York: Macmillan.

Gompers, Samuel. 1917. "Shall Education Be Rockefellerized?" In *The American Federationist* XXIV (March): 206–8.

Goulden, Joseph. 1971. *The Money Givers.* New York: Random House.

Hall, Peter Dobkin. 1992. *Inventing the Nonprofit Sector And Other Essays on Philanthropy, Voluntarism, and Nonprofit Organizations.* Baltimore, Md.: The Johns Hopkins University Press.

Hammack, David C. 1989. "Community Foundations: The Delicate Question of Purpose." In *An Agile Servant,* edited by Richard Magat. New York: The Foundation Center.

———, ed. 1998. *Making the Nonprofit Sector in the United States: A Reader.* Bloomington: Indiana University Press.

———. 1999. "Foundations in the American Polity." In *Philanthropic Foundations: New Scholarship, New Possibilities,* edited by Ellen Condliffe Lagemann, Bloomington: Indiana University Press.

———. 2002. "Nonprofit Organizations in American History: Research Opportunities and Sources." *The American Behavioral Scientist* 45(11): 1638–674.

———. 2005. "Community Foundations." In *Philanthropy in America: A Comprehensive Historical Encyclopedia,* edited by Dwight F. Burlingame. Santa Barbara: ABC-Clio.

Hammack, David C., and Stanton Wheeler. 1994. *Social Science in the Making: Essays on the Russell Sage Foundation, 1907–1947.* New York: Russell Sage Foundation.

Harlan, Louis R. 1958. *Separate and Unequal: Public School Campaigns and Racism in the Southern Seaboard States, 1901–1915* Chapel Hill: University of North Carolina Press.

Harrison, Shelby, and F. Emerson Andrews. 1946. *American Foundations for Social Welfare.* New York: Russell Sage Foundation.

Harvey, McGehee, and Susan L. Abrams. 1986. *"For the Welfare of Mankind": The Commonwealth Fund and American Medicine.* Baltimore, Md.: Johns Hopkins University Press.

Haskell, Thomas. 1977. *The Emergence of Professional Social Science: The American Social Science Association and the Nineteenth-Century Crisis of Authority.* Urbana: The University of Illinois Press, 1977.

Hirschmann, Ira. 1981. *The Awakening: The Story of the Jewish National Fund.* New York: Shengold.

Hobhouse, Arthur. 1880. *The Dead Hand: Addresses on the Subject of Endowments and Settlements of Property.* London: Chatto and Windus.

Hohner, Robert A. 1987. "Southern Education in Transition: William Waugh Smith, the Carnegie Foundation, and the Methodist Church." *History of Education Quarterly* 27(2): 181–203.

Holcombe, Randall G. 2000. *Writing Off Ideas: Taxation, Foundations, and Philanthropy in America.* New Brunswick, N.J.: Transaction Publishers.

Hollis, Ernest Victor. 1938. *Philanthropic Foundations and Higher Education.* New York: Columbia University Press.

Hopkins, Bruce R. 1979. *The Law of Tax-Exempt Organizations.* New York: John Wiley & Sons.

Howard, Nathaniel R. 1963. *Trust for All Time: The Story of the Cleveland Foundation and the Community Trust Movement.* Cleveland: The Cleveland Foundation.

Jarchow, Merrill E. 1981. *Amherst H. Wilder and His Enduring Legacy to Saint Paul.* St. Paul, Minn.: The Amherst H. Wilder Foundation.

Jenkins, Edward C. 1950. *Philanthropy in America: An Introduction to the Practices and Prospects of Organizations Supported by Gifts and Endowments, 1924–1948.* New York: Association Press.

Jordan, W. K. 1960. *The Charities of London, 1480–1660: The Aspirations and the Achievements of the Urban Society.* New York: Russell Sage Foundation.

———. 1961. *The Charities of Rural England, 1480–1660.* London: Allen & Unwin.

Joselit, Jenna Weissman. 1996. *Aspiring Women: A History of the Jewish Foundation for Education of Women.* New York: Jewish Foundation for Education of Women.

Joseph, Samuel. 1935. *History of the Baron de Hirsch Fund: The Americanization of the Jewish Immigrant.* New York: Jewish Publication Society.

Josephson, Emanuel Mann. 1952. *Rockefeller, "Internationalist," The Man Who Misrules the World.* New York: Chedney Press.

Karl, Barry D., and Stanley N. Katz. 1981. "The American Private Philanthropic Foundation and the Public Sphere, 1890–1930." *Minerva* 19(2): 236–70.

Katz, S. N. 1988. "The Legal Framework of American Pluralism: Liberal Constitutionalism and the Protection of Groups." In *Beyond Pluralism: The Conception of Groups and Group Identities in America,* edited by Wendy F. Katkin, Ned Landsman, and Andrea Tyree. Chicago: University of Illinois Press.

Katz, Stanley N., Barry Sullivan, and C. Paul Beach. 1985. "Legal Change and Legal Autonomy: Charitable Trusts in New York, 1777–1893." *Law and History Review* 3(1985): 51–89.

Keele, Harold M., and Joseph C. Kiger, eds. 1984. *Foundations.* Westport, Conn.: Greenwood Press.

Kelley, Mary L. 2004. *The Foundations of Texan Philanthropy.* 1st ed. College Station: Texas A&M University Press.

Keppel, Frederick P. 1930. *The Foundation: Its Place in American Life: An Account of the Development of Philanthropic Endowments and Their Present Activities in Relation to Education and Scientific and Social Progress.* New York: Macmillan.

Kiger, Joseph C. 1954. *Operating Principles of the Larger Foundations.* New York: Russell Sage Foundation.

Kiser, Clyde Vernon. 1975. *The Milbank Memorial Fund; Its Leaders and Its Work, 1905–1974.* New York: Milbank Memorial Fund.

Klepper, Michael, and Robert Gunther. 1996. *The Wealthy 100.* Secaucus, N.J.: Carol Publishing Group.

Kohler, Robert E. 1991. *Partners in Science: Foundations and Natural Science, 1900–1945.* Chicago: University of Chicago Press.

Lagemann, Ellen Condliffe. 1983. *Private Power For the Public Good: A History of the Carnegie Foundation for the Advancement of Teaching.* Middletown, Conn.: Wesleyan University Press.

———. 1989. *The Politics of Knowledge: The Carnegie Corporation, Philanthropy, and Public Policy.* Middletown, Conn.: Wesleyan University Press.

———, ed. 1999. *Philanthropic Foundations: New Scholarship, New Possibilities.* Bloomington: Indiana University Press.

Lankford, John. 1964. *Congress and the Foundations in the Twentieth Century.* River Falls, Wis.: Wisconsin State University.

Lindeman, Eduard C. 1939. *Wealth and Culture.* New York: Harcourt, Brace.

Lomask, Milton. 1964. *Seed Money: The Guggenheim Story.* New York: Farrar, Straus.

Lundberg, Ferdinand. 1937. *America's 60 Families.* New York: Vanguard Press.

———. 1969. *The Rich and the Super-Rich.* New York: Bantam Books.

McPherson, James. 1975. *The Abolitionist Legacy: From Reconstruction to the NAACP.* Princeton, N.J.: Princeton University Press.

Milbank Memorial Fund. 1940. *Milbank Memorial Fund 1905–1940: Thirty-Five Years in Review.* New York: Milbank Memorial Fund.

Miller, Howard S. 1961. *The Legal Foundations of American Philanthropy, 1776–1844.* Madison: State Historical Society of Wisconsin.

———. 1970. *Dollars for Research: Science and Its Patrons in Nineteenth-Century America.* Seattle: University of Washington Press.

National Association of Social Workers. 1929–1960. *Social Work Year Book,* vol. 1–14. New York: Russell Sage Foundation.

National Commission on Philanthropy and Civic Renewal. 1997. *Giving Better, Giving Smarter: Renewing Philanthropy in America.* Milwaukee, Wis.: The Harry and Lynde Bradley Foundation. http://pcr.hudson.org/index.cfm?fuseaction=book_giving.

Nielsen, Waldemar A. 1972. *The Big Foundations.* New York: Columbia University Press.

———. 1985. *The Golden Donors: A New Anatomy of the Great Foundations.* New York: E. P. Dutton.

Noble, David F. 1977. *America By Design: Science, Technology, and the Rise of Corporate Capitalism.* New York: Alfred A. Knopf.

Noel, Thomas J. 2000. *A Pikes Peak Partnership: the Penroses and the Tutts.* Boulder: University Press of Colorado.

Oates, Mary J. 1995. *The Catholic Philanthropic Tradition in America.* Bloomington: University of Indiana Press.

O'Connor, Alice. 2001. *Poverty Knowledge: Social Science, Social Policy, and The Poor in Twentieth-Century U.S. History.* Princeton, N.J.: Princeton University Press.

Odendahl, Teresa, ed. 1990. *Charity Begins at Home: Generosity and Self-Interest Among The Philanthropic Elite.* New York: Basic Books

Ogg, Frederic A. 1928. "Foundations and Endowments in Relation to Research." In *Research in the Humanistic and Social Sciences.* New York: Century Company for the American Council of Learned Societies.

Olasky, Marvin. 1992. *The Tragedy of American Compassion.* Washington, D.C.: Regnery Publishing.

Owen, David. 1964. *English Philanthropy, 1660–1960.* Cambridge, Mass.: Harvard University Press.

Parmar, Inderjeet. 2004. "Selling Americanism, Combatting Anti-Americanism: The Historical Role of American Foundations." In *Anti-Americanism Working Papers.* Budapest: Center for Policy Studies, Central European University.

Pattillo, Jr., Manning M., and Donald M. Mackenzie. 1965. *Church-Sponsored Higher Education in the United States.* Washington, D.C.: American Council on Education.

Princeton Review. 1860/2002. "Presbyterianism." *Princeton Review* 32(3)(July 1860): 546–67. Making of America Journal Series. Ann Arbor: University of Michigan and the Andrew W. Mellon Foundation. http://www.hti.umich.edu/m/moagrp.

Quigley, Carroll. 1981. *The Anglo-American Establishment.* New York: Books in Focus.

Rabinowitz, Alan. 1990. *Social Change Philanthropy in America.* Westport, Conn.: Quorum.

Ransom, David. 1975. "Ford Country: Building an Elite for Indonesia." In *The Trojan Horse: A Radical Look at Foreign Aid,* edited by Steve Weissman. Palo Alto, Calif.: Ramparts Press.

Raymond Rich Associates. 1939. *American Foundations and Their Fields.* New York: Raymond Rich Associates.

———. 1942. *American Foundations and Their Fields,* vol. 5. New York: Raymond Rich Associates.

Rich, Wilmer Shields, and Neva R. Deardorff. 1948. *American Foundations and Their Fields,* vol. 6. New York: Raymond Rich Associates.

Richards, William C., and William J. Norton. 1957. *Biography of a Foundation: The Story of the Children's Fund of Michigan, 1929–1954: A Terminal Philanthropic Foundation.* Detroit: The Fund.

Rockefeller Foundation. 1972. *Directory of Fellowships and Scholarships, 1917–1970.* New York: The Foundation.

Roelofs, Joan. 1987. "Foundations and Social Change Organizations: The Mask of Pluralism." *Insurgent Sociologist* 12(Fall): 31–72

———. 2003. *Foundations and Public Policy: The Mask of Pluralism.* Albany: State University of New York Press.

Rosenwald, Julius. 1929. "Principles of Public Giving." *The Atlantic Monthly,* May 1929.

Rudolph, Frederick. 1962. *The American College and University: A History.* New York: Alfred A. Knopf.

Russell Sage Foundation. 1915. "American Foundations." *Library Bulletin* 11 (June).

———. 1920. "American Foundations." *Library Bulletin.*

———. 1924. "American Foundations." *Library Bulletin.*

———. 1926. "American Foundations." *Library Bulletin.*

———. 1930. *American Foundations for Social Welfare.* New York: Russell Sage Foundation.

———. 1938. *American Foundations for Social Welfare.* New York: Russell Sage Foundation.

————. 1956. *Report of the Princeton Conference on the History of Philanthropy in the United States.* New York: Russell Sage Foundation.

Saunders, Frances Stonor. 2000. *The Cultural Cold War: The CIA and the World of Arts and Letters.* New York: The New Press

Savage, Howard W. 1956. *The First Twenty-Five Years: The Story of a Foundation.* Battle Creek, Mich.: The W. K. Kellogg Foundation.

Schaff, Philip. 1879. "Progress of Christianity in the United States." *The Princeton Review* LX(2): 209–52.

Schenkel, Albert F. 1995. *The Rich Man and the Kingdom: John D. Rockefeller, Jr., and the Protestant Establishment.* Harvard Theological Studies 39. Minneapolis: Fortress Press.

Shulman, Jay, Carol Brown, and Roger Kahn. 1972. "Report on the Russell Sage Foundation." *Insurgent Sociologist* 2(4, Summer): 6–34.

Sitton, Tom. 1999. *The Haynes Foundation and Urban Reform Philanthropy in Los Angeles: A History of the John Randolph Haynes and Dora Haynes Foundation.* Los Angeles: The Historical Society of Southern California.

Smart, Kenneth. 1970. *A Sacred Trust: The Story of the Baptist Foundation of Texas.* Dallas: Baptist Foundation of Texas.

Society for the Promotion of Collegiate and Theological Education at the West. 1867. *Annual Report* for 1867.

Spencer, Rae MacCollum. 1972. *The Gift of Imaginative Leadership: Harry Galpin Stoddard, Affectionately Known as "Mr. Worcester" 1873–1969.* Worcester, Mass.: privately printed.

Stanfield, John H. 1985. *Philanthropy and Jim Crow in American Social Science.* Westport, Conn.: Greenwood Press.

Starrett, Agnes Lynch. 1966. *The Maurice and Laura Falk Foundation: A Private Fortune, A Public Trust.* Pittsburgh: Historical Society of Western Pennsylvania.

State of New York. 1893. Laws of the State of New York Passed at the One Hundred and Sixteenth Session of the Legislature, Begun January Third, 1893, and Ended April Twentieth, 1893, in the City of Albany. Albany, N.Y.: James B. Lyon, Printer.

Stefancic, Jean, and Richard Delgado. 1996. *No Mercy: How Conservative Think Tanks and Foundations Changed America's Social Agenda.* Philadelphia: Temple University Press.

Strom, Stephanie. 2004. "Charities Face Increased Reviews by I.R.S. as Senate Considers Strengthening Oversight." *New York Times,* June 23, 2004.

Taylor, Eleanor K. 1953. *Public Accountability of Foundations and Charitable Trusts.* New York: Russell Sage Foundation.

Thwing, C. F. 1897. *The American College.* London: G. P. Putnam's Sons.

Tittle, Diana. 1992. *Rebuilding Cleveland: The Cleveland Foundation and its Evolving Urban Strategy.* Columbus: Ohio State University Press.

Troyer, Thomas A. 2000. "The 1969 Private Foundation Law: Historical Perspective on Its Origins and Underpinnings." *The Exempt Organization Tax Review* 27(1): 52–65.

Turner, James. 1985. *Without God, Without Creed: The Origins of Unbelief in America.* Baltimore, Md.: The Johns Hopkins University Press.

Twentieth Century Fund. 1928. "Survey of Foundations." New York: Twentieth Century Fund.

U.S. Census Bureau. 2001. "Time Series of State Population Estimates: April 1, 2000, to July 1, 2001." Available at: http://www.census.gov/popest/archives/2000svintage_2001/ST-2001EST-01.html (accessed May 11, 2006).

U.S. Senate. 1916. Industrial Relations: Final Report and Testimony Submitted to Congress by the Commission on Industrial Relations. 64th Cong., 1st sess., August 23, 1912. S. Doc. 415. Washington: Government Printing Office.

Urofsky, Melvin I. 1982/1994. "Proposed Federal Incorporation in the Progressive Era," *American Journal of Legal History* 26. Reprinted in *Growth of the Regulatory State, 1900–1917,* edited by Robert F. Himmelberg. New York: Garland Publishing.

Wall, Joseph Frazier. 1989. *Andrew Carnegie.* Pittsburgh, Pa.: University of Pittsburgh Press.

Walsh, Frank. 1915. "Perilous Philanthropy." *The Independent* LXXXIII, August 23.

Weaver, Glenn. 1975. *Hartford Foundation for Public Giving: The First Fifty Years.* Hartford: Hartford Foundation for Public Giving.

Weaver, Warren, with George M. Beadle et al. 1967. *U.S. Philanthropic Foundations; Their History, Structure, Management, and Record.* New York: Harper and Row.

Weissman, Steve, ed. 1975. *The Trojan Horse: A Radical Look at Foreign Aid.* Palo Alto, Calif.: Ramparts Press.

Wheatley, Steven. 1988. *The Politics of Philanthropy: Abraham Flexner and Medical Education.* Madison: University of Wisconsin Press.

Wickey, Gould, and Ruth E. Anderson, eds. 1940. *Christian Higher Education: A Handbook for 1940.* Washington, D.C.: Council of Church Boards of Education.

Wolverton, Brad. 2004. "Rethinking Charity Rules." *The Chronicle of Philanthropy* (July). Available at: http://philanthropy.com/premium/articles/v16/i19/19003101.htm (accessed May 11, 2006).

Wood, Struthers & Company. 1932. *Trusteeship of American Endowments: With Comparative Analyses of the Investment Experience of Leading Universities.* New York: Macmillan.

Wooster, Martin Morse. 1994. *The Great Philanthropists and the Problem of "Donor Intent."* Washington, D.C.: Capital Research Center.

Wormser, René Albert. 1958. *Foundations: Their Power and Influence.* New York: Devin-Adair Co.

Wyllie, I. G. 1959. "The Search for an American Law of Charity." *Mississippi Valley Historical Review* 46(2): 203–21.

Young, James C. 1926. "The Dead Hand in Philanthropy." *Current History* (March): 837–42.

Zurcher, Arnold, and Jane Dustan. 1972. *The Foundation Administrator.* New York: Russell Sage Foundation.

Chapter 4

Accountability and Legitimacy in American Foundation Philanthropy

Peter Frumkin

A central problem in American philanthropy is whether donors are ever held adequately accountable for their giving. This issue arises in part from the tax deduction that donors receive for their giving, but is also connected to the power donors have to use resources to enact their agendas. Interestingly, the issue is more pressing in some parts of the field of American philanthropy than others. For individual donors who operate quietly or who give only modest amounts of money, only rarely do groups complain about access, transparency, and fairness. For large institutional donors, including private, corporate, and community foundations, accountability is far more pressing. Foundations face several organized and mobilized watchdog groups that do nothing but monitor and critique foundation practices. At the center of the accountability issue is the concern that philanthropy's fundamental power asymmetry between donor and recipient makes it very hard to create accountability systems appropriate for a field that delivers billions of dollars a year.

Accountability

It is important to step back from operational issues and ask a more basic question related to how foundations are or are not accountable. Why should foundations worry about being accountable for how philanthropic funds are given away? After all, no one is held accountable for how private wealth is spent when it comes to the consumption of real estate, automobiles, food, clothing, entertainment, or any other good or service (Frank 1999). Some might ask why the expenditure of philanthropic funds should raise any issues related to accountability given that the decision to give is a private and voluntary one about how to expend wealth. The answer lies in the fact that philanthropy has several features that make it distinct from ordinary private consumption decisions. Foundation philanthropy in particular has at least three features that expose it to accountability demands.[1]

First, giving is often accompanied by a tax break, which can take the form of a deduction on personal income taxes, lower estate taxes if gifts are made upon death, and lower taxes on foundation investment income. When money passes from private hands into the charitable world, government rewards donors and bestows on them privileges and benefits that other citizens do not enjoy. Along with these subsidies, one might argue, comes a responsibility to use philanthropic funds wisely and effectively, because at least part of the cost of philanthropy is borne by government in the form of forgone tax revenue. Accepting subsidies creates responsibilities, at least in the minds of some. Thus, the first argument for accountability stems from the fact that, unlike many forms of private consumption, philanthropy is accompanied by a substantial public subsidy (Brody 1998).

The second feature of giving that makes philanthropy quite different from other forms of private consumption stems from the effect it has on other people. The purchase and use of private goods in the market tend to be personal and carry only limited consequences for others because few private goods are shared or have significant externalities. In philanthropy—particularly large-scale foundation philanthropy—the opposite is the case. Donors use funds in public ways and the nature of their work in communities and neighborhoods unavoidably influences others. Sometimes these effects are direct, such as when human services are being offered, other times the effects are more indirectly felt, such as when a policy is being researched and advocated (Ferris and Mintrom 2002; Smith 2002). The fact, however, that philanthropy is public in its intentions and seeks to enact a private vision of the common good raises accountability issues precisely because the act of giving projects private values and commitments into the public sphere. The individuals and communities on which these values are projected can and do make accountability demands on donors (Collins, Rogers, and Garner 2000).

All of this raises the third common argument for philanthropic accountability. Unavoidable power asymmetries result when one person or institution gives money to another. Although many foundations work hard to break down some of the boundaries of class and race that philanthropy often raises, these cleavages are real and cause many to worry about the intentions and methods of foundations. Few grant applicants are at ease around foundations, and often feel as though they must tread lightly. Although it would be useful if foundations and recipients could talk openly about projects together, the reality is that the wealth and power differential makes this kind of conversation difficult (Ostrander and Schervish 1990). In light of these barriers and the fundamentally unequal position that givers and recipients occupy in the philanthropic exchange, accountability concerns naturally arise—though they may have to be raised by third parties who have some distance from the particular philanthropic transaction in question.

Given these three more or less compelling arguments and the amount of money now involved in philanthropy, nonprofit organizations, local communities, government agencies, and increasingly, certain segments of the public have taken the stance that foundations should be held accountable for how they use charitable funds. One reason there has been a growing interest in resources controlled by private foundations stems from political and budgetary shifts that have occurred in recent decades. As large entitlement programs such as Social Security and Medicare have come to consume greater and greater proportions of the national budget, the amount of money available for discretionary social spending has declined proportionally. This has made it harder for government to support the creation of major new domestic programs and pushed some of their responsibilities to state and local government, and even to charities (Smith and Lipsky 1993). In many fields of nonprofit activity, the importance of charitable dollars has increased substantially. Foundation grants are one of the key ways that nonprofits launch new program initiatives, which only later attempt to achieve sustainability through the charging of program fees or through other forms of long-term financing (Letts, Ryan, and Grossman 1999).

In many ways, accountability remains a confused and conflicted concept, even if it is prominent in public debate about philanthropy.

Part of the problem stems from the fact that we have at least two dominant conceptions of accountability, and neither quite applies to the world of foundations. One is rooted in democratic theory. It holds that accountability becomes a reality when the tether of the vote is established between representatives and constituents. In politics, for example, citizens can exercise the right to vote, allowing them both to select those who will represent them and hold these persons accountable for the decision they take in government. The right to vote breathes meaning into the idea of accountability because it expresses consent and creates a sanctioning mechanism that can be applied if the behavior of the representative is not faithful to the interest of constituents. Of course, democratic accountability requires that citizens vote and keep abreast of political debates and issues, something that does not always occur. Still, by arming citizens with a tool to keep their representatives responsive, democratic accountability succeeds in keeping those granted power responsive to those who have delegated this power.

Attractive as it might be, democratic accountability is not an option in the field of philanthropy, or at least not for the majority of foundations and institutions. Foundations are profoundly undemocratic in that they do not give their grant recipients or the communities in which they operate the ability to recall them or reverse their behavior. In fact, almost all philanthropy is profoundly undemocratic in that wealthy elite use their resources to enact their personal vision of the public good (Nielsen 1985). Some foundations may convene experts and listen to the opinions of others before making major commitments, but, by and large, philanthropic decision making is a private affair. The meetings of foundation boards are not open to the public, board members do not stand for public election, and these organizations operate largely as they see fit, or how their founders, families, or trustees judge most efficacious.

A second kind of accountability is substantially different from the democratic variety. It is mutual accountability—a commitment among parties that each party to an agreement or collective effort will hold the other side accountable and vice versa. In the nonprofit world, such systems have been established in a wide array of fields, ranging from community development to welfare to work services. One of the most clear examples of how mutual accountability works is in the emerging field of microfinance. At least one of the more prominent nonprofits making small loans for business development around the world relies on a special form of mutual accountability in many of its loan programs in Latin America. Instead of lending to one person, money is lent to groups of five. The members of these "solidarity circles" are responsible not just individually for the loans they have taken out, but as a group. If one person defaults, the others are held responsible for the debt (Buntin and Letts 1996). This system has allowed microfinance organizations to achieve low default rates. It builds solidarity and trust among the parties to the agreements. It is also a way to cultivate commitment and enforce rules.

Unfortunately, grants are not loans and mainstream philanthropy largely operates as a one-way street. The idea of implementing a system of mutual accountability runs counter to the basic precept that foundations provide capital and nonprofit organizations are responsible for implementation. There is little room in most philanthropy for mutual accountability either among a group of nonprofits or between foundations and recipients. Nonprofits generally guard their independence fiercely, few would want to cast their lot with that of other organizations, and givers and getters generally do not view themselves as part of common enterprise.[2] Mutual accountability construed broadly would demand that nonprofits take responsibility for the performance of other organizations, not just their own. Given the huge pressures and harried conditions under which many nonprofits operate, it is hard to imagine this ever happening. Construed more narrowly, mutual accountability would mean that funders would have responsibilities to nonprofits after a grant is issued. And though foundations do sometimes make multiyear commitments, funding is often limited to a few years and foundations rarely deny themselves the freedom to cut off a nonprofit should it perform poorly initially or should the interests and focus of the funder change.

There is yet another possible way to construe the concept of mutual accountability in the world of philanthropy, one that connects foundations to other foundations. The idea might have some traction within two different contexts. The first is the tightly bound geographical communities of foundations. In some cities, such as Minneapolis, Chicago, and San Francisco, foundations are part of tight professional networks organized around regional associations of grant makers. Within these local groupings, institutional donors might reasonably feel some sense of peer accountability and could develop learning networks around frank peer assessments. A second context in which donors might respond to mutual accountability claims are issue areas in which groups of foundations are concentrated, such as health and arts, where large affinity groups of foundations are already organized. Within such groups, foundations might be willing to engage one another in a system of mutual accountability aimed at fostering dynamic learning.

In recent decades, there have been a few isolated examples of foundations that have tried to overcome the lack of either democratic or mutual accountability by changing the fundamental rules of the game. The work of the alternative funds is the most obvious such example (Ostrander 1995). Unhappy with the hierarchy and detachment of conventional private and community foundation, a movement was started in the 1960s to transform institutional philanthropy from the ground up. Groups of wealthy individuals with progressive political outlooks started alternative funds to disburse philanthropic money in a new way. Rather than have donors sit on the board of these new funds and control the use of the money collected, the alternative funds brought in community members, organizers, and representatives from nonprofit organizations to serve on the grants committees, where funding decisions were made. By turning the tables in philanthropy and by placing power in the hands of the grassroots, these progressive philanthropists believed that they had broken through the accountability trap in which conventional philanthropy had long been mired (Odendahl 1990). These funds created both democratic accountability and mutual forms of accountability between and among community leaders and funders. Not surprisingly, the profile of the alternative fund movement reached its apex in the 1970s at the height of progressivism and has been on the decline since, never constituting more than a minuscule fraction of the philanthropic universe. Mainstream individual and institutional philanthropy, having taken note of this utopian vision of shared governance, decided that this vision was simply not that attractive in the end. For the vast majority of foundations, the loss of power and control inherent in alternative funds has proven too extreme and final.

If the models of democratic and mutual accountability do not apply well to the field of philanthropy, it may be useful to analyze exactly how accountability is currently practiced in the field. Instead of taking the fateful step of actually building accountability structures upon which voice and action are possible, the vast majority of foundations have taken less radical steps, the most significant of which has been the movement to offer up increased transparency in the place of accountability (Frumkin 1999). If accountability involves a noisy and contentious dialogue between the world of philanthropy and its many stakeholders, transparency can be pursued by foundations as a long and uninterrupted monologue. It involves pushing out toward the world information and details about philanthropy, and makes no real commitment to listen or respond. Transparency is far less threatening to foundations than accountability and, as a consequence, has emerged as an attractive alternative strategy. A substantial increase in the transparency of foundations has in fact been achieved in recent decades. Foundations have taken a host of information sharing steps aimed at ensuring that questions about philanthropy are readily answerable (McIlnay 1998). This transparency work has led to greater understanding of the field of foundations among the general public and allowed nonprofit organizations to research and direct their funding proposals more efficiently (Bernholz 2004).

Although moving information out into the open is laudable, it is neither the functional nor moral equivalent of creating a real accountability mechanism. As traffic on this one-way street of information has increased, there remain strikingly few meaningful feedback loops bringing information back to foundations. To be sure, a few large foundations have experimented with surveys of their grant recipients. These efforts have ended up looking like simple customer satisfaction surveys in which issues of process and procedures have dominated (Bolduc, Buchanan, and Huang 2004). Even with a promise of anonymity to respondents, these surveys have struggled to elicit honest comments and are only a modest step toward making foundations accountable for the procedural side of their work. Grantee surveys may provide some insight into how nonprofits are treated by foundation staff, but they provide no information on the substantive issue of whether wise philanthropic choices and effective grants are being made. Other foundations, particularly those with a flair for theatrics, have experimented with open houses and town hall events, in which nonprofits are invited to pose any question they wish to the foundation's leaders, who typically sit on stage in such sessions. Like shareholder meetings of large companies, these events can have a staged and surreal quality to them. But, unlike shareholder meetings, which can be contentious, foundation open houses are quiet affairs, because few nonprofits are able to express themselves candidly in such a situation, even if they have major complaints and concerns.

The most common transparency device involves the simple release of information. Foundations have set up elaborate and informative Web pages, published annual reports in ever greater numbers, issued concise grant-making guidelines explaining what they intend to fund, and released concept papers laying out assumptions and preferred approaches to particular problems. Although this information flow has certainly made it easier to understand what givers are thinking and what they are seeking to support, it is a broad but shallow form of disclosure. Releasing information can and does make the grant-making process appear less mysterious, but it is still a weak proxy for real accountability systems.

Perhaps the most visible response of the philanthropic community to the accountability challenge has been to hire professional staff to manage the grant-making process.[3] Foundation staff act as a mix of talent scouts, evaluators, and public relations specialists, providing a buffer between the foundation board, which may include the founder and family member, and the public. Beyond what they do, professionals within philanthropy represent something more significant: a commitment to taking philanthropy seriously. In many ways, the rise of professional grant makers represents the single most significant development in the field of philanthropy in recent decades. Only with professionalization have the issues of effectiveness and accountability truly risen to the surface and become amplified. Professionals in philanthropy have worked to create fieldwide norms and standards for conduct, training programs aimed at developing grant-making skills, and a body of expert knowledge to guide practice. All this work has focused on fulfilling the instrumental dimension in philanthropy by ratcheting up the technology around giving, rationalizing practices and building administrative structures, generally strengthening the field in the eyes of the nonprofit community and the public.

When carried out by individual donors who simply enact their values and connect them to public needs, philanthropy is an expressive exercise through which donors project their commitments and beliefs onto the world (Mason 1996; Frumkin 2002). Although it may aim at achieving clear goals and producing tangible public benefits, the stakes of individual giving tend to be relatively modest, especially when the amounts of money involved are small. Giving is an experience for donors that allows them to make a connection to an organization or cause that means something to them. It is not surprising that hospitals and universities receive large numbers of gifts from alumni and former patients, who want to give something back. When giving is done by professionals on behalf of a donor, the relative mix of expressiveness and instrumentalism shifts in favor of the latter (Barry and Manno 1997). Few foundation staff, particularly those who come onto the scene long after the donor is gone, understand their work as anything other than using philanthropic resources as effectively as possible in support of the mission.[4] Being effective is also a way for professionals to achieve recognition within the field and to advance to positions of greater responsibility. Because they are giving away money that they did not earn themselves, professionals within philanthropy are also instinctively concerned about accountability. Though solutions to the accountability quagmire remain elusive, it is possible to interpret the related move to greater levels of transparency as being largely driven by professionals seeking to document and publicize their own work.

The overall effect of professionalization in philanthropy has been mixed. On the one hand, the process has certainly contributed to boundaries between foundations and recipients being lowered, and it has removed some of the caprice and personalization inherent in donor-controlled giving. My contention is that this shift has had more subtle effects that have gone largely unexamined. Professionalization has also impoverished the field in many ways by robbing it of an important part of what makes philanthropy distinctive, namely the convergence—and at times collision—of private values with public purposes (Frumkin 1999). By focusing on maximizing the impact of giving, the pronounced shift toward professional grant making that has taken place in recent decades may have ultimately made it harder to achieve the most important form of strategic alignment, namely connecting private values to public purposes. It is this connection that differentiates private philanthropy's work from government's and that often leads philanthropy to support new and untested approaches to long-standing public problems. In the end, the infusion of professional grant makers throughout foundation philanthropy hardly solves the core accountability question and actually raises a number of new and difficult issues.

The Past and Future of Foundation Accountability

As foundations wrestle with finding solutions to the challenge of accountability, the threat of new government regulation and oversight of the field still remains. Attempts to make foundations appear more accessible and better managed fall to the wayside when a few instances of perceived abuse, partisanship, or indulgence appear. Although foundations have enjoyed a largely charmed existence over the past century, Congress has at times shown an interest in foundations, focusing not on whether such organizations were making good use of their resources, but rather whether they were engaged in excessive political activity (Edie 1987). In fact, the history of congressional scrutiny of the perceived partisanship of large foundations over the past century is critical to why the central problems in foundation philanthropy remain unaddressed and thus unresolved. Recently, Congress turned its attention back to foundations. In 2003, it had asked difficult questions about how foundations were managed and how accountable they were to the communities they serve. It took an interest in the administrative expenses of foundations and even proposed a revision to the payout rule that determines the minimum level of distributions demanded of foundations. This new public scrutiny sent shivers throughout the field, led foundations to mount an expensive lobbying effort to thwart any change to the existing regulations, and generally put the field on the defensive for the first time in a long time.

The conflict over the administrative expenses of foundations started with an article in San Jose's *Mercury News,* which reported on the salary and retirement package of the James Irvine Foundation's recently retired president. This prompted Senator Grassley, chair of the Finance Committee, to note: "Every dollar that featherbeds a foundation executive doesn't help a person in need. You have to wonder how excessive executive salaries and retirement packages fulfill the vision of those who left their money to set up foundations."[5] It was not long before others voiced similar concern regarding money being spent on foundation salaries and overhead, especially at a time when foundation giving had slowed and the public funds available for discretionary social spending were dwindling. As legislation bearing on a broad range of issues related to charitable giving of all kinds was winding its way through Congress, the House of Representatives introduced a bill (HR7), which provided that the mandated payout of foundations—

set at 5 percent of the average monthly value of the endowment during the preceding year—be altered in one small way. Specifically, administrative expenses could no longer be counted as qualifying distributions and credited toward the payout minimum.

As the debate unfolded in the press and in professional meetings, two developments were surprising. The first was that the foundation community never articulated a clear and compelling argument for expenditures on professional salaries rather than grants. To win over their critics, foundations needed to make the case that the grants they made were either more effective than they would have been without the presence of substantial staffs, particularly in the larger foundations, or that staff expense was critical to the field being accessible and accountable. To make this argument, the foundations or their trade associations should have come forward with concrete cases and illustrations of how the cost of foundation overhead and staffing expenditures were more than offset by better performance and accountability. No such cost benefit analysis was ever advanced, not even conceptually. Instead, foundation spokesmen fell back on overblown claims that the proposed changes would endanger the foundation community's long-term viability. The intellectual laziness of the field in the face of an important challenge was stunning.

The second surprising development was the silence of many nonprofit leaders in the middle of this important debate and the willingness of several nonprofit groups to speak out against the proposed change to the payout rule. For a field that prides itself on its advocacy work and its commitment to the most needy, the spectacle was remarkable. Faced with the prospect of increasing the level of foundation funding that reach nonprofits by billions of dollars, most of the sector's leaders were either trying to stay clear of the controversy or cowering at the thought of offending their funders by speaking out. Of course, reasonable people can disagree about whether the change proposed in HR7 is wise. There is no reason, however, that the issue should have elicited such thundering silence within the sector.

At this interesting and contentious juncture in the evolution of private foundations, it is important to see that the field has periodically found itself in the public spotlight because under all the political posturing is the issue of accountability. Endowed in perpetuity and enjoying considerable power over their many stakeholders, foundations remain comfortably adrift. There are few forces pushing foundations to solve the field's core problem. Even Congress is unlikely to pursue the matter very aggressively or successfully, given the substantial lobbying effort the field mounts whenever government regulators begin to hover in the doorways.

For headway to be made on the core problems in philanthropy, a new movement within the field is needed. One idea floated at various times is a foundation accrediting system comparable to that used by colleges and universities. And although there is much to criticize in such a formal model, at least one element of such an approach bears serious consideration. A system of peer review would at least vest responsibility for improving foundation behavior within the field, rather than look unrealistically to any of philanthropy's stakeholders to do so. If nothing else, this would represent an acceptance of the reality that perpetual foundations are unlike most other institutions. Foundations can and will make progress on the accountability issue when pressure—either formal or informal—from their peers becomes meaningful. This will involve establishing norms that make it more difficult and more costly for foundations to operate without taking accountability seriously. These norms could be cultivated and promoted through peer review and interorganizational consultation. For the process to begin, however, leadership within the field is critical, given that foundations are likely to remain immune to outside reform. If nothing else, real leadership would remind foundations that perpetuity and power are not ends in themselves.

From Accountability to Legitimacy

The accountability woes of foundations do not exist in a vacuum. They interact with and exacerbate the related problem of legitimacy, a question that is hard to avoid when considering philanthropy. After all, giving projects out into the public sphere the power and resources of a few people and allows private parties to act on the behalf of the public. Because donors have more power and opportunities than non-donors to shape the lives of others, there is a natural question of what makes the exercise of this power legitimate. By legitimate I mean initially simply being perceived as legitimate by stakeholders—not actually acting in a way that renders these perceptions of the fair and just exercise of power meaningful and credible. The answer to the legitimacy question in philanthropy requires that one plumb the multiple sources of support and acceptance from which philanthropy can potentially draw. It also demands that the distinction between individual givers and institutional funders be examined. The issue of legitimacy arises sharply once funds are domiciled in institutions that enjoy tax-exemption and operate for public purposes (Bremner 1987; Weaver 1967). Although individual givers may feel some pressure to act in ways perceived to be as legitimate as some of the large foundations, they are in fact often able to give with relative impunity and remain well under the radar screen. Principals are also protected to some extent by the fact that philanthropic funds are really "their money" to be deployed as the person who earned the funds sees fit. When professional staff take on the responsibility of disbursing the funds of donors, legitimacy challenges surface and tough questions emerge about the choices made in the name of a donor often long deceased, but whose impact on the public is still being interpreted by a few, though felt by many.

What are the possible sources of foundation legitimacy? It can be drawn from government, even when philanthropy lobbies against reform and obstructs policy changes. Many donors who create foundations start with the impulse to seek the benefit of a major tax deduction, a reduction of estate taxes, or simply the ability to operate as a tax-exempt organization. In so doing, they point to one aspect of foundations that appears to confer some legitimacy on institutional philanthropy, namely that public policy supports this activity indirectly. For those who want to question the right of foundations to make decisions that might determine the survival or collapse of charitable organizations and have important human consequences for those who depend on programs funded with philanthropic dollars, the presence of government policy—affirming the idea of private action in the public good—creates some political cover and supports the legitimacy of foundations. If philanthropy were not legitimate, government would not endorse it and support it through public policy.[6] Of course, there are some problems with this argument, namely that many goals supported by policy may not ultimately be meritorious or legitimate.

Legitimacy can also be drawn from the organizations that philanthropy supports. Nonprofit organizations are in a unique position to see foundations do their work. The grant-seeking process may humiliate and infuriate nonprofit managers if too many hoops must be jumped through or if the process appears capricious or stacked in favor

of certain organizations. However, foundations can handle the difficult challenge of sifting through requests and choosing among them in
ways that create greater levels of trust, and, ultimately, greater levels
of legitimacy. Attending to procedural issues, including returning tele-
phone calls, promptly acknowledging proposals, and sending credible
letters explaining board decisions are all part of what it takes to make
a donor appear to be rightly and justly exercising control over philanthropic resources. Although it would be difficult for foundations if the
legitimacy of their work boiled down to the frequency with which they
selected the most qualified and highest impact organizations for funding, in practice, the most significant thing foundations can do is garner
the acceptance and respect of the organizations they work most closely
with. Funding nonprofits and treating grantees fairly is a meaningful
measure of support and legitimacy.

The legitimacy of philanthropy can also be bolstered by consulting
with peers, collaborating with entities that already have legitimacy,
and securing the approbation of leaders in the field. Given the profound imbalance of power between givers and receivers, few channels
of redress are open to nonprofit organizations that may have been
denied support or that may have a grievance. To create the semblance
of an open system in which foundations are able to receive and act on
information about their grant-making processes and policies not only
from the nonprofits that have gotten grants but also from a more neu-
tral group of observers, foundations can create networks of collaboration and consultation, which build the appearance that they are
legitimately exercising philanthropic power.

Finally, enterprising and aggressive foundations can legitimate
themselves. That is, through their own actions, particularly by giving
grants to organizations that contribute to the public interest in significant and visible ways, foundations can bask in the reflected
light of the good work done by grant recipients. This form of self-
legitimization—strategic grant making to organizations that occupy
visible positions in the sector and that shape public opinion—
is appealing because it does not require much work beyond processing requests for funding and initiating programs with a high potential
return value. Philanthropy can act and give in ways that build public support and understanding, creating a reservoir of goodwill that
can later be tapped should challenges arise. The main problem with
this model of self-legitimization is that it depends to some extent on

what grantees do with grants, and does not speak to the larger issue of mission effectiveness, or how well foundations achieve their philanthropic objectives.

There is a major problem with this framing of the legitimacy question in philanthropy, however. It is a problem that raises a host of complex issues that many foundations would prefer to ignore out of convenience. Legitimacy in philanthropy must mean more than the narrow descriptive claim that foundations are legitimate when they are perceived or thought to rightly possess the power and position to enact their commitments through giving. It must also have a normative dimension (Applbaum 2004). It needs to reflect the rightful discharge of philanthropic duties. It must have a substantive dimension that allows those on the outside to note not only that large individual donors and foundations in America legally and legitimately have great wealth they can deploy however they see fit, but also that these individuals and institutions are discharging their responsibilities wisely. The obstacle to defining philanthropic legitimacy so that it sets standards for the just use of philanthropic power and resources is clear. It inevitably leads to confusion about standards for legitimate philanthropic work. The minimal existing standards for giving hardly provide much real guidance or assurance that philanthropic resources are being used wisely and effectively.[7]

It is fair to say that philanthropy has made substantial progress in defining the conditions under which descriptive claims about its legitimacy as a field can be supported. On the whole, however, it has made far less progress in understanding and spelling out any normative framework and its leaders have fiddled with and stumbled over the concept of effective philanthropy as a centerpiece in their case for a greater and deeper claim related to legitimacy (Walker and Grossman 1999).

Government and Foundations

As foundations work through some of the accountability and legitimacy challenges, they cannot avoid the deeper contextual question of what the proper relationship is between philanthropy's quest to contribute to the public good and government's work to meet public needs? The question relates to both accountability and legitimacy. Accountability appears to imply—at least at some level—a relationship with government and the constituencies it represents. Legitimacy also appears—in some measure—to demand that foundations craft a relationship with the public sector, though there are, as I have suggested, additional bases for it. In the end, however, the relationship of foundations to government is more complex than it first appears. There is not a positive and linear relationship between strong foundation-government relations and either greater accountability or legitimacy.

Philanthropy is shaped by government through regulation and the application of subsidies. Still, philanthropy has many ways—at least four[8]—in which it can turn around and frame its working relationship with government (Ylvisaker 1999). Each of the four has its advantages and disadvantages and each has consequences for the nature of the actual philanthropic work that foundations are to do (Young 1999).

The first option is to see giving as being engaged in a supplementary relationship to government. If government at the federal, state, or local level happens to be working in the same programmatic area as a donor, the supplementary model would suggest that philanthropy track what the public sector is doing and look for opportunities to add funds where needed to strengthen the public sector's ability to meet those needs. In this conception of the relationship, government is driving the process and has the primary responsibility for choosing causes and issues. Philanthropy's role is to dutifully add to this agenda by working in fields and in places where government, for one reason or another, is not able or willing to do so. Seeing philanthropy as supplementary eases some of the burdens on foundations because it does not ask that philanthropy break new ground or solve long-standing problems: Instead it focuses on the question of resources and works toward greater scale and reach. Whether philanthropic resources are adequate to this task is difficult to know because accounts vary greatly, in terms of both which government programs need to be privately supplemented and how large philanthropic resources are likely to be over time. Lingering doubts about this concept have been explored empirically by examining whether government funding actually crowds out private giving. Far from inviting giving into areas where government is working, the crowding-out hypothesis suggests that public funding will drive away foundations and work against a supplementary relationship. Evidence suggests that even though this effect may exist, its magnitude is relatively small (Kingma 1989).

Regardless of its feasibility or significance, the idea of philanthropy mirroring government is problematic, at least in terms of the consequences it would have for the expressive and instrumental content in giving. Even the most ardent advocate for greater equity and efficiency in philanthropy would blanch at the idea that philanthropy's unfettered resources should be principally devoted to doing what government could do through taxation. The argument against a supplementary role for philanthropy in social provision is that it would push giving too far away from its expressive, personalistic side and shut down a major motive behind giving: the desire to enact one's values through charitable action. Although there might be plenty of overlap between public priorities and private charitable interests, this coincidence in purposes takes on a different form depending on whether it is the happy result of circumstances or the product of directive public policy designed to achieve it through new subsidies or regulation.

Philanthropy can assume a second posture in relation to government by defining a complementary role for itself. Instead of simply tracking government priorities and supplementing public expenditures where needed, it can try to define a relationship whose central feature is the sensible and productive division of labor between sectors. As government does its work, it inevitably leaves many public needs unattended, not only because funds are limited for discretionary programs, but also because some groups are more able to press their case for support. Lobbying and advocacy can shape how public funds are allocated in ways that may not be entirely equitable. For philanthropy, this problem can be an opportunity. Locating significant gaps in funding and helping groups that have been left outside the political process voice their concerns and needs can be a potent and valuable role for philanthropy. When foundations seek out and fill gaps left by government, they can correct for those gaps and bring into public view needs that may have been obscured for some time. If successful in crafting a complementary role to government, philanthropy can thus serve both as a funder of last resort and as a social spotlight, shining attention on issues and problems that have not been seen or heard enough.

There is at least one significant problem, however, with the idea of philanthropy complementing government. Philanthropy cannot be effective if its agenda is driven by forces outside the field or if its primary mode of operation is reactive. There is some danger that an important element in creative philanthropy would be lost: the capacity to shape the public agenda in ways that those inside and outside government might have never considered. In this sense, the challenge for funders who adopt a complementary role in relation to government is to hold on to the power of initiative that allows foundations to move ahead with ideas and projects even when evidence and support for their work is just emerging or not even present. Philanthropy should be thinking thoughts, drawing up plans, and supporting programs that government has not thought of supporting. It is very hard for foundations to be in the vanguard if they are simply looking for gaps in the current landscape.

To counter the pacifying character of complementary relations, foundations can take a third and different approach to structuring their relations with government. They can strike up and maintain an adversarial relationship with government, one in which philanthropy actively challenges the assumptions of the public sector and works to counter its influence. Thus, rather than look either to supplement or complement, foundations can pursue philanthropic agendas actively geared toward counterbalancing and reversing wrong government directions and poor government choices. As an adversary, philanthropy may have to rely to some extent on government to set the direction, albeit in a contrarian sort of way. As an adversary, philanthropy needs to know what government's priorities and programs are to be able to work in the opposite direction, be it by delivering services differently or supporting policies that run counter to the dominant paradigm. There is a relatively small component of organized philanthropy that has in fact adopted an adversarial position. With a heavy emphasis on radical politics, community empowerment, and progressive policies, some funders of social change have declared that there is already plenty of money supporting mainstream approaches to political and social problems and that the real opportunities lie in supporting causes in opposition to the status quo.

The problem with an adversarial stance is that it assumes disagreement about policy as a starting point and builds an agenda based on that assumption. Not only is it limiting for philanthropy to focus on what government does, it also makes little sense. Rather than starting with the question "What do I oppose?" foundations are probably much better off, all things considered, with the more basic question, "What do I believe in, what do I stand for?" It is unlikely that remaining in an adversarial role indefinitely will produce the kind of psychic feedback needed to generate long-lasting enthusiasm for giving. Just as supplementary and complementary roles are too limiting, so too is an adversarial approach. Given the tremendous freedom of philanthropy, it would be a shame to give over large amounts of this freedom to the narrow cause of opposition.

Thankfully, a fourth option is open. Philanthropy can define for itself an autonomous relationship from government, one in which the direction of giving is sheltered from government policy directives (Frumkin 2000). Autonomy in absolute terms is hard to achieve, of course. By its very nature, philanthropy is active in the public sphere and will frequently collide, overlap, and interact with government programs and policies. However, there is a meaningful difference when these points of intersection are the result of mission pursuit grounded in independent consideration of philanthropic interests and opportunities, rather than the product of a careful calculus grounded in the decisions taken by public sector agencies. Still, in defining a posture in relation to government, both individual and institutional donors can consciously craft for themselves a relationship in which plenty of distance is maintained and in which philanthropy is able to act positively to address the social problems that emerge. To do so requires more work than any of the other three postures, all of which are more reactive. To act autonomously, philanthropy needs the guidance not only of efficient administrators, but also of visionary leaders capable of analyzing community needs creatively and then developing innovative responses.

Several good arguments encourage philanthropy to doggedly guard its autonomy and resist capitulation on the basis of accountability and legitimacy worries. The first is that any of the first three options for philanthropy's interaction with government essentially put giving at something of a disadvantage: public policy is seen as the trigger and benchmark that drives private giving, in one direction or another. Looking too closely at what other actors are doing, even when it is an actor as significant as government, can be a significant mistake, akin to looking under the lamppost simply because that is where the light is located. Foundations can reserve for themselves the right to work in areas that government has not yet even identified as worthy of public sector attention or that are too controversial for policy to address. To preserve the capacity of the field to innovate—at the level not only of the design of intervention but also of the conceptualization of public needs—foundations need some space between their work and government's.

In the end, foundations can trade away much of their autonomy to partner closely with government, or jealously guard their independence and maintain some distance. The choice has profound consequences not only for how they conceive of their work, but where philanthropic energies are focused. How foundations understand their relationship with government can lead them to focus on very different things. When autonomy is a starting assumption, the philanthropic challenge will start with defining the core public problems worthy of attention. For foundations, this is an invitation to reflect on the question of how best to find a provocative intersection of public purposes and private values, the heart of philanthropic strategy. When a close partnership with government is sought, philanthropic energy will be focused further down the process to the crafting of better programs. If the fundamental value proposition is defined by government, the role of the donor is changed and rendered far more technical. The task becomes one of assessing what government is currently doing and then devising a plan either to amplify and expand successful programs or to devise a new model of service delivery that will produce even greater value. Operating in a supporting role to government entails an unacceptable attenuation of the freedom and potential of foundations. How then can foundations sensibly navigate this terrain and establish a relationship between their giving and existing public priorities? Although there are many ways in which government and philanthropy can and do interact productively through partnerships, the probability of alignment and fit will be higher if foundations claim— at least during their early stages—a fair amount of autonomy. Freedom from external constraints and expectations is critical to foundations being able to deliver on the promise of more effective forms of giving.[9]

If foundations can maintain some programmatic autonomy from government, plenty of room will still be available for accountability between the sectors. There need not be a zero-sum game between autonomy and accountability, or between autonomy and legitimacy. Instead of associating the two issues with cumbersome collaborations and attempts at policy integration, foundations need to see the broader picture. Accountability for administering charitable funds is far less onerous than substantively coordinating grant-making programs. Foundations should count themselves fortunate in the freedom they enjoy, especially if they strategically maintain some distance between their work and government's. Accountability for procedural matters can also enhance the legitimacy of foundations in the eyes of the field's many stakeholders.

Will accountability and legitimacy ever be perfect in foundation philanthropy? Probably not. Freedom is a profound privilege, one that foundations should guard jealously. If they succeed in holding on to the special role and identity, the public will ultimately benefit because foundations will be able to fulfill their potential as contributors to a vibrant and pluralistic society. Living with some accountability and legitimacy ambiguity may turn out to be a fundamental attribute of the foundation field, rather than a problem that can or should be remedied anytime soon.[10]

Notes

1. For an international and comparative perspective on the issue of foundation accountability, see Anheier and Toepler (1999) and Bertelsmann Foundation (2000) where the nature of public oversight of organized philanthropy is shown to take many different forms.
2. Part of the independence of nonprofits can be traced to their increasing commerciality and the rise of earned income as prime source of agency finance. On the freedom that this funding source can create and its connection to more traditional charitable sources of support, see Dees (1988).
3. For an overview of the procedural issues in foundation grant making, see Orosz (2000). A more reflective consideration of the challenge of managing foundations can be found in Fleischman (2004).
4. The issue of donor intent and the obstacles to its preservation over the long haul is taken up in Bork (1993) and Wooster (1998). The issue central to conservatives who worry that professionals tend to overlook the philanthropic intentions of founders over time.
5. Quoted in Nadler (2003). Ahn, Eisenberg, and Khamvongsa (2003) present a broader perspective on the controversy over self-interested transactions and trustee fees.
6. A comprehensive review of the legal framework surrounding foundations can be found in Fremont-Smith (2004), where the history and evolution of government's stance toward giving are also presented.
7. Interest in nature of philanthropic effectiveness is growing. For an empirical perspective on how foundation staff construct the concept of effectiveness, see Ostrower (2004). A framework for increasing effectiveness in foundations is developed in Porter and Kramer (1999).

8. Young (1999) develops a threefold typology that I draw upon and then extend here.
9. On the many different ways to construe the possible purposes of philanthropy against which to measure its effectiveness, see Prewitt (1999).
10. For a fuller discussion of the challenges facing philanthropy today, see Frumkin (2006).

References

Ahn, Christine, Pablo Eisenberg, and Channapha Khamvongsa. 2003. "Foundation Trustee Fees: Use and Abuse." Washington, D.C.: The Center for Public and Nonprofit Leadership, Georgetown Public Policy Institute.

Anheier, Helmut K. and Stephan Toepler, eds. 1999. *Private Funds, Public Purpose*. New York: Kluwer Academic/Plenum Publishers.

Applbaum, Arthur Isak. 2004. "Legitimacy in a Bastard Kingdom." Working Paper, Center for Public Leadership, Kennedy School of Government. Cambridge, Mass.: Harvard University.

Barry, John W., and Bruno V. Manno, eds. 1997. *Giving Better, Giving Smarter*. Washington, D.C.: National Commission on Philanthropy and Civic Renewal.

Bernholz, Lucy. 2004. *Creating Philanthropic Capital Markets*. New York: John Wiley & Sons.

Bertelsmann Foundation. 2000. *Striving for Philanthropic Success: Effectiveness and Evaluation in Foundations*. Gutersloh, Germany: Bertelsmann Foundation Publishers.

Bolduc, Kevin, Phil Buchanan, and Judy Huang. 2004. *Listening to Grantees: What Nonprofits Value in their Foundation Founders*. Boston, Mass.: Center for Effective Philanthropy.

Bork, Robert H. 1993. "Interpreting the Founder's Vision." In *Donor Intent*. Washington, D.C.: Philanthropy Roundtable.

Bremner, Robert H. 1987. *American Philanthropy*. Chicago: University of Chicago Press.

Brody, Evelyn. 1998. "Of Sovereignty and Subsidy: Conceptualizing the Charity Tax Exemption." *The Journal of Corporation Law* 23(4): 585–629.

Buntin, John, and Christine W. Letts. 1996. "Accion International." Kennedy School of Government Case #1354.0. Cambridge, Mass.: Harvard University.

Collins, Chuck, and Pam Rogers, with Joan P. Garner. 2000. *Robin Hood Was Right: A Guide to Giving Your Money for Social Change*. New York: W. W. Norton.

Dees, J. Gregory. 1988. "Enterprising Nonprofits." *Harvard Business Review* 64(1)(Jan./Feb.): 55–67.

DiMaggio, Paul. 2001. "Measuring the Impact of the Nonprofit Sector on Society is Probably Impossible but Possibly Useful: A Sociological Perspective." In *Measuring the Impact of the Nonprofit Sector*, edited by Patrice Flynn and Virginia A. Hodgkinson. New York: Kluwer Academic.

Edie, John A. 1987. "Congress and Foundations: Historical Summary." In *America's Wealthy and the Future of Foundations,* edited by Teresa Odendahl. New York: Foundation Center.

Ferris, James M., and Michael Mintrom. 2002. "Foundations and Public Policymaking: A Conceptual Framework." Research Report #10. Los Angeles: University of Southern California, School of Policy, Planning, and Development.

Fleishman, Joel L. 2004. "Simply Doing Good or Doing Good Well." In *Just Money: A Critique of Contemporary American Philanthropy,* edited by H. Peter Karoff. Boston, Mass.: TPI Editions.

Frank, Robert T. 1999. *Luxury Fever.* Princeton, N.J.: Princeton University Press.

Fremont-Smith, Marion. 2004. *Governing Nonprofit Organizations.* Cambridge, Mass.: Harvard University Press.

Frumkin, Peter. 1999. "Private Foundations as Public Institutions: Regulation, Professionalization, and the Redefinition of Organized Philanthropy." In *Philanthropic Foundations: New Scholarship, New Possibilities,* edited by Ellen Condliffe Lagemann. Bloomington: Indiana University Press.

———. 2000. "After Partnership: Rethinking Public-Nonprofit Relations." In *Who Provides? Religion and the Future of Social Welfare in American Democracy,* edited by Mary Jo Bane, Brent Coffin, and Ronald Thiemann. Boulder, Colo.: Westview Press.

———. 2002. *On Being Nonprofit.* Cambridge, Mass.: Harvard University Press.

———. 2006. *Strategic Giving.* Chicago: University of Chicago Press.

Kingma, Bruce R. 1989. "An Accurate Measurement of the Crowd-Out Effect, Income Effect and Price Effect for Charitable Contributions." *Journal of Political Economy* 97(5): 1197–207.

Letts, Christine W., William P. Ryan, and Allen Grossman. 1999. "Virtuous Capital: What Foundations Can Learn from Venture Capitalists." *Harvard Business Review* 75(2): 36–44.

Mason, David E. 1996. *Leading and Managing the Expressive Dimension: Harnessing the Hidden Power Source of the Nonprofit Sector.* San Francisco, Calif.: Jossey-Bass Publishers.

McIlnay, Dennis P. 1998. *How Foundations Work.* San Francisco, Calif.: Jossey-Bass Publishers.

Nadler, Eric. 2003. "Nonprofit Foundations: Perks Spur Debate in Congress." *Mercury News,* May 1, 2003.

Nielsen, Waldemar A. 1985. *The Golden Donors: A New Anatomy of the Great Foundations.* New York: Truman Talley Books and E. P. Dutton.

Odendahl, Teresa. 1990. *Charity Begins At Home: Generosity and Self-Interest Among the Philanthropic Elite.* New York: Basic Books.

Orosz, Joel J. 2000. *The Insider's Guide to Grantmaking.* San Francisco, Calif.: Jossey-Bass Publishers.

Ostrander, Susan A. 1995. *Money For Change.* Philadelphia, Pa.: Temple University Press.

Ostrander, Susan A., and Paul G. Schervish. 1990. "Giving and Getting: Philanthropy as a Social Relation." In *Critical Issues in American Philanthropy,* edited by John Van Til et al. San Francisco, Calif: Jossey-Bass Publishers.

Ostrower, Francie. 2004. *Attitudes and Practices Concerning Effective Philanthropy: Executive Summary.* Center on Nonprofits and Philanthropy, Washington, D.C.: Urban Institute.

Porter, Michael E., and Mark Kramer. 1999. "Philanthropy's New Agenda: Creating Value." *Harvard Business Review* 77(6): 121–30.

Prewitt, Kenneth. 1999. "Foundations as Mirrors of Public Culture." *American Behavioral Scientist* 42(6): 977–86.

Rockefeller, John D. 1909. *Random Reminiscences of Men and Events.* New York: Doubleday.

Smith, James Allen. 2002. "Foundations and Public Policy Making: A Historical Perspective." Working paper. Los Angeles: University of Southern California, School of Policy, Planning, and Development.

Smith, Steven Rathgeb, and Michael Lipsky. 1993. *Nonprofits for Hire.* Cambridge, Mass.: Harvard University Press.

Walker, Gary, and Jean Grossman. 1999. "Philanthropy and Outcomes: Dilemmas in the Quest for Accountability." In *Philanthropy and the Nonprofit Sector in the United States,* Charles T. Clotfelter and Thomas Ehrlich. Bloomington: Indiana University Press.

Weaver, Warren. 1967. *U.S. Philanthropic Foundations.* New York: Harper and Row.

Wooster, Martin Morse. 1998. *The Great Philanthropists and the Problem of Donor Intent.* Washington, D.C.: Capital Research Center.

Ylvisaker, Paul. 1999. "The Relationship Between Private Philanthropy and Government." In *Conscience and Community: The Legacy of Paul Ylvisaker,* edited by Virginia Esposito. New York: Peter Lang.

Young, Dennis R. 1999. "Complementary, Supplementary or Adversarial? A Theoretical and Historical Examination of Nonprofit-Government Relations in the United States." In *Government and Nonprofits,* edited by Elizabeth T. Boris and C. Eugene Steuerle. Washington, D.C.: Urban Institute.

Chapter 5

Redistributional Effects of America's Private Foundations

Julian Wolpert

Grants by America's 62,000 private foundations, with assets of $477 billion, totaled $30.3 billion in the year 2002 (Foundation Center 2003). Those are substantial numbers, but of themselves do not indicate whether the grants are redistributive and how their distributive targeting compares to government transfers and assistance programs. These questions are the focus of analysis in this chapter. However, the issues are complex and some preliminary discussion is needed about the concept of redistribution when applied to foundations. Little would be learned, for example, from merely calculating short-term changes in the income or the wealth distribution of Americans that can be traced to foundation activities, even if that were technically feasible. The related issue is whether foundations have legitimate longer-run functions, other than redistribution, that yield even greater social benefit.

Some of the major conceptual issues can be identified. Redistribution of "what, to whom, over what period, how much, to what end, and at what rate of progressivity" remain central questions for a comprehensive assessment. Does redistribution properly apply to the macro body of the foundation sector or the micro activities of individual foundations; to the deployment of foundation assets or just revenues; to immediate or long-term effects; to local, national, or global benefits; or to future generations? Alternatively, can an assessment of redistribution effects apply to the before and after well-being of the most disadvantaged beneficiaries even if relative disparities increase as a result of foundation grants? Does redistribution refer just to outcomes of foundation activities or to the process for distributing funds as well? How are distributive outcomes assessed when foundations broaden the narrow monetary notions of charity and redistribution to more general social benefit objectives that may have long-term consequences on welfare, such as improving levels of home ownership, safety and security of neighborhoods, environmental sustainability, good mental health, freedom from malaria and other disabling diseases, access to good public schools and higher education, or even appreciation of classical music, and the like?

Are Foundations Redistributive?

Policy makers would be gratified by a progressive pattern of foundation grants achieved without stringent government regulations. Sophisticated observers of American politics never seriously believed that the great fortunes that created foundations could have been taxed at a highly progressive rate or that foundation philanthropy would fundamentally alter the distribution of wealth (Colwell 1993; Dowie 2001; Edie 1987). Officials would be happy to learn that at least some social benefit and amelioration of disparities still do result from those "taxing opportunities that have been forgone." Thus, the counterfactual is not the unrealistic assumption "what would government have accomplished if the wealth that created foundations had been taxed?" The more pragmatic distributive perspective for policy makers is "which modest legislative or regulatory changes can be made at the margin that supplement self-regulation to induce somewhat better outcomes from foundation activities for the nation's neediest residents?"

Analysts decry the shortage of data for rigorous analysis of "who benefits," but their assessments (albeit partial) do confirm a modestly progressive flow of transfers (Clotfelter 1996.) We cannot reliably determine, for example, the share of direct or indirect benefits received by the less well-off. Foundation grants are awarded to nonprofit organizations and rarely to individuals. In 2001, 51,000 organizations received 125,000 grants. However, few if any nonprofits collect information about the income or wealth of clients who benefit from the services funded solely by foundation grants.

The Foundation Niche in Social Welfare Spending

A number of earlier studies have probed data on the distribution of grants by service sector as potential gross indicators of distributive impacts (Clotfelter 1992). The prevailing assumption is that grants targeted to social services are more distributive than those dedicated to the arts, health, or higher education. The data are derived for the 80 percent of private foundation grant dollars tracked by the Foundation Center, as well as some information from the large number of community, corporate, and smaller private foundations. These analyses have generally concluded that foundation impacts are mildly redistributive and are becoming somewhat more so, though little or no funding is transferred directly to households in need (Margo 1992). The private foundation share of annual total U.S. contributions (about 8 percent) is dwarfed by individual giving (77 percent). The foundation share of total nonprofit revenues ($1.6 trillion) varies by service sector but averages about 1.7 percent (2.2 percent for all types of foundations) (AAFRC 2003).

In 2003, the nation's gross domestic product (GDP) was $11 trillion and federal spending alone (without expenditures by state and local government) was $2.1 trillion—19.5 percent of GDP and ten times the total amount of charitable contributions from all sources. Therefore, foundations (with annual grants of only 1 percent of federal spending) must search for opportunities to be instrumental in a service arena in which they are generally minor players. Federal, state, and local government as well as individual and corporate donors have much more prominent roles in supporting the services delivered by nonprofits. Furthermore, many nonprofit recipients of foundation grants receive greater shares of their revenues from service fees, other grants and contracts, and endowment income. Still, the $30 billion of private foundation grants are critically important, especially in selective service sectors, such as higher education and the arts.

Data Sources and Gaps

Existing data are inadequate for rigorous comparative analyses of beneficiaries from government social welfare programs or other charitable modes like individual donations, bequests, trusts, corporate donations, or grants from corporate foundations. Furthermore, no systematic data are available about individual cash donations to the needy. However, such tallies, even if feasible, would provide a notably incomplete perspective of comparative effectiveness as agents of distributive justice.

Relative to the minimum information thresholds for a rigorous longitudinal study of the distributive effects of foundations, analysts can point to very little data. The difficulties in assessing the distributive agenda of foundations from their grant-making activities is illustrated from the data shown in table 5.1 and figure 5.1. These data (the best available) are derived from the Foundation Center's analysis of grants of $10,000 or more by the nation's 1,007 largest foundations, which represent more than half total grant dollars. The current information (since the 1990s) is only roughly comparable to the earlier data because of shifts in the classification procedures. The service sectors targeted for grants undoubtedly differ by the share of beneficiaries in low income groups.

Targeting by Sector

Margo's 1990 analysis of the distributional effects of foundation grants showed a pre-World War II pattern that emphasized the health, education, and scientific research categories with little attention devoted to the arts, social services, or religion (Margo 1992). The assumption here is the poor are prominent direct beneficiaries only of the social service sector and the other sectors serve mainly middle- and upper-income households. Yet a case can be made that some portion of grants for education are targeted to scholarships for lower-income students; health grants have significant longer-term benefits for the poor; and some of the funds for the arts and religion provide cross-subsidization of services for lower-income beneficiaries. A shift toward the education and arts categories occurred by the late 1950s and 1960s and the share of grants declined in health, welfare, and scientific research, after which grants for education declined and health increased somewhat. Margo concludes that the distribution of grant dollars has varied in response to social trends and government activity, has probably been quite regressive in its targeting in the past, and has bypassed certain population groups (especially minorities). The data record in the late 1980s shows consistent emphasis on higher education and somewhat more progressive tendencies especially among the very large and the regionally focused foundations.

More recent data reveal that support for specific populations reached 40 percent of grant dollars in 2001. The largest targeted groups for grants included children and youth, disadvantaged groups, ethnic and racial minorities, and women and girls. The largest increases between 2000 and 2001 were for offenders and ex-offenders, the disabled, people with AIDS, single parents, crime or abuse victims, substance abusers, the military and veterans, and senior citizens.

Table 5.1   Percentage of Foundation Grants by Major Area of Funding

Year	2001	1997	1996	1995	1993	1991	1987	1977	1966	1957	1931
Arts	12	13	12	12	15	14	15	13	17	4	3
Education	27	24	25	25	24	25	18	25	42	53	26
Health	21	17	16	17	18	17	18	24	10	16	32
Human services	24	15	17	17	15	14	27	21	13	10	14
Public affairs and social benefits	11	12	12	12	11	13					
Science and technology	3	5	4	5	4	6					
Social science	2	3	3	2	3	1	21	15	12	14	23
Environment	6	5	5	5	5						
International	2	4	3	4	4						
Religion	2	2	2	2	2	2	2	2	5	3	1
Other	0	0	0	0	0	0	0	0	2	0	1
	100	100	100	100	100	100	100	100	100	100	100

Source: See figure 5.1.

Figure 5.1 Percentage of Foundation Grants by Major Area of Funding

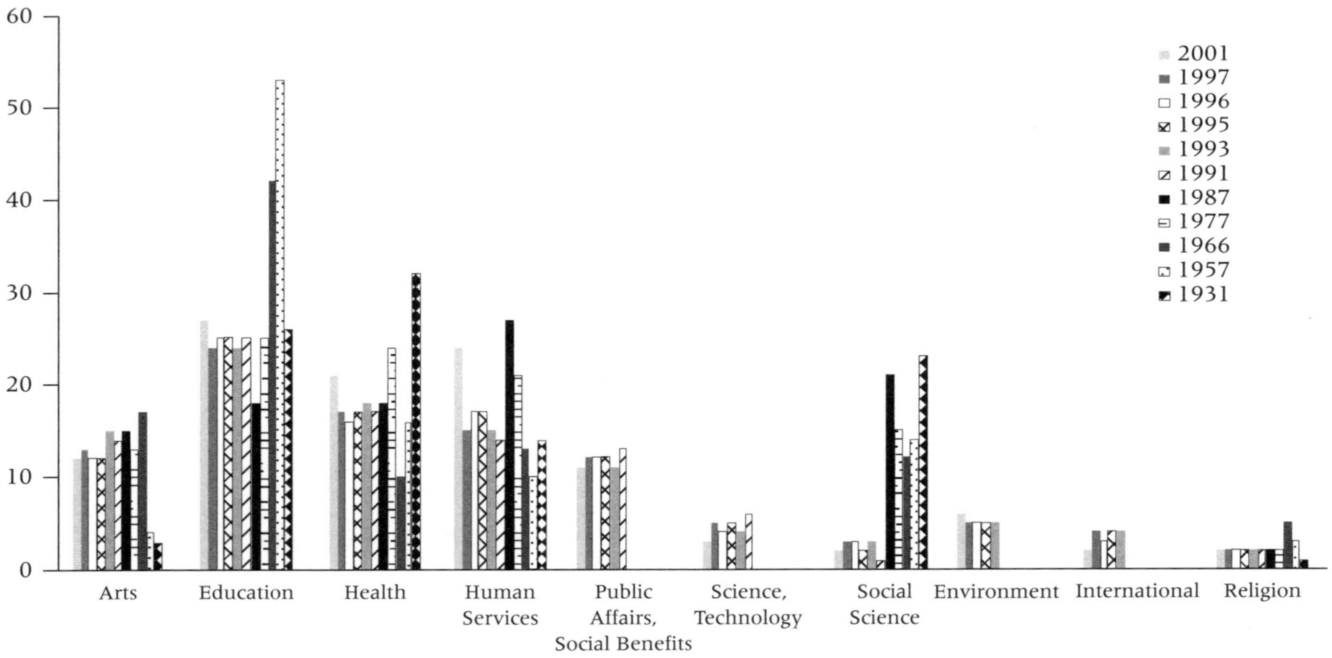

Legend:
2001
1997
1996
1995
1993
1991
1987
1977
1966
1957
1931

Categories: Arts, Education, Health, Human Services, Public Affairs, Social Benefits, Science, Technology, Social Science, Environment, International, Religion

Source: Foundation Center (2003); Margo (1992, table 7.5, 221).

Substantial increases in specific grant-making programs of a few top funders, such as the Gates, Robert Wood Johnson, MacArthur, and Ford foundations, helped to raise support for many of these population groups (Foundation Center 2003).

In contrast to private donors who devote half of their giving to religious institutions, the foundation share is only 2.2 percent. Only 1 percent of foundation grants went to agencies that serve the homeless, and 2 to 3 percent were made to support advocacy activities. Advocacy implies "giving a voice" through grant support for convenings, coalition-building, lobbying, and partnering with government. The overwhelming majority, 90 percent, of foundations restrict their grants to their local community. International giving by foundations in the sample, primarily for U.S.-based programs, increased to $2.5 billion in 2001 in 12,000 grants, up from $1.07 billion in 1998. Direct grants for overseas agencies decreased to $771 million. The pattern reveals a focus on support primarily for major institutions, especially the elite universities, major museums and symphony orchestras, and teaching hospitals, and secondarily for social services, the environment, advocacy, and international aid. Disadvantaged households are not prominent as clients but could be affected indirectly. A localism bias is quite evident, especially among community foundations that are also larger supporters of social service agencies.

Redistribution

The analysis requires that we briefly review basic public finance and tax policy issues, redefine concepts of redistribution and charity, and consider prominent counterfactuals. We begin with the public finance issues.

Taxes and Public Sector Programs

Theory tells us that income redistribution within a nation is probably best achieved coercively by government and not voluntarily through philanthropy or charitable donations. Government establishes criteria for "entitlements" for its assistance to the needy, whereas foundations have a "license to be selective and discriminatory." Progressive and centralized taxing authority of income and wealth has also been accompanied by policies and programs that promote upward mobility through education, job training, and the like. Instrumental assistance for Third World residents also requires the level of resources available only to the federal government.

A considerable body of theory and policy analysis has focused on the distribution of income or wealth as a public good and the consequences of extreme disparities, for example, the political and social repercussions of concentrated and inherited wealth. Income inequality has spill-over effects on the distribution of health, education, housing, and crime victimization. Distinctions are also made in the literature between shorter- and longer-run approaches for accomplishing some degree of income and wealth redistribution to lessen the impacts of disparities (Murphy and Nagel 2002).

Governments such as the United States devise tax policies that specify the share of household resources to be made available for government collection. Taxes generate revenues for public goods that presumably benefit everyone. However, a share of the tax revenues is also dedicated not to the needy per se but to selected surrogates for the needy, such as children in single-parent households, the physically and mentally handicapped, the unemployed, and the elderly infirm. Targeting needy groups directly to reduce disparities through cash transfers has been politically more feasible for the elderly and the unemployed than for the working poor or single parents (Murphy and Nagel 2002).

Government tax policies also establish the degree of progressiveness and the allowable exemptions and deductions within its income, estate, personal property, and other taxes. Societies determine tax policies and programs to finance national government, giving state and local governments authority to raise revenues according to their preferences for public goods and programs for targeted groups.

National governments have the leading shorter-term role in adjusting income extremes through progressive taxation and transfer of benefits to selected groups. Some income redistribution occurs as a result of progressive tax policies. However, governments generally make much greater shorter-term progress in reducing disparities through transfers and targeted appropriations to lift minimum floor levels than from paring income and wealth at the high end of the distribution through taxation. Such policies help to reduce the stigma of visible poverty without fundamental change in income distribution.

These government allocations take the form of cash transfers and payments for in-kind social, health, employment training, and educational services, delivered for the most part through contracts with non-profit service providers. Presumably, the cash payments are intended to cover the immediate short-term needs for food, shelter, and other essentials among the neediest. On the other hand, the financing of in-kind services can be seen as a form of government philanthropy, that is, a longer-term investment in creating a service infrastructure for remedying or at least mitigating the problems of the neediest population groups. These are again attempts to reduce impediments to the "equalization of opportunity" but without necessarily leveling the proverbial playing field.

Alternatively, these expenditures for in-kind services may be viewed as a paternalistic attempt to distort the consumption of the poor to what is good for them, such as through service programs that foster work effort, acquisition of job skills, drug and alcohol abuse prevention, and the like. According to either perspective, government's tax and spending policies are currently targeted more toward relieving poverty conditions among distinct groups of the neediest (children, the elderly, and the underemployed, for example) than to redistributing wealth.

Private Charity and Philanthropy

Citizens may not be content with government's distributive policies and the level and targeting of its expenditures for benefits to special population groups. However, there is little reason to believe that the same citizens who resist progressive government taxing or liberal transfer programs would be more generous in their charitable contributions or less paternalistic about their disposition. Individuals can, of course, donate money directly as charity to needy people who may or may not receive transfers from government, although these sums are generally not very substantial, except in cases of major short-term disasters, like the tragedy of September 11. The donations are officially recorded and counted as charity and deductible from donors' income taxes, however, only when they are transferred through a recognized nonprofit organization.

The deductions are forgone government revenue and therefore a public subsidy for the charitable purpose selected by the donor. Just as the national government decentralizes responsibility for financing certain public goods and transfers to state and local government, government at both federal and state levels delegates individuals to select

worthy charitable agencies. The decentralization of grant-making discretion from government to donors assumes that society's needs could
be more knowledgeably and more generously addressed through this
fragmented approach. Reliance on the donor to make sound targeting
decisions may be justified at least partially, given that the tax deduction
for the donation does not fully compensate the contributor. However,
the delegation of authority to donors may also be seen as a "license to
be self-serving." One observer argues that "those empowered to make
grants should not assume that they have the wisdom to solve serious
problems simply because they control the money" (Dowie 2001).
Donors presumably contribute to those nonprofits with services they
know well, sanction, and may use themselves. Large donors may even
be able to dedicate their gifts to some targeted purpose, originate new
services, or even help to establish new nonprofits or NGOs.

Foundation Philanthropy as an Agent of Redistribution

How conducive are foundations to a shorter- or longer-term distributive agenda relative to the public sector's approach? Related questions
must also be revisited, including whether income redistribution is the
most appropriate metric for assessing foundation impacts and how
suitable the comparisons with the counterfactual alternatives are.

Private foundations are not ideally suited to redistributing wealth,
especially in the short run. Some of the major constraints include:

- limited assets relative to income inequalities,

- relative autonomy and fragmentation in targeting,

- restrictions related to donor intent,

- gaps in the regulatory environment,

- a shortage in appropriate nonprofits to whom grants can be made
  and difficulties in monitoring and evaluating project outcomes, and

- a localism bias.

On the other hand, these handicaps become virtues for foundations
in pursuit of their other philanthropic goals that may or may not yield
greater redistribution (Abramson and Spann 1998; Karl and Katz 1987;
Prewitt 1999).

American foundations are fragmented and largely autonomous without stringent regulation of their grant-making operations. Their grants can be disbursed to an immense variety of nonprofit organizations with distributive agendas that differ significantly. For the most part, their emphasis has shifted over the years from charity to philanthropy. They now concentrate primarily on building and supporting an infrastructure for societal well-being through grants to intermediaries, that is, nonprofit providers of in-kind services. The service clients of these nonprofits are then the primary beneficiaries, but presumably ripple effects extend the range of those who benefit.

The donors who establish foundations are willing to surrender some very limited degree of autonomy in determining how and at what pace the wealth can be put to best use in return for the tax privileges. In the trade-off, society—represented by governmental institutions—determines the price of giving by donors through its income and estate tax laws and exercises some control over the operations of the foundation through regulations, audits, and the threat of court action.

Concern with the distributive effects of American foundations would be a less important issue if multimillionaires over the past century had submitted voluntarily and graciously to highly progressive income and estate taxes. The issue would furthermore be of little consequence if they and their political allies were advocates for a vigorous government-sponsored agenda for promoting social benefit and redistributing income and wealth. It should come as no surprise that neither of these opportunities was enticing. Congress also recognized early on that well-financed lobbying for changes in tax policy and the use of tax dodges could easily subvert any scheme for taxing a significant share of income and wealth. The private foundation has emerged over the past century as a compromise and concession to tap wealth that politics determined would not be fully available to be taxed (Boris and Wolpert 2001).

In addition, the aspiration of Congress for foundations has been widened from charity and redistribution to the broader goal of social benefit. Implicit here is the assumption that permitting greater donor authority for targeting of foundation funds under the somewhat ambiguous umbrella of social benefit would elicit greater generosity. The hope was that the contributions to establish foundations would exceed the revenues anticipated from a very progressive system of taxation. Optimism also suggested the skill and wisdom necessary to create large fortunes could be tapped to devise strategies and programs for social benefit that would be at least as effective as those originating with government and perhaps even better.

Why would donors opt to establish a foundation rather than simply make donations directly to nonprofit organizations? The decision has two possibly independent steps: first, whether to start the foundation and, second, determining the mission and targeting agenda. One prominent hypothesis links both steps, the prospect of "perpetuity of control." Donors have their names attached to the foundations, hence acknowledgment and recognition (and sometimes even absolution) occur not just once but can continue. The minimum 5 percent payout regulation virtually guarantees the donor, heirs, or chosen professional managers the latitude for "perpetual grant-making and targeting authority." The donor essentially retains control of his or her money that can be targeted to his or her vision of a better society, for example, lofty goals to help level the playing field for children, foster a more egalitarian society, experiment with different forms of social experimentation, or greater appreciation of classical music. The targeting can also enable the donor to foster efforts for regressive tax policy and to restrict the scope of government in matters dealing with the poor. However, the constraints of donor intent can often be moderated by trustees, professional managers, or court action when necessary. Furthermore, the desire to exercise control is often moderated by the parallel aspiration for recognition and approval by peers in the donor and foundation communities for the humanitarian implications of the grant activities (Dowie 2001). Unfortunately, we lack information to determine if the transfer of foundation control from donors and their families to independent trustees and professional managers results in more distributive outcomes.

The fortunes made by start-up entrepreneurs and by the stock market run-up has augmented the number of foundations and their assets enormously in the past several decades, especially relative to government revenues set aside for transfers and programs targeted to reduce income disparities. A substantial rebound in foundation growth occurred after the decline following the 1969 Tax Reform Act that had increased regulation and taxation of foundations. Some modest setbacks have also occurred during market corrections and following recent tax legislation that has "raised the price of giving" by lowering tax rates at the high income end and established a schedule for gradual elimination of estate taxes.

If foundations have not been effective agents of redistribution in the short run, then have their activities been instrumental in other ways—for example, addressing long-term needs, undertaking unpopular projects, helping empower disadvantaged groups, and funding projects that have created new ideas and approaches to societal well-being?

Foundation Response to Inequalities in the Shorter and Longer Term

An example illustrates many of the complexities in assessing the time dimension of foundation impacts. The appropriately named Robin Hood Foundation in New York City, founded by a commodities trader and two Wall Street colleagues, supports local programs that help prevent poverty and serve the needy. Board members underwrite the administrative costs so that all donations go directly to help those in need.

The foundation seeks to "prevent poverty and its suffering, and to do that, we want to support what works, not what appeals to our ideologies." Its "philosophy is simple: to significantly affect people living in poverty you have to attack its root causes. We believe that if there is a need no one is meeting, we need to brainstorm, pool resources, and create a program that not only meets that need but works toward eliminating the problem" (http://www.robinhood.org/approach/source.cfm).

Based on the origin and destination of the funding, the foundation easily passes the redistribution test, at least so far as needy New Yorkers are concerned. Yet, the capacity of the Robin Hood and other foundations that carry on similar local humanitarian projects is dwarfed both by the magnitude of need and by the much larger potential resources of federal, state, and local government. The needs identified by Robin Hood represent "public sector failures" more than individual gaps and the foundation role, therefore, can only be peripheral and sometimes prejudicial to addressing root causes. The so-called non-ideological approach of Robin Hood according to critics leads to a focus on the victims and inhibits it from advocating causes such as a living wage, progressive income and estate taxes, extended unemployment coverage, and affordable housing. Critics suggest that Robin Hood's efforts would be better deployed by challenging the firms of their Wall

Street colleagues to refrain from seeking exemption from city taxes that provide revenues for city services, public schools, and many safety net programs.

Could the well-intentioned and efficacious founders and board members of Robin Hood accomplish more on behalf of the needy in New York and elsewhere through lobbying business and legislative officials for revenue-raising policies that would enable the public sector to be more generous? If Robin Hood funding had been diverted to policy think tanks and public action groups, they would fail the conventional, narrow definition of redistribution but could likely have a far greater long-term impact on distributive justice. On the other hand, a more politicized progressive agenda might not attract nearly as much foundation funding and therefore less humanitarian assistance.

If short-term lessening of disparities requires government's much greater access to financial resources, what then is the longer term niche for charity and philanthropy in addressing income distribution issues, especially when income and wealth gaps are widening? In the short term, private charity currently has the capacity and potential for only peripheral, immediate, and local relief efforts. Furthermore, charity and philanthropy, judging by their current targeting of donations and grants, are only mildly distributive and have been largely crowded out from relief of current poverty conditions. This evidence would appear to suggest that philanthropy's distributive role must be assessed principally from the longer-run perspective of achieving structural and institutional impacts. In fact, a substantial focus by foundations, or other charitable instruments, on direct assistance to the worst-off groups in society would appear to usurp government's role and imply backsliding from progress toward distributive justice. But does that mean that philanthropy is excused from a distributive agenda?

Persistent and severe longer-term inequalities are assumed to require structural change in civil and governmental institutions. In the United States, for example, racial disparities in income could not be reduced without lessening racism and implementing electoral and civil rights reform. Progress in upward mobility has required investing public education and institutions of higher learning and advocacy to raise minimum wages. Advocacy and lobbying for progressive estate taxes were needed to foster legislation to limit intergenerational transfers of wealth. These efforts have involved establishing an "infrastructure with a distributive justice agenda" inside and outside government to balance forces opposed to equity interventions. Here, progress in changing public attitudes and revamping civil and governmental institutions has benefited significantly from philanthropy channeled through foundation support of progressive think tanks and education of the electorate. The recent backsliding to a reduced role for government as the principal agent for greater parity in society has also found support from conservative think tanks that have been assisted by grants from selected foundations. The open debate on embedded equity issues fostered by the independent voices of foundations has been highly informative and productive.

The Arguments of Foundation Advocates and Critics

Foundations are free to develop program areas and target their grants as they choose, as long as the activities fall within the governmental definition of charitable purposes—educational, religious, scientific, literary, relief of poverty, and other public benefit activities. Still, the media are very attentive to occasions when foundations in highly distressed communities make substantial grants to distant organizations that serve very narrow constituencies, such as in the humanities, high culture, and higher education. Although they can legitimately be as responsive or unresponsive as they choose, many foundations have adjusted in response to changing perceptions of how they can best meet emerging societal needs and seize opportunities for effective involvement.

Donors and professional staff of some of the larger foundations are generally more sensitive to their reputation for achieving some good in areas recognized as important among society's leaders and the foundations they see as peers. They are also likely to be more proactive in eliminating abusive practices. Their grants policies, annual reports, and public pronouncements typically reflect their concern with accountability and transparency. Greater openness and willingness to provide a rationale for their grant-making activity are promising milestones toward more beneficial outcomes.

On the one hand, philanthropic foundations can be marvelously effective in capturing wealth in large chunks that can then be directed into civic betterment. Foundations are especially useful in tapping civic-minded donors who have accumulated more wealth than they can or want to spend on consumption, reinvestment, or passing on to heirs. Donors and societies both benefit from the trade-offs that emerge from this partnership. The concentration of assets in the hands of foundations enables them to undertake ambitious projects, initiate and sustain charitable institutions and their services, finance the construction of buildings, provide educational opportunities through scholarships and fellowships, create a service infrastructure, and support diverse societal perspectives as well as unpopular causes. Foundations also perpetuate philanthropic dynasties and enhance the reputations of their founders.

Wealthy potential donors may not necessarily define their philanthropic preferences along narrow ideological and class lines. Many are motivated by religious, political, and stewardship values (Odendahl 1987). They may in fact prefer that their wealth be dedicated to humanitarian and civic purposes that match broad societal goals or even be used in a compensatory or redistributive fashion. Many donors have also been willing, after identifying a set of broad philanthropic objectives, to surrender control over management to an independent board of trustees and a professional staff.

If society's agenda for civic, social, and cultural progress and that of donors coincide, then the donors spend their assets through the foundations that are established as government would have preferred had the wealth been taxed. In this happy state, government is inclined to reduce the price of giving and loosen its regulatory discretion. How much better it is to tax and regulate less and still have private wealth be dedicated to the public interest.

Encouraging signs are evident in Dowie's (2001) review of the history of American foundations, where he identifies some positive role models for "a new and imaginative era of philanthropy." He credits Ted Turner, Walter Annenberg, and George Soros (among others) who "imagined worlds without AIDS, strife, ignorance, and tyrants, then made massive and immediate financial efforts to make these worlds real."

On the other hand, societies are generally diverse and rarely represented by unitary notions of the public interest or common good. Critics argue that the preferences of those who have accumulated enormous wealth are certain to be different from those of the general populace and conflicts are therefore inevitable. Wealthy individuals in a relatively unregulated free enterprise system with a weak governmental structure could try to impose their ideology, agenda, and priorities on society through the foundations they control. Financial success is often accompanied by paternalism and arrogance. Some donors establish foundations because they feel that government (or the average voter) is seriously flawed or deficient and that successful entrepreneurs like themselves are better equipped to determine how the funds are spent. Many have also felt that existing charities were run inefficiently by "feel-good" social workers. Early foundation donors recognized that planning of societal institutions was essential but were alarmed by the growth of state-sponsored planning in European countries. Critics alternatively berate proactive and partisan practices of some foundations and decry among others their lack of engagement and leadership to help shape government policy on behalf of distributive justice (Dowie 2001). The collective assets, networks, and grant-making experience of foundations are being applied either too effectively or insufficiently to influence public debates and policy makers.

Yet the larger foundations often perceive themselves as innovators and initiators of program activity and are not inclined to adopt new roles proposed for them, for example, simply compensating for government cutbacks of safety net programs or bailing out nonprofits when their revenues from other sources are jeopardized. Salamon (1997) has shown very convincingly that foundation resources, even if retargeted strategically and spent at an accelerated level, could not compensate for federal cutbacks. Furthermore, reducing the discretion that foundations now have—to decide how their resources can best be used to enhance the quality and variety of American life—could deprive society of a badly needed independent voice.

Criticism of foundation practices have come from both conservative and liberal sources. Foundations are either "tools of reaction and privilege" or "endangering our existing capitalistic structure." Some analysts and critics suggest a biased political slant is observable in grants that support social engineering, incremental rather than fundamental societal change, encouragement for change agents, citizen participation and engagement, protection of civil liberties and voting rights, building civil infrastructure, and population planning.

Conservatives have attacked the big foundations for violating the values and intentions of the original donors with their grants; for being trendy and politically correct; for their involvement in issues such as family planning, abortion rights, gender preferences, voter registration, and welfare rights. They accuse foundations and their recipient nonprofit agencies of improper advocacy, lobbying, and political involvement.

The National Committee for Responsive Philanthropy (NCRP) proposed in the late 1980s that foundations be publicly challenged by evaluating and rating their performance through studies of board composition and risk-taking in grant making and publicly reward them for good performance in assisting the economically disadvantaged and politically disenfranchised. NCRP's recent analysis of twelve "right wing" foundations shows that they are making large grants to conservative think tanks, advocacy groups, and colleges for conservative projects on free-market economics and ways to limit government (Covington 1997). These foundations support groups attempting to influence national policy and the next generation of politicians and voters. The conservative foundations maintain that they are only reacting to the so-called liberal bias of the large foundations.

Regulation to Enhance Equity Outcomes

Why should society and government monitor foundation operations and governance and continue to review policies for regulating their establishment and activities, especially if self-regulation does not seem to be working? Disagreement arises currently in very limited areas (involving potential abuse) including fiscal accountability, disclosure and transparency of operations, use of foundation resources for private gain, excessive administrative expenditures, political partisanship and lobbying, and payout rates. Some of the issues of concern to government are likely to be remedied by the foundations themselves; others are structural or pertain to a minority of organizations and may require revised legislation or greater enforcement of existing laws.

Policymakers at federal and state levels do not seem concerned at present with other problematic issues, including the targeting of foundation grants relative to societal needs and priorities, enhanced incentives for attracting more new wealth to foundations, and the potential hazards of concentrated foundation assets in few hands. Yet the limited focus of policymakers and self-regulation in addressing only the most blatant foundation abuses misses opportunities to promote positive reforms that could make grant making more effective and equitable.

The Competing Alternative Approach

The conventional methods and metrics for assessing the distributive effects of American foundations for regulatory purposes have significant and obvious flaws. Categorizing the targeting by service sectors tells us too little about the direct and indirect beneficiaries and the effectiveness of the programs that have been supported. Assessments of payout rates and administrative expenses also entail no firm standards that could apply across the variety of contexts.

Longer-term outcomes are more appropriate for analysis because of foundations' comparative advantage in probing root causes that are amenable to constructive intervention. For example, the Gates and Annenberg grants to improve public school instruction may have a delayed income effect for current pupils that will only unfold over many years, similar to the lag in improving well-being from the public health grants to Third World nations. Monitoring and evaluation will determine whether these program experiments yield the greatest benefits to the neediest populations and whether they inadvertently induce government to divert funding away from these sectors. A highly successful parallel example of public sector philanthropy is the government's National Science Foundation, which provides grants competitively to researchers and helps develop and support the science infrastructure. Analyses have revealed that at least some of the supported projects have developed insights about root causes that could be applied effectively in policy interventions.

An appropriate set of criteria for assessing foundation contribution to distributive justice would include criteria relevant to both operating procedures and short- and longer-term outcomes. Data that go beyond grants by service sector, fiscal data, and payout rates to document grant-making practices and some formatted detail about their outcomes would be ideal. According to a proposed competing alternative approach outlined next, the distributive agenda of foundations would ideally be monitored by the foundation community or else by regulators. This monitoring would document actual or anticipated impacts of recent targeting of grants and payout levels. It would include evidence that foundations have met specified criteria:

- Made a good faith attempt to examine the most pressing service gaps affecting the disadvantaged population in their own communities (for large foundations, their communities are national or world-wide)

- Determined that these gaps are addressed adequately by government or other funders

- Investigated opportunities for collaborative efforts with other potential funders to devise satisfactory means for intervening

- Participated in an assessment of their community's complement of nonprofit organizations and capacity to deliver appropriate services

- Helped (within the limits of their targeting agenda) to improve the capacity of high-risk and start-up agencies to address the service gaps

- Determined that their grants to nonprofit agencies are likely to be sufficient to yield instrumental outcomes or to fall short of these objectives

- Encouraged their nonprofit grantees to monitor service beneficiaries and evaluate long-term impacts of the services that are provided

- Disseminated findings of the effectiveness of the programs they support to policy officials, public interest groups, and the media

- Adjusted payout levels to the demand for high priority projects

- Documented their grant decisions in widely available reports

- Showed evidence of appropriate gender and minority representation among trustees and management staff

The proposed guidelines are intended to help induce in foundations a somewhat higher long-term progressiveness, but not necessarily divert them from their established mission. The rationale for the guidelines is the importance of challenging foundations and other philanthropists periodically to justify "who is likely to benefit and how" from their current agenda and why the most vulnerable population groups are not included as beneficiaries. Foundations should not be coerced to become more redistributive, even if that were politically possible, but challenged to be more transparent about the social benefit anticipated from their current grant-making efforts.

In some communities, donors' forums and nonprofit umbrella groups currently collaborate with the local community foundation to carry out assessments of significant service gaps affecting disadvantaged groups. The findings are used to make allocation decisions more equitable by helping ensure that high priority services do not fall between the cracks. At the same time, government officials at all levels and the media are made aware of the gaps between funding needs and the available charitable resources.

The procedural steps are too demanding to expect broad voluntary compliance and not likely to be readily adopted by federal or state regulators, but are quite consistent with current practices of a number or the larger well-managed foundations. The guidelines could also win acceptance by foundations anxious to satisfy legislators' expectations about the deployment of funds deducted as charitable contributions. Others might comply to gain greater recognition from respected philanthropic and professional peers and the influential media.

Compliance is likely to be less prevalent among smaller foundations unwilling or unable to collaborate in assessing community priorities or to monitor, evaluate, and disseminate the outcomes of their funding support. However, some of these smaller foundations may be induced to collaborate in their grant making with local community foundations that do carry out systematic analyses of service priorities. Other likely omissions include foundations that are gun-shy about making policymakers aware of the high priority service gaps that exceed the capacity of philanthropy to remedy and would require advocacy and lobbying for greater public funding. Some others, for competitive reasons, forgo opportunities to address important equity issues that would requiring leveraging their assets through collaboration.

The most serious impediment to this approach, however, is inflexibility among a substantial share of foundation donors and professional staff about their mission and the targeting agenda for their grant making. This constraint limits their ability to reallocate resources to service areas where they can be deployed more effectively for social benefit. For example, foundation agendas established in the Great Society period of generous funding for social programs are not in tune with the current sustained emphasis on shrinking government.

Another significant impediment is the community and regional imbalance between the needs of the most disadvantaged population and the capacity of both philanthropic and local government sectors. The combination of the clustering of large foundations in a few large cities and their localism bias inhibits attention to depressed areas where charitable resources are minimal and local government is overwhelmed.

The guidelines are only suggestive, but a very similar informal set of procedures were implemented in New York City following the 9/11 crisis. The aftermath of 9/11 collapsed into a very short period the need for donor organizations to demonstrate how they could collaborate with each other and government to fulfill community expectations. The success of their efforts provides important clues about best practices that should be helpful in responding to longer-term issues such as poverty among children, affordable health care, safe neighborhoods, and so on.

Summary and Discussion

The federal government alone has the potential authority and capacity to bring about a more equitable distribution of income and wealth. In recent years, however, the modestly progressive tax and spending policies of government have reinforced both income and wealth disparities. Relative to government's resources and annual expenditures, charitable giving and philanthropy in all its forms, including foundations, cannot have an instrumental role in reducing even the most prominent disparities, at least in the short run. Furthermore, the evidence shows that most foundation grants are targeted to supporting major institutions and quality of life services that have little to do with income or social inequality. Their distributive impacts in the short run are modest and peripheral.

The longer-term trends show somewhat greater responsiveness by foundations (with some lag) to an equity agenda combined with sporadic attempts to advance public discourse and advocacy on a range of controversial social issues. Why then fault foundations for not being more effective agents of redistribution? Why not just be grateful that they have captured considerable wealth that could not be taxed for political reasons and are doing some good work that benefit Americans and many in Third World nations? Why scare off potential donors with additional restrictions on foundation activities? Why face the risk of having to forgo all these resources when foundation donors and professional managers are becoming more committed to targeting structural impediments to improved standards of living?

The evidence demonstrates some reason for optimism about an enhanced equity agenda for parts of the foundation community. The optimism stems from the greater advocacy efforts of some foundation donors and professional managers for policy interventions on poverty and related issues based on evidence from the many experimental and demonstration projects they themselves have supported over the years. Reinforcement of these advocacy and lobbying efforts has come from foundation and other partners in collaborative support projects, favorable media coverage, greater acclaim from other donors and peers, and the effects of greater pressure for accountability and transparency.

With neither private nor public sectors in the United States currently preoccupied with equity issues, foundations have much preparatory work to have a more influential role. More hard evidence is needed of what has been learned from foundation grant making about the roots of sustained inequality and how the imperatives identified from the findings can be implemented through public policy and programs. Foundations can best "make a difference" by having their diverse accumulated experience, independent voice, and influence included in the policy debates about causes and remedies for persistent deprivation and inequality.

Appendix

1. Fundamental Questions

The foundation redistribution issues raise some fundamental questions that unfortunately cannot be addressed rigorously with currently available data. The absence of critical data on distributive impacts can perhaps be attributed to the inherent complexity of monitoring "who benefits" or perhaps to society and policy makers' forbearance about the prospect of long-term foundation effects on societal well-being. Several of these primary issues merit study:

Which criteria, standards, and data reporting requirements are most appropriate for evaluating the distributive impacts of America's foundations and their contributions to an egalitarian society?

Have private foundations been able to capture a significant share of the nation's concentrated private wealth and, if so, "at what price"?

Have foundations been more effective distributive instruments than government, private charitable giving, or corporate or community foundations?

Have foundations established from the assets of America's wealthiest families been more distributive than government policy and thus subject to evaluation based on a higher standard of equity?

Why hasn't the philanthropy of elites channeled through foundations not favored their own interests, institutions, political orientations, and preferred strategies for assisting the needy? Have foundations been more distributive when discretion has been transferred from donors and their families to independent trustees and professional managers?

Alternatively, if foundations are primarily charitable instruments, have they been directing their assets to compensate for business and government failure to reduce disparities and their ripple effects on the quality of life of the neediest groups?

Given their limited resources, grant-making preferences, and modest oversight by government, have foundations still contributed significantly to greater equity in American society?

2. Significant Propositions

Improved data would make it possible to examine a number of propositions about the distributive effects of America's foundations:

Distributional impacts (as transfers of income and wealth from the affluent to the needy) are mildly redistributive over the long term.

Much of the wealth that has created foundations could not feasibly have been taxed by the federal government and made available for public sector programs.

Redistribution via foundations, no matter how generous and humanitarian the motive, has been counterproductive when attempts have been made to usurp and crowd out government's primary role as the agent of redistribution.

Foundations have promoted distributive justice effectively by using their political influence, networks, resources, and experience (gained from supporting instrumental programs in which government and other donors have not been active) to guide funders and policy makers about root causes of deprivation and workable means for their remediation through public sector efforts.

The independence and autonomy of foundations have been major assets in America's democratic society when deployed to examine the functional and dysfunctional activities of public and private sector activities as they affect income and wealth distribution. Inappropriate government regulation of foundations has curtailed or limited their independent voice, or alternatively made them a less attractive instrument for potential donors.

3. Data Requirements

Analysts would ideally like to have access to time series data on

the distribution of income and wealth among affluent households (for example, the wealthiest 5 percent) that have (and have not) established and contributed to foundations

the same distributions for households that contribute no charity or target their donations directly to individuals or nonprofit groups (to determine if the foundation outlet for philanthropy leads to larger donations and more distributive targeting)

the amount of forgone revenues for federal and state governments represented by the tax deductions for these contributions

the payout levels and administrative expenditures of the foundations, including salary levels and payments to trustees

the service activities and income distribution of direct beneficiaries of the nonprofit organizations which have received foundation funding (separated from the revenues and clientele served by the same organizations that were financed from other sources to determine if foundation grants are more distributive than other contributions)

long-term changes in the income distribution of all the indirect beneficiaries of foundation grants

virtually the same information for beneficiaries of government expenditures for public goods and special payments for targeted populations (for example, the unemployed, elderly poor, handicapped children, and the like)

4. Counterfactual Arguments

Analysts insist that a foundation's distributive effects be examined relative to the impacts that could have been achieved if the funds had been taxed and deployed by government. Supplementary information would be needed to probe the counterfactuals.

How else would the fortunes of industrialists and entrepreneurs have been deployed if there were no foundations?

What if the United States had fewer foundations, their assets had been lower, they had been regulated differently, or tax policy were altering the incentives for creating new foundations?

What would government do with the revenues if tax deductions to establish foundations did not exist and the wealth had been taxed at a progressive rate?

What if these wealthy individuals had simply made donations to their favorite charities or community chests or disbursed contributions through their businesses or corporations rather than establishing foundations? Would the outcomes of these contingencies have yielded greater distributive impacts (for example, less disparity in income and wealth)?

What, then, is the relative or comparative effectiveness of foundations as instruments of redistribution in democratic societies with well established three sector economies (that is, private, public, and nonprofit sectors), the answer to which can be used to address the incremental question, i.e., is expansion or contraction of foundation activities at the present time likely to contribute to a more equitable society?

How feasible would it be for government to alter the incentives and regulatory environment for foundations to yield more progressive outcomes?

References

Abramson, Alan J., and J. Spann. 1998. *Foundations: Exploring Their Unique Roles and Impacts on Society.* Washington, D.C.: Aspen Institute.

American Association of Fundraising Counsel. 2003. *Giving USA: The Annual Report on Philanthropy for the Year 2003.* New York: AAFRC.

Boris, Elizabeth, and Julian Wolpert. 2001. "The role of philanthropic foundations: Lessons from America's Experience with Private Foundations." In *Third Sector Policy at the Crossroads,* edited by Helmut K. Anheier and Jeremy Kendall. London: Routledge.

Clotfelter, Charles T., ed. 1992. *Who Benefits from the Nonprofit Sector?* Chicago: University of Chicago Press.

———. 1996. *Buying the Best: Cost Escalation in Elite Higher Education*. Princeton, N.J.: Princeton University Press.

Colwell, Mary A. 1993. *Private Foundations and Public Policy*. New York: Garland Press.

Covington, Sally. 1997. *Moving a Public Policy Agenda: The Strategic Philanthropy of Conservative Foundations*. Washington, D.C.: National Committee for Responsive Philanthropy.

Dowie, Mark. 2001. *American Foundations: An Investigative History*. Cambridge, Mass.: MIT Press.

Edie, John A. 1987. *Congress and Private Foundations: A Historical Analysis*. Washington, D.C.: Council on Foundations.

The Foundation Center. 2003. *Foundation Giving Trends, 2003*. New York: The Foundation Center.

Karl, Barry D., and Stanley N. Katz. 1987. "Foundations and Ruling Class Elites." *Daedalus* 116(Winter): 1–40.

Margo, Robert A. 1992. "The Distributional Impact of Foundations: A Historical Perspective." In *Who Benefits from the Nonprofit Sector?* edited by Charles T. Clotfelter. Chicago: University of Chicago Press.

Murphy, Liam, and Thomas Nagel. 2002. *The Myth of Ownership: Taxes and Justice*. New York: Oxford University Press.

Odendahl, Teresa. 1987. "Wealthy Donors and Their Charitable Attitudes." In *America's Wealthy and the Future of Foundations,* edited by Teresa Odendahl. New York: The Foundation Center.

Prewitt, Kenneth. 1999. "The Importance of Foundations in an Open Society." In *The Future of Foundations in a Free Society*. Gütersloh: Bertelsmann Foundation Publishers.

Salamon, Lester M. 1997. *Holding the Center: America's Nonprofit Sector at a Crossroad*. New York: Nathan Cummings Foundation

Chapter 6

Foundation Legitimacy at the Community Level in the United States

Kirsten A. Grønbjerg

Community Foundations occupy a strategic place among U.S. foundations. Although they make grants like other nonoperating foundations, they are classified as public charities rather than private foundations because they raise funds on an ongoing basis from many donors rather than just a few (such as a sponsoring corporation or founding family). Although most grant-making foundations have a regional focus, community foundations have so more explicitly. They pursue broader community issues, solicit donors with special connections to one community, pool funds for the benefit of that community, and include community representatives on their boards or fund distribution committees (not just donors as do family or corporate foundations).

Community foundations therefore face more explicit challenges to their community legitimacy than other grant makers. Indeed, as I show, they make more deliberate efforts to assess community needs so as to prioritize grant making and to structure their grant making on an open, competitive basis. At the same time, they face growing competition from other fundraising organizations (United Way [UW], women's, or other special funds) and donor advised funds (DAFs) offered by major investment companies, such as Fidelity or Merrill Lynch (Lenkowsky 2002).

Community Foundations—A Special Type of Funder

In the United States, community foundations are recognized as public charities under Section 501(c)(3) of the Internal Revenue Code and therefore pay no federal income tax (nor most state or local taxes)[1] on their annual surplus.[2] They can also receive contributions that are deductible (within limits) from the taxable income of individual or corporate donors. This important tax incentive is not available to exempt entities recognized under other 501(c) subsections (labor unions, social clubs, business groups, fraternal organizations),[3] and is justified on the argument that charities benefit the broader community (not just their own members) and relieve the need for government efforts.

Community foundations share these tax advantages with other public charities. Some (hospitals, schools, churches, literary societies, prevention of cruelty to children or animals, or testing for public safety) are routinely granted charitable status. Others must meet tests of purpose (community benefit) and public support (not rely primarily on assets or relatively few donors) as community foundations do when they obtain contributions from many donors. While other grantmaking foundations are recognized as tax-exempt charities when they meet the purpose-mission test, most are considered private foundations because they fail to meet the public support test. Thus, family and independent foundations depend primarily on income from assets donated by a few founders,[4] whereas corporate foundations receive their revenues (and assets, if any) from a single business or corporation. This legal distinction dates to the Tax Reform Act of 1969, which sought to address concerns about abuses (especially self-dealing) by private foundations (Hammack 1989, 39–41).[5] Granting public charities favorable legal treatment—greater tax deductions for donors, no excise tax on investment income, and fewer operational requirements (see table 6.1)—encourages wealthy individuals to channel charitable trusts or endowments to community foundations rather than create family foundations (Hammack 1989, 41; Clontz 2001).

Community foundations are less easily distinguished from other public charities that also raise and pool contributions from donors and support other charities financially (UW, Catholic Charities, Jewish Federation, and alternative funds—black UW, Women's Funds). Although all may focus on a geographic region, community foundations have broader funding priorities and seek endowments,[6] not just annual support. On both counts community foundations are becoming less distinctive now that other fundraising organizations also seek endowments and allow donors to designate which charities should receive their contributions.

Table 6.1 Key Attributes of Private and Community Foundations

Attributes	Private Foundations	Community Foundations
Amounts deductible for donor		
Publicly traded securities	Fair market value	Fair market value
Other appreciated property	Limited to cost basis	Fair market value
Limits on contributions for donor		
Cash contributions	30 percent of donor's adjusted gross income	50 percent of donor's adjusted gross income
Gifts of appreciated property	20 percent of donor's adjusted gross income	30 percent of donor's adjusted gross income
Administrative requirements		
Payment of excise tax	1 to 2 percent of investment income	None
Required payout levels	5 percent of assets or more	No minimum requirement
Limits on excess business holdings	Yes	None
Donor control	Legal	Advisory
Anonymity	No; must file detailed returns on grants, fees, investments, salaries	Yes; donors and grants can be private; foundation may buffer donors from grant seekers
Other features		
Primary advantages to donors	Control, independence, family identity, focus, employment of relatives	Deductibility, flexibility, access to expertise, permanence, no administrative duties, anonymity
Distinctive structures	Single fund, may focus on designated region(s), board has full authority	Pooled funds, focus on named region, separation of investment and allocations decisions

Source: Adapted from Clontz (2001).

The rapid growth of DAFs managed by commercial mutual funds as a service to investors, but recognized as charities by the IRS, has muddied the waters. Twelve of the largest commercial DAFs (including those established by Fidelity, Merrill Lynch, and Vanguard) had accumulated more than $3.4 billion in assets in 39,000 individual DAFs and distributed almost $1 billion in funds to charities in 2003 (Larose and Wolverton 2003). Although the combined assets were down slightly from the previous year (reflecting the continued erosion of the stock market) the number of donors and the distribution to charities increased by respectively 14 and 11 percent.[7] Because the oldest (and largest) of these funds, Fidelity Investments Charitable Gift Fund,[8] is only twelve years old, the accumulated assets and volume of distribution to charities is truly impressive.

Most commercial DAFs operate as low-frills, pass-through mechanisms where donors instruct fund managers on support for specific charities. The strong marketing and technological capacity of the parent companies means that these funds compete aggressively with community foundations in catering to the interests of well-to-do donors (Clyde 2003; Carson 2002). Because these funds do not assess community needs or review grant applicants, overhead costs are low and donors may pay less for the services (Greene 2003). Indeed, Dot Ridings, president and CEO of the Council of Foundations, made veiled references to this when she pointed to " 'bottom feeders' at work, abusing the community foundation model" (2002).[9] The line is blurring, however. Since 2003, Merrill Lynch Community Charitable Fund has announced contracts with a growing number of community foundations to benefit from their understanding of charities and community needs (Berry-Helmlinger 2003). Some charities, including community foundations, now contract with commercial investor funds to manage "private-label gift funds" on their behalf (Blum 2002).

Evolution and Growth of Community Foundations

The first U.S. community foundation was established in Cleveland in 1914 at the initiative of banker, lawyer, and civic leader Frederick Goff, who emphasized a permanent charitable endowment (rather than annual operating funds), pooled contributions from many donors (rather than the wealthy few), focus on varied and changing needs of a particular community (rather than narrow or preconceived ones endorsed by individual donors), and leadership in identifying new opportunities and challenges in the community (Newman 1989, 74–75). Under Goff's leadership, the Cleveland Foundation separated investment management (controlled by financial experts) from fund distribution (controlled by a committee appointed by key bank and public officials), thus ensuring public representation, rather than donor control. Among its first actions, the foundation commissioned nationally prominent investigators to undertake extensive studies of the city's elementary and secondary education, recreation, and criminal justice systems (Hammack 1989, 25–27).

Early community foundations in Pittsburgh, Buffalo, Chicago, and other midwestern cities undertook similar projects—the Chicago Community Trust commissioned surveys on Americanization services to new immigrants, housing facilities for young women, prenatal care, and conditions at Cook County Jail (Grønbjerg 1983)—thereby creating visibility, legitimacy, and a leadership agenda. By contrast, many in northeastern cities, such as the New York Community Trust, initially focused on managing and distributing charitable funds on behalf of donors, but later became active in broader community reform efforts (Hammack 1989, 30–31).

These two models—the community- and donor-oriented approaches—are still evident among community foundations, with major implications for how they raise and manage funds and for accountability to the local community (Leonard 1989, 95–99). The former model places a premium on community leadership, participation in community collaborative initiatives, and access to unrestricted funds to target high priority needs; the latter focuses on serving the interests and needs of donors and on managing donor advised funds.[10] The latter have grown more rapidly, but are more threatened by commercial DAFs, though Leonard (1989) argues that the most successful community foundations incorporate both models—as well as careful attention to grant making.

Community foundations expanded rapidly in the 1920s, came to a virtual standstill in the 1930s, and then grew rapidly in the 1950s (Hammack 1989, 25). Their growth resumed in the 1970s and since then their numbers have more than tripled to reach more than 600 in 2002 and assets have grown seven-fold in constant dollars to $30 billion. Indeed, community foundation assets have grown faster than those of other foundations—up by 201 percent (more than tripled) in constant dollars over the 1992 to 2002 period, compared to 132 percent for private foundations and 67 percent for corporate foundations—accounting for 6.4 percent of all foundation assets in 2002, up from 4.6 percent in 1981 (Lawrence, Atienza, and Marino 2003, 70–71, 49, 14, 72).

Throughout, a disproportionate number have been small. The largest six (of 650) now account for "only" 21 percent of the $30 billion dollars in assets,[11] down from 40 percent in the 1941 to 1987 period and over 75 percent in 1921 (Hammack 1989, 42).[12] Community foundations have spread to all fifty states, the Virgin Islands, and Puerto Rico, but are still concentrated in the Midwest and Northeast, with Indiana and Michigan almost fully saturated, thanks to initiatives by the Mott, Lilly, and Kellogg foundations.

Community Foundations and Legitimacy

The overall growth in community foundations is prima facie evidence that they are meeting important needs or have some competitive advantages. Devolution and the shift of policy initiatives from the federal to the state and local level have placed a premium on mobilizing local resources to address community issues while the decline of locally owned businesses may have created a leadership vacuum. Indeed, community foundations have several advantages in responding to these challenges (Hammack 2004). Many work closely with financial institutions and know investment alternatives and tax regulations. Many have professional staffs with expert knowledge of community issues and local nonprofits. Many have worked with business, government, or other philanthropic institutions to develop new initiatives, taking a leadership role on selected issues (Lawrence, Atienza, and Marino 2003, 67).

By playing leadership roles in addressing complex local problems, community foundations enhance their legitimacy—provided, of course, they do so with reasonable skill and effectiveness. The historic growth in their numbers, assets, and gifts has provided the visibility—and resources—to take on new initiatives. It is too early to assess the impact of encroaching commercial DAFs, which directly challenge their efforts to serve donors, but not (yet) their community leadership or grant making.

Community Legitimacy: Standards and Expectations

Not surprisingly, there are numerous efforts to articulate standards or expectations for community foundations (beyond the legal criteria outlined), including certification standards. Most include fairly elaborate operational standards relating to accountability to stakeholders[13] and build on efforts to identify areas of competency and common characteristics (Council on Foundations 1988, 1992). The latter fall into three categories: legal—purpose, status, geographic area, common instrument, permanence, stewardship, fiduciary role; operational—inclusiveness, responsiveness, community involvement, governance (representative of the community); and philosophical—grant making, leadership, growth, disclosure, representation (equity and diversity of staff and board). Most of the second two types of characteristics relate directly to community accountability. The National Committee for Responsive Philanthropy (NCRP 1994, 2–3), concerned with how philanthropy addresses disenfranchised groups, includes promoting grassroots community development, fostering community cohesion, and contributing to principles of social justice, equity, and diversity—concepts that relate explicitly to community legitimacy.

I combine several of these criteria, but in less detail, and view them as preconditions for and mechanisms by which community foundations can play a leadership role and meet expectations of community legitimacy: ensure community representation and inclusiveness in governance, staff, and volunteers; disseminate information about activities; assess community needs and establish funding priorities to lay the foundation for a community leadership role; track public policy developments and respond to those that affect the mission; monitor the role and activities of other funders and participate in external planning and networking; monitor the capacities and challenges faced by local nonprofits; and structure the grant-making process as a proactive, open, competitive process. (I ignore generic practices in marketing or managing investments, donors, or human resources.)

Community Legitimacy: The Evidence

The significant growth in community foundations for sustained periods during most of the twentieth century demonstrates their value to donors (or perhaps just the weakness of other community institutions). To determine whether community foundations meet expectations of community legitimacy, I review first several efforts to determine their performance across localities or at different stages of development before comparing them to other philanthropic funders.

Variations in Community Foundation Practices

A variety of studies have examined the extent to which community foundations meet the types of standards outlined above. Thus Agard's (1992) survey of eighty-nine U.S. community foundations examined whether differences in administrative, social, strategic, and technical systems was related to age, asset level, and size of community served. She found that the number of geographic affiliates and supporting organizations (indicating complexity and external engagement) increases some with age and size, as does the number of pages in the annual report (indicating efforts to communicate), but not the number of advisory committees or their members, or the type of mission.

A second approach, self-assessments by community foundations, include the Lilly Endowment (LEI) efforts to evaluate its GIFT (Giving Indiana Funds for Tomorrow) initiative launched in 1990 to build and strengthen Indiana community foundations. The initiative—two rounds of challenge grants and one round of organizational development grants—is generally credited with a significant growth in the number (from fifteen to more than ninety) and assets (from $100 million to over $1 billion) of Indiana community foundations since 1990. As a result, virtually every county has a community foundation, though some share managers.

In 2000, to "take stock" of GIFT, LEI offered technical and financial assistance to Indiana community foundations for an extensive self-assessment of ethical and operational standards. All ninety-two participated. The "Taking Stock" findings (Lilly Endowment 2001) suggest that most (especially older and larger ones) have key organizational components in place, but many struggle to meet operating costs or secure reliable revenues. A majority reported strong boards, grant making, ethical standards, and collaboration with others, but many lack visibility and face challenges in public awareness, external communication, citizen participation, and strategic planning and evaluation (most likely because most are young and small).

A third approach, case studies, focuses on fewer and less representative community foundations in order to examine issues in greater depth. Magat's *An Agile Servant* (1989) highlight ways in which six-teen community foundations selected for diversity in geography and size, categories of leadership, thematic elements, and replicability have acted as conveners on community needs or as catalysts on crit-ical issues, assisted nonprofit organizations, promoted neighborhood developments, and built assets.

NCRP's evaluation of ten large community foundations presents more critical findings. Over the 1988 to 1994 period NCRP scored each on its responsiveness to disenfranchised groups on the use of volun-teers in the grant-making process and discretion over distribution of funds; services to local nonprofits; effective communications with grant seekers, grantees, and the larger community; pattern of giving with regard to disenfranchised groups; leadership-catalytic role in addressing critical community problems; risk taking in giving and serv-ing the community; active fundraising; and diversity of board and staff. The project revealed substantial variations among the ten community foundations on almost all of the indicators, with the Boston and Philadelphia community foundations held out as models for embrac-ing citizen empowerment.[14]

Overall, these studies suggest that community foundations vary considerably in how they carry out their activities and in whether they meet expectations of community legitimacy as defined. The unsur-prising finding that younger and smaller community foundations face greater challenges provides a cautionary context for the many that are new and small. They, like many larger more established ones, may find it difficult to demonstrate strong community leadership, effective grant making, and constructive attention to donor needs and interests—let alone the catalytic role envisioned for them by watchdog organizations such as the National Committee for Responsive Philanthropy (NCRP).

Community Foundations Versus Other Philanthropic Funders

This still leaves the question of how community foundations compare to other types of foundations in terms of practices that strengthen community legitimacy. There are reasons to think that they might compare favorably because they are more likely to make information about themselves available to the general public than other funders. Thus 84 percent of community foundations issued publications (ver-sus 32 and 13 percent respectively for corporate and other grant-making foundations)[15] or annual reports (79 percent versus 15 and 5 percent respectively) or maintained Web sites (65 percent versus 18 and 5 percent respectively) in 2003 (Atienza and Marino 2003b, 4, 7, 11). Such practices generally increase with the size and age of the foundation. Overall, community foundations as a group out-performed the largest (assets of $100 million or more) and the oldest (established before 1950) foundations regardless of type on all three dimensions.[16] Similarly, Ostrower (2004) reports that 68 percent of community foundations engaged in six or more communications activities, while only 17 percent of corporate and 11 percent of other private foundations do.

They also have larger staff and boards. Thus 82 percent employ staff, compared to only 24 percent of corporate foundations and 14 percent of other private foundations, and those with staff employ more than corporate and other private foundations (median of 4 compared to 2 and average of 7.4 versus 3.4 and 4.3 respectively). Community foundations have also larger boards of directors (average of 12.4) than corporate (5.6) or other private grant-making foundations (3.8) (Atienza and Marino 2003a, 12–14). Large staffs allow community foundations to maintain activities essential for community leadership and large boards help them build broader relationships with external stakeholders.

But community legitimacy involves other considerations as well. To address those issues, I turn now to findings from a project that examined philanthropic and public human service funders in Chicago.[17] In the mid-1990s, my students and I completed in-depth interviews with forty-six philanthropic funders representing a stratified sample of foundations fairly evenly divided among four major types—independent, family, corporate, and community and public foundations[18]— and four size categories.[19] The community and public foundation type included all community foundations in the Chicago metropolitan region as well as one UW and several special funds (for example, women's fund).

The purpose of the study was to examine how different types of funders in one community (thus holding community conditions constant) position themselves with regard to changes in the broader human service environment by examining how they assessed the human service environment (broadly defined), relationships with funded agencies, and participation in planning structures.[20] Here, I

highlight how community foundations compare to other philanthropic funders on these dimensions.

There are good reasons to expect differences among types of funders.
Resource dependency theory (Pfeffer and Salancik 1978) posits that
organizations must secure resources from the environment to survive
but also seek to lessen or otherwise manage the impact of their dependency on external organizations. Philanthropic funders need two types
of resources: financial resources to pay grants and human resources to
manage operations and decide what to fund. Of course, they also need
a cadre of willing grant recipients to meet legal pay-out requirements.

Public charities such as community foundations (hereafter community and public foundations) and corporate foundations and giving
programs[21] (hereafter corporate funders)—depend on external sources
for the funding they award, but differ in their reliance on external decision makers. Community and public foundations and UW[22] obtain
donations from the public and use community boards in making
awards, which is why they have larger boards. Corporate funders
depend on profits from a single business firm (hence sales to external
customers), whose leaders control fund distribution. Family and independent foundations obtain most or all grant dollars from sources
they control (Nielsen 1996)—mainly investment income from
endowments—but differ in governance structures. In family foundations (most private foundations), founders or descendants directly
control investment and grant decisions. For independent foundations,
control rests with an independent, self-perpetuating board of directors
expected to adhere to the founder's directives, but with little direct
accountability to founders or their descendants.

Population ecology theory (Hannan and Freeman, 1977, 1984)
argues that obligations to prior commitments and routine patterns of
interaction restrict the ability of organizations to respond to rapidly
changing environments. Many philanthropic funders face such structural inertia. For family and independent foundations, articles of incorporation may specify priorities and limit what can be funded, whereas
the charters of community foundations usually allow for greater flexibility and changes over time (less so for DAFs) and corporate funders
are subject to shifts in corporate priorities and business strategies. Most
philanthropic funders, especially family foundations, are governed
by relatively few individuals with long tenure, thus favoring well-
established routines and decision preferences, whereas corporate

Table 6.2   Types of Foundations by Grant Source and
Governance Structure

Typical Governance Structure	Typical Source of Grant Funding	
	Existing Sources	Newly Generated Sources
Direct donor control (internal)	Family: donor and donor's family directly control existing endowment	Corporate: corporate executives directly control allocation of recent or current corporate profit
Deputy or indirect donor control (external)	Independent: independent board (and staff) controls existing endowment	Community: community board controls mix of newly raised funds and existing endowment

Source: Author's compilations.

funders and community and public foundations are likely to have greater turnover among key decision makers.

Funders who depend most on financial and human resources from the external environment should be more closely attuned to external developments and demonstrate less structural inertia than those with few such linkages. Community and public foundations exemplify the former pattern, family foundations the latter. Independent foundations and corporate funders are intermediary, sharing one, but not both, elements of external resource dependency (see table 6.2).

At the time of the study, several major changes were underway in the human service environment. Demographic, social and economic trends were aggravating community needs, especially in inner cities. Changes in public policy—welfare reform, managed care, and devolution—brought cuts in social spending programs, changes to the social safety net, and shifts in intergovernmental relations. UW and corporate funders faced major corporate restructuring, and stock market growth increased assets for family, independent, and community foundations. In addition, human service nonprofits faced their own operational challenges because of the trends noted above and growing competition.

Community Needs
One of the great strengths of American philanthropy is the range of missions and approaches that philanthropic funders pursue. But do

such funders have mechanisms in place to recognize and respond to community changes? They must, if they are to meet expectations of community legitimacy.

BROADER HUMAN SERVICE FOCI   Community and public foundations have notably broader areas of funding interests than other funders. For many family but also some independent foundations, the underlying philosophy and related activities were so tightly circumscribed by founders that changes in community needs had no practical impact on grant activities, while corporate funders focused their philosophy on specific business objectives. This is consistent with a recent survey, which found that 63 percent of community foundations, but only 12 percent of corporate and other private foundations, say that maintaining a broad grants program is very important to effectiveness (Ostrower 2004).

MORE COMPREHENSIVE VIEWS OF COMMUNITY NEEDS   As expected, community and public funders expressed more comprehensive, in-depth views on community needs and monitored these systematically, consistent with their broader scope of external linkages. Others, mainly family foundations and smaller corporate funders, found it difficult to articulate clear views on community needs, and some paid no attention to these issues at all. Only a handful of the largest made proactive efforts to establish funding priorities through research, read aggressively in the field, or participated in networks of researchers, public agencies, private funders, and advocacy organizations at the national or local levels. The rest relied on a combination of efforts to keep informed (occasional newsletters, the media) and more reactive approaches, such as grant applications. The latter is likely to result in selective and incomplete understandings of community needs given that information is filtered through the interests of grant seekers.

MORE RESPONSIVE TO CHANGING NEEDS   By their own account, trends in community needs affected only about half the philanthropic funders including all community and public foundations. The rest were locked into funding patterns that allowed for no adaptation or said that the nonprofits they funded were not significantly affected by changes in community needs. Of those that adapted, a small minority, including most community and public funders, had sought to become more open and accommodating: handling more requests, speeding up the grant process itself, providing education in affected areas, taking greater risks, or attempting to organize constituency groups. The rest limited their funding by focusing grant making on particular populations or issues, reducing multiyear funding to avoid ties to vulnerable agencies, insisting on greater accountability, or seeking long-term planning from funded agencies.

Public Policy Developments

Federal and state policy developments add further complexities. When we began our interviews in July 1996, the scope of changes under way in public policy promised to significantly alter the environment for nonprofit human service providers: welfare reform, federal budget cuts, reforms of immigration laws, reductions in social benefits for aliens, and devolution of program responsibilities from federal to state levels. In Illinois, this process was confounded with the state's extension of performance based or managed care contracting to health and human services and a significant restructuring of the state's human service system.[23] There were also regulatory initiatives at the federal level to limit nonprofit advocacy, expand government contracting to sectarian organizations, and modify tax-deductible donations.[24] In short, philanthropic funders active in the human service field might have been expected to pay close attention to these developments since the changes were likely to affect them or at least their grant recipients.

GREATER AWARENESS OF POLICY ISSUES   Although philanthropic funders had more articulate views on public policy developments than community needs, only a handful—mainly community and public foundations, UW, large independent or corporate funders—were informed and thoughtful about these issues. Most of the rest discussed welfare reform (then nearing a final vote) but usually focused on issues related to their particular arena of grant making. When prompted, some did comment on such issues as regulation of advocacy or the state's human service reorganization, but small independent, family, or corporate foundations or giving programs found these topics entirely irrelevant—they said they paid no attention, were unaware of them, or didn't want to talk about them.

MORE ENGAGED IN POLICY DEVELOPMENTS   Most community and public and some independent foundations were clearly engaged in public policy developments, viewing them as integral to their own environment and making substantial efforts to shape the public policy debate. Overall, larger funders, including some family foundations, were more aware of public policy developments, perceived more impact on their own activities, and took more proactive stances. They made efforts to think strategically to influence the overall system, award larger grants to have more impact on funded agencies, or support advocacy efforts. Others took a wait-and-see stance, expecting increased requests as agencies lost public funding. Some considered narrowing their focus, looked for stronger projects or more "viable" agencies, and worried about fragile grantees. However, many thought public policy developments were irrelevant and paid no attention them.

Philanthropic Developments

There were also important developments under way in philanthropy. As noted, community foundations grew rapidly and UW of Chicago funding declined 28 percent between 1992 and 1993 (Grønbjerg et al. 1996) due partly to the Aramony scandal in the early 1990s (Bothwell 1993), but mainly because of structural changes in the UW resource system[25] and regional conflicts with the UW of suburban Chicago. Corporate contributions programs became more aligned with marketing or public relations, and corporate restructuring created havoc with the operation of many such programs. Family and independent foundations, closely tied to corporate profits, saw rapid growth in assets, and increases in corporate executive compensation and corporate mergers and acquisitions created new wealth and family foundations. Such developments matter to philanthropic funders, since without mutual awareness they cannot coordinate responses to community changes.

GREATER LEGITIMACY   We found a great variety of perspectives on philanthropic funders—and reluctance to generalize—but views were generally consistent with resource dependency theory. Those who were comfortable talking about public and community foundations[26] emphasized the ongoing need to pool smaller bequests and thought this made these funders more responsive to the community and concerned with broader policy issues than other funders.[27] They, especially Chicago Community Trust (CCT),[28] were seen as important to the philanthropic community, helping to identify and solve issues by bringing people together and attracting a critical mass of highly qualified staff. Some paid close attention to which agencies CCT supported or dropped, although several were critical of CCT, questioning its leadership, elitism, and "tortuous" grant process.

A few funders thought that the need to raise funds continuously made community and public foundations less willing to take risks. Others worried that these efforts created direct competition with funded agencies. When asked about notable trends, several funders pointed to more intensive, "desperate," fundraising efforts by community and public foundations. Others noted the growth of new community foundations as a result of matching grants from major foundations or a vacuum in community leadership as banks and other local businesses were bought out and no longer locally owned. Overall, though community foundations were not particularly visible to most funders, they had considerable community legitimacy among those who knew of them.

Most also recognized UW, though with mixed assessments, but were reluctant to express views on other philanthropic funders. Those who did noted greater self-interest among corporate funders, diversity and idiosyncrasies of family foundations (exemplifying "heart of philanthropy" but also funding pet projects), and the freedom of independent foundations to act. However, most, especially smaller ones, work in isolation and found it not worth the effort to interact with other funders. Others were so constrained by their mission, mandates by key decision makers, or prior commitments that they deliberately circumscribed their efforts. A few, mainly large independent ones, spoke of the need for collaboration or for greater capacity among funders, but few elaborated or engaged in any related planning.

Agency Operational Challenges

Legitimacy also requires efforts to respond to operational challenges faced by nonprofit agencies. We focused on agency amounts and sources of funding; legal requirements or regulation; licensing or reporting requirements; accessibility or facility-related issues; staff development and compensation; management or administrative capacity; program development and evaluation; governance structure and capacity; and mergers, collaborations, and other interorganizational relations.

More Responsive   Compared to views on community needs, public policy, and philanthropic developments, community and public foundations do not stand out when it comes to operational problems of human service agencies. Almost all funders agreed that challenges centered on funding (as a cause or an effect of other challenges). Their agreement and detailed assessment is not surprising—funders want assurances that agencies have the capacity to carry out the promised objectives and spend much of their time interacting with agencies. When asked the more difficult question of how to address the problems, a handful of community, public, and independent foundations thought that funders themselves should change: develop better understanding of what it takes to run an agency, collaborate and share results of evaluating grantees, and fund organizational development. Most pointed the finger at public funders. For the rest, responses were limited and rarely went beyond additional training and technical assistance.

Grantee Selection Practices

Philanthropic funders award grants to both individuals (scholarships) and nonprofits. To meet expectations of community legitimacy, the grant-making process should be relatively open and grants awarded to appropriate recipients. We asked funders to describe the major criteria or principles they used in making funding decisions and how they process requests. We probed also for informal considerations (see Grønbjerg and Martell 2000).

Formal Screening Processes   Although funders used eclectic review criteria, reflecting the special niches they have sought for themselves, five broad themes emerged: geography (agency locations, program focus), personal connections to the funder, fiscal status and budgets, performance or reputation, and mission. The selection processes also varied widely, ranging from entirely unstructured and informal reviews to highly systematic ones with formal requests for proposals (RFPs), point scoring systems linked to formal criteria, multiple review levels, and site visits. Overall, we rated the processes followed by roughly a quarter of the funders as fairly informal and about a fifth as formal, with the rest somewhere between the two.

Virtually all community and public foundations used formalized review processes, regardless of size, including formal RFPs, point scoring systems linked to formal criteria, multiple review levels, and site visits. This helps them portray themselves as responding systematically to community needs and support their efforts to raise funds from the general public on an ongoing basis. Some relied extensively on volunteer review panels, others used structures that invited systematic scrutiny. For one large funder, this involved four levels of staff review, including a semi-adversarial process, before reaching the board for final review and decision. When asked about personal relationships between applicant agencies and board members, some acknowledged rare instances where board members had "interfered" in the review process.

A handful of large or medium-sized corporate and independent foundations also used formal review processes, but most other funders used notably informal processes and directed their funding mainly— or entirely—at agencies that were part of the personal networks of board members or other key individuals directly associated with the funder. This is, of course, why the process can be so informal—the funder already knows the agency and feels no need to undertake any systematic investigations. By the same token, agencies unfamiliar to these funders have little opportunity to make their case heard or become part of the system.

RELATIVE HIGH TURNOVER RATES   We also asked funders about the annual turnover in funded agencies. Overall, reflecting the widespread use of informal selection processes, most funders reported very modest turnover rates. Of those able to give an estimate,[29] more than a third (37 percent) said their turnover was usually no more than 10 percent. Another 42 percent gave rates that, though higher, still fell below 30 percent. Only 16 percent had turnover rates that exceeded 50 percent, including 8 percent with rates of 75 percent or higher. Note that some defined turnover as funding new programs, not new agencies, whereas others included grantees rotating off for a period of time (usually a year).

Community and public foundations had the highest turnover rates, averaging 40 percent (range of 20 to 70 percent), consistent with their greater reliance on formalized selection procedures, and most saw turnover as entirely appropriate and desirable. Independent foundations were next, averaging turnover rates of about 27 percent, but with a wider range (10 to 80 percent). Family foundations and corporate funders had notably lower turnover rates, averaging 17 and 11 percent respectively, and none exceeded 30 percent—consistent with their informal selection processes.

MORE EXTENSIVE EVALUATIONS   Finally, we asked funders to describe how they evaluated grantees and how effective they thought the process was. Although the overwhelming majority of funders do not formally evaluate the programs or agencies they fund, community and public foundations do, though they mainly rely on self-reports and rarely look at them unless the agency is seeking renewed funding. Other funders did not find evaluations particularly valuable, arguing that the small size of their grants did not warrant evaluations or that reputation and personal contacts provided them with all the information they needed. In fact, most felt overwhelmed by processing requests for funding and put their efforts into screening applicants, making site visits to those they did not know well.

These findings are consistent with Ostrower's (2004) analysis of foundation responses to questions about proactive grant making, technical assistance and capacity building for grantees, social policy and advocacy, and internal staff development. She found that most large foundations scored high on these dimensions, but so did 46 percent of community foundations regardless of size, compared to 21 percent of all other types of grant-making foundations.

New Challenges, New Linkages?

The rapid growth in community foundations undoubtedly reflects and reinforces their legitimacy. Certainly, they have more structures in place to meet expectations of community legitimacy than other philanthropic funders, except perhaps for the largest of those. Overall, these findings are broadly consistent with resource dependency theory. First, funders most exposed to external resource constraints (community and public foundations) have more comprehensive views of the external environment and respond more systematically to perceived changes than those which rely least on decision makers recruited from the outside (family foundations, corporate funders). Second, sheer size is associated with more extensive efforts to keep informed and operate formally, perhaps because of greater staff capacity and higher volume of grants. It is important to recognize, however, that the funders most insulated structurally from the external environment, such as family foundations, by the same token are also at greater liberty to pursue highly risky strategies and therefore may have greater community impact than those needing to appease broader constituency groups.

The competitive pressures community foundations now face from commercial DAFs (Lenkowsky 2002) may modify the role they play in local communities and challenge their community legitimacy. Recent efforts to form partnerships between community foundations and some commercial DAFs, however, suggest that such relationships may take many forms. They will, however, need to articulate their distinctive contributions and the larger ones, at least, may be able to highlight their strengths in community leadership and grant-making. But there are limits to this approach if donors are intent on having their wishes followed, because efforts to modify donor intent raise legal issues of trustee fidelity and weaken donors' trust in the institutions (Frumkin 1997). The many new and small community foundations may be hard-pressed to get beyond their initial focus on meeting donor interests and take on community leadership roles.

Continuing devolution and cuts in public spending will present a host of new community challenges for community foundations to address. Lack of resources may force them to develop innovative strategies and collaborative relationships, but they will need flexible and discretionary funding if they are to live up to promises. Perhaps the greatest challenges they face are the highly fragmented approaches and planning efforts among philanthropic funders and their own isolation from public funders. Although there is growing, but far from universal, recognition that philanthropy does not have the financial capacity to compensate for shifts in public policies, philanthropic funders may also lack the institutional capacity to play a decisive role. Only a small minority of funders appear to be true cosmopolitans in their consideration of a wide range of issues and in their interests in coordination. Community foundations are disproportionately in that category, but some, especially smaller ones, are not.

I thank Patricia Borntrager Tennen for her help in identifying relevant literature and data sources and Gerald Suttles, Richard Clerkin, Francie Ostrower, Theo Schuyt, the editors and two anonymous reviewers for comments on earlier drafts. They do not necessarily agree with my analysis nor are they responsible for any remaining errors.

Notes

1. This may include state and local sales taxes and local property taxes on real estate holdings.
2. Earnings derived from activities not directly related to the organization's tax-exempt mission (unrelated business income) are taxable at the same rate as for commercial entities.
3. Some of these are eligible to receive tax-deductible contributions for specific public benefit purposes.
4. As do the so-called operating foundations that use earnings from endowments to operate their own programs rather than support other charities.
5. For some political observers, abuses included perceptions that foundations pursued aggressive leftist political agendas.
6. Most focus on planned or deferred gifts (Regenovich 2003), such as simple bequests in wills, beneficiary designations on retirement or life insurance plans, trusts (charitable lead trusts, charitable remainder unitrusts, charitable remainder annuity trust), and contractual arrangements (pooled income fund, deferred payment gift annuities, charitable gift annuities, retained life interest).
7. The previous year, data from sixteen such funds (Larose 2002) reveal dramatic increases over the 2000 to 2001 period in total assets (up 21 percent), amounts distributed (up 40 percent), and number of individual DAFs (up 31 percent).
8. Fidelity Investments Charitable Gift Fund, the first (established in 1992, Lenkowsky 2002)—and largest—of these funds, accounted for the bulk of assets (69 percent), distributions (77 percent), and individual DAFs (78 percent).
9. If commercial funds do not screen designated charities, they may violate regulations imposed by the Homeland Security Act to prevent U.S. charities from supporting terrorist activities (Silber 2002).
10. Leonard (1989) identifies also a third model—grant making—that focuses on relationships with grantees.
11. This analysis of assets, gifts, and grants by 650 community foundations is based a 2002 Survey of Community Foundations (Columbus Foundation 2004).
12. Nationally, only 44 percent of 650 community foundations had assets of more than $10 million in 2002 (with estimated annual budgets of $500,000 for all operations, assuming earnings of 5 percent) and only 9 percent had assets of $100 million or more. Of $2.5 billion in grants awarded, the 11 percent that awarded $10 million or more accounted for three-fourths of the total. The 10 percent that received $10 million in gifts that year accounted for 71 percent of the total ($3.3 billion), while 2 percent reported no gifts in 2002 (data are missing for another 10 percent) and 5 percent made no grants (data are missing for another 8 percent).
13. An international meeting in 1998 of community foundations identified the following: serving as a mechanism for addressing local issues and problems by making grants and undertaking community leadership to

address a wide variety of critical needs, being accessible to grant-seekers and donors, and targeting a defined geographic area (Community Foundations of Canada 2000, 8). It also highlighted four broad characteristics of community foundations with implications for accountability to local communities: core values of neutrality, mutual responsibility, inclusiveness, accessibility, and accountability; multiple functions of building endowment, stewarding donated funds, serving donors, making grants, and engaging in community leadership; good management practices with regard to internal governance, fundraising, marketing, grant making, and community relations; and efforts to document outcomes of what has been accomplished and when.

14. NCRP issued a report for each of the ten foundations, describing the community context, along with detailed findings for each of the assessment areas, comparisons to the other foundations examined, and recommendations. For an example, see National Committee for Responsive Philanthropy (1994). For a summary, see National Committee for Responsive Philanthropy (1995).

15. The Foundation Center distinguishes between corporate, community, and other private foundations, but does not separate the latter into family and independent foundations.

16. Compared to the largest foundations: publications (84 versus 70 percent), annual reports (79 versus 52 percent), and Web site (65 versus 58 percent); compared to the oldest foundations: publications (84 versus 42 percent), annual reports (79 versus 23 percent), and Web site (65 versus 20 percent).

17. For a description of the project and methodology see Grønbjerg and Martell (2000). The analysis presented here is based on Grønbjerg and Jones (1997). I gratefully acknowledge financial support from the Nonprofit Sector Research Fund at the Aspen Institute, the Chicago Community Foundation, Woods Fund of Chicago, the Field Foundation of Illinois, Loyola University Chicago, and the Center on Philanthropy at Indiana University as well as research assistance by Todd Campbell, Colleen Carpenter, Edde Jones, Laura Martell, and Laurie Paarlberg.

18. We interviewed twelve family foundations, twelve independent foundations, twelve corporate funders, nine community and public foundations, and five other funders, selecting at random three of each type within each of four size categories, in some cases exhausting the size/type category before reaching the count of three.

19. We defined as large those awarding $5 million in grants or more, as medium those with grants between $1 million and $4.9 million, as small those with total grants between $500,000 and $999,999, and as tiny those with less than $500,000 in grants.

20. There were corresponding interviews with government funders not referenced here.

21. We combined corporate foundations and corporate giving programs, although there are important differences between the two. Corporate foundations must meet reporting, minimum pay-out, and excise tax

requirements that apply to all private foundations. Corporate giving programs are exempt from these regulations, but cannot award in excess of 10 percent of annual taxable income and must support only charities.

22. We included UW organizations here because they raise funds on an ongoing basis as do community/public foundations. Although UW is not eligible for membership in the Council on Foundations (Joanne Scanlan, personal communication), some are members of regional associations of grantmakers or undertake endowment campaigns.

23. Although less ambitious than originally planned, this involved merging three existing state agencies and components of three others to create a new Department of Human Services with 20,000 employees and a budget of $4 billion, and consolidating 147 existing programs with 4,500 grants and contracts.

24. Key proposals included the Istook (Republican member of the House of Representatives from Oklahoma) budget amendment to limit nonprofit advocacy (summer, 1995), the "charitable choice" provision of the 1996 Welfare Reform Act, and efforts to change appreciation rules for in-kind donations and extend the deductibility of charitable donations for people who do not itemize their tax returns.

25. These include new corporate interest in strategic philanthropy, shift from manufacturing to service jobs with lower wages and less established traditions for supporting United Way, and corporate restructuring (for example, takeovers, downsizing, and dominance of multinational corporations).

26. We had to name and explain the Chicago Community Trust or the Chicago Foundation for Women as examples before most recognized at least the former.

27. As one family foundation official observed, they are accountable to everyone and no one because there is no particular donor to whom they have to answer.

28. Although eclipsed by UW in the amount of funds it awards on an annual basis, CCT is the largest community foundation in the region, and second only to the MacArthur Foundation in total foundation assets.

29. Not included here are nine funders who were unwilling or unable to do more than say they had a "fair" amount of turnover. They were spread about evenly across the four types of funders.

References

Agard, Kathryn A. 1992. "Characteristics of Community Foundations at Different Ages and Asset Sizes." Ed.D. diss. Michigan State University.

Atienza, Josefina, and Leslie Marino. 2003a. *Foundation Reporting: Update on Public Reporting Trends of Private and Community Foundations.* New York: The Foundation Center.

———. 2003b. *Foundation Staffing: Update on Staffing Trends of Private and Community Foundations.* New York: The Foundation Center.

Berry-Helmlinger, Lyn. 2003. "Merrill Lynch starts nonprofit fund." *Denver Business Journal* (April 4, 2003). http://www.bizjournals.com/denver/stories/2003/04/07/story7.html.

Blum, Debra E. 2002. "Tailor-Made for Charity." *Chronicle of Philanthropy* 14(16, May 30): n.p. Available at: http://philanthropy.com/free/articles/v14/i16/16000701.htm.

Bothwell, Robert O. 1993. *Federated Giving: Recent History, Current Issues.* Washington D.C.: National Committee for Responsive Philanthropy,

Carson, Emmett D. 2002. "Community Foundations Facing Crossroads." *Chronicle of Philanthropy* 14(15)(May 16, 2002): 39.

Clontz, Bryan. 2001. "Check Out Local Community Foundations." *National Underwriter/Life and Health Financial Services* 105(49): 35–36.

Clyde, Allan R. 2003. "Cover Story: A Conversation with Steven Minter." *Foundation News & Commentary* 44(2)(March/April): 1.

Columbus Foundation. 2004. *Survey of Community Foundations, 2003.* Columbus, Ohio. http://www.columbusfoundation.org.

Community Foundations of Canada. 2000. *Building the Worldwide Community Foundation Movement.* Ottawa, Canada. http://www.community-fnd.ca

Council on Foundations. 1988. *Community Foundation Competency Guide.* Washington, D.C.: Council on Foundations.

———. 1992. *Common Characteristics of Community Foundations.* Washington, D.C.: Council on Foundations.

Frumkin, Peter. 1997. "Fidelity in Philanthropy: Two Challenges to Community Foundations." *Nonprofit Management and Leadership* 8(Fall)(1): 65–76.

Greene, Stephen G. 2003. "Community Foundations Consider New Approaches for Financial Stability." *Chronicle of Philanthropy* 16(1)(October 16, 2003): 21.

Grønbjerg, Kirsten A. 1983. "Historical Perspectives on Chicago Nonprofit Sectors." Research Guide III. *The Nonprofit Sector in an Era of Governmental Retrenchment.* Washington, D.C.: The Urban Institute.

Grønbjerg, Kirsten A., Lori Harmon, Aida Olkkonen, and Asif Raza. 1996. "The United Way System at the Crossroads: Community Planning and Allocation." *Nonprofit and Voluntary Sector Quarterly* 25(4)(December): 428–52.

Grønbjerg, Kirsten A., and Edwina Jones. 1997. "Philanthropic Human Service Funders in a Changing Environment." Paper presented at the Annual ARNOVA Meetings. Indianapolis, Ind. (December 3–6, 1997).

Grønbjerg, Kirsten A., and Laura Martell. 2000. "Philanthropic Funding of Human Services: Solving Ambiguity Through the Two-Stage Competitive Process" *Nonprofit and Voluntary Sector Quarterly* 29(1)(Supplement): 9–40.

Hammack, David. 1989. "Community Foundations: The Delicate Question of Purpose." In *An Agile Servant: Community Leadership by Community Foundations,* edited by Richard Magat. New York: The Foundation Center.

———. 2004. "Community Foundations." Unpublished paper.

Hannan, Michael T., and John H. Freeman. 1977. "The Population Ecology of Organizations." *American Journal of Sociology* 82(5): 929–64.

————. 1984. "Structural Inertia and Organizational Change." *American Sociological Review* 49(2): 149–64.

Larose, Marni D. 2002. "Assets of Donor-Advised Funds Totaled $12.3 Billion, Last Year, Survey Finds." *Chronicle of Philanthropy* 14(16)(May 30): n.p.

Larose, Marni D., and Brad Wolverton. 2003. "Donor-Advised Funds Experience Drop in Contributions, Survey Finds." *Chronicle of Philanthropy* 15(15)(May 15): n.p.

Lawrence, Steven, Josefina Atienza, and Leslie Marino. 2003. *Foundation Yearbook: Facts and Figures on Private and Community Foundations, 2003.* New York: The Foundation Center.

Lenkowsky, Leslie. 2002. "Foundations and Corporate Philanthropy." In *The State of Nonprofit America,* edited by Lester M. Salamon. Washington, D.C.: Brookings Institution.

Leonard, Jennifer, 1989. "Creating Community Capital: Birth and Growth of Community Foundations." In *An Agile Servant: Community Leadership by Community Foundations,* edited by Richard Magat. New York: The Foundation Center.

Lilly Endowment. 2001. "Taking Stock." A Program of the GIFT Initiative. Executive Summary. Indianapolis, Ind.: Lilly Endowment Inc.

Magat, Richard, ed. 1989. *An Agile Servant: Community Leadership by Community Foundations.* New York: The Foundation Center.

National Committee for Responsive Philanthropy (NCRP). 1994. *The Denver Foundation and the Disenfranchised: High Response Grantmaking, But Taking No Risks.* A Report of the Community Foundations Responsiveness Project. Washington, D.C.: National Committee for Responsive Philanthropy.

————. 1995. "Community Foundations and Citizen Empowerment: NOT!" *Responsive Philanthropy* (Spring).

Newman, Bruce. 1989. "Pioneers of the Community Foundation Movement." In *An Agile Servant: Community Leadership by Community Foundations,* edited by Richard Magat. New York: The Foundation Center.

Nielsen, Waldemar A. 1996. *Inside American Philanthropy: The Dramas of Donorship.* Norman: University of Oklahoma Press.

Ostrower, Francie. 2004. *Attitudes and Practices Concerning Effective Philanthropy: Executive Summary.* Washington, D.C.: The Urban Institute.

Pfeffer, Jeffrey, and Gerald R. Salancik. 1978. *The External Control of Organizations: A Resource Dependence Perspective.* New York: Harper and Row.

Regenovich, Dean. 2003. "Establishing a Planned Giving Program." In *Hank Rosso's Achieving Excellence in Fund Raising,* 2nd ed., edited by Eugene R. Tempel. San Francisco: Jossey-Bass.

Ridings, Dorothy S. 2002. "From the President: Standard-bearer." *Foundation News & Commentary* 43(5)(September/October): n.p.

Silber, Norman I. 2002. "Donor-Advised Funds Can Be Terrorism Tools." *Chronicle of Philanthropy* 14(7)(January 24, 2002): n.p.

Part III

European Perspectives

Chapter 7

Historical Changes in Foundation Functions and Legitimacy in Europe

Giuliana Gemelli

Historically, foundations are among the oldest of social institutions, having been with us for nearly 3,000 years. From the Greek and Roman period to the Middle Ages, in the Christian and the Islamic and Jewish traditions, their raison d'être has been to preserve memoria, both sacred and profane.

This concept—perpetuating fame and glory after the founder's death, establishing an afterlife, and maintaining the social relation between founder and beneficiaries—is implicit in the Arabic word waqf, which refers to philanthropic foundations in the Islamic world and is derived from the root verb waquafa, which means to "cause a thing to stop and stand still." In the Jewish tradition, the practice and the rigorously defined rules of the Zedaka indicate both the path to perpetuating the act of giving after the death of the giver and the community's responsibility to support the poorest by giving them the opportunity to create income and help themselves, to the ultimate benefit of the community. "Religion and giving," Wuthnow observes, "are never private issues" (2003).

In fact, by articulating individual freedom and social responsibility, foundations extend the concept of legacy as a relationship between the founder and the beneficiaries to the principle of responsibility toward the next generation. In so doing, they establish the tradition of applying private wealth for public purpose and benefit, which has proved such a fundamental need of societies to preserve their identity and sustain their development.

Foundations, as institutions devoted to giving through legacy, thus have a generally universal aim, though they are of course highly differentiated in the particulars of organization and mission. The concept on which they as institutions are based, differentiated iso-morphism,[1] implies just this, that their structural patterns and social functions are remarkably similar, but that their configuration, aims, and organizational models change with historical and social context.

As path-dependent institutions, foundations demonstrate the evo-lutionary patterns of societies and cultures in respect to universal needs, such as using private wealth for public purposes in the quest for social justice and economic redistribution. From a long-term perspec-tive, the legitimacy of foundations is strictly related to how these two aspects—universal aims and specific social needs—are articulated.

Several paradoxes are at work. Foundations are both deeply rooted in specific cultural and social tradition yet the agent of social change; they operate in preserving values and social identity of a specific soci-ety and constitute a framework for cultural hybridization. "Middle Eastern Jewish patterns may have been reinforced by the example of the Islamic *waqf* and its popularity as a nutriment for building mosques and schools," Cohen points out. "In Europe some transfor-mation, perhaps influenced by Christian models, seems to have occurred" (2003).

The process of differentiated isomorphism of foundations has increased in the modern era when different patterns of articulation between states and societies emerged. Initially, from the deterioration of the Roman Empire onward, the role of the church was strong, with monasteries filling the role and showing many traits of modern foun-dations, such as a governing bodies, specific regulations, and endow-ments. Toward the late nineteenth century, however, secularization began to limit the legitimacy of the church as the institution to deal with social issues.

It became progressively more difficult to define foundations gener-ally in such a way to hold true across cultures, economic frameworks, and political borders. If it is difficult to speak of a Western model of a foundation, it is even more difficult to define a common European vision of the role, vision, and practices of foundations. Both institu-tional configuration and legitimacy are embedded in a triangle of rela-tions involving the state, the market, and local, regional, and national communities.

Foundations in Europe underwent several dramatic changes between the sixteenth century and the twentieth. First was the Reformation, which effectively partitioned the continent. In the Protestant north, Anglo-Saxon-Germanic traditions influenced the dissemination of the foundation concept to North America. In the Catholic south, foundations essentially did not exist. In time, as the Industrial Revolution got under way in the eighteenth and nineteenth centuries, foundations emerged in the north in the framework of new institutional drivers, created by the interests of a dynamic elite and emerging middle class. The rights and responsibilities of the citizens in the north were a driving force in social change. In the south, on the contrary, the state arrogated power to become that force. The emergence of a social economy sector during the nineteenth century, however, led to a compromise between the state and the market. This entailed legalizing organizations such as mutual companies and associations whose aim was to generate mutual interest and collective wealth rather than return on individual investment. Paradoxically, in several countries, particularly in France despite specific evolutionary patterns, the development of foundations as legitimate institutions was limited by the development of associations in the framework of social economy, which includes both charities and voluntary service as well as enterprises of social redistribution.

Generalizations, however, such as the division between north and south, can be misleading. Limits to foundations' legitimacy existed in Germany in the nineteenth century, for example, when, according to the German legal theorist Carl von Savigny, they could exist only if they were under state control. It was the state's task to define priorities and regulatory bodies were established to supervise the behavior of foundations. In most European countries, the role of foundations was questioned, albeit for different reasons, and their legitimacy was the result of a very dynamic process with periods of systematic decline. This was the case in Revolutionary France, where the Loi Le Chapelier of 1791 led to a Janus-like effect—abolishing the ancien régime institutions on the one hand, and impeding the growth of new intermediate institutions on the other. In England as well, at least in certain periods, charities were subject to regulatory pressures. One well-known example is the Charitable Uses Act of 1601, which entitled citizens to take legal action against charities if they suspected them of malfeasance. In 1736, English Mortmain Act abolished the right of corporate bodies, especially churches and charities, to hold land. Charities were even considered detrimental to security of the state. The legislation reproved the pride and vanity of donors to prevent and limit them in giving.

The Enlightenment did not, as one might expect, foster the development of foundations. In Diderot's *Encyclopédie* in 1755, for example, Turgot wrote about foundations as a total waste of time because he considered their assets inert money: foundations, Turgot stated, were by definition devoted to obsolescence and immorality because the purpose they were created for would not last indefinitely. The government, he maintained, had an incontestable right to suppress foundations entirely, and should do just that.

In the nineteenth century, the fate of foundations depended on the configuration of the national state and the way in which it assumed responsibility to shape the relations between the market and society. In the twentieth century, the differentiated isomorphism of European institutions was overwhelmed by an emerging new model of foundation in the Western world characterized by three factors: the integration of philanthropy and corporate institutions, the professionalization of philanthropy through the creation of endowed foundations and their bureaucracies, and the beginning of a process of internationalization of philanthropy. The development of so-called American style scientific philanthropy shifted the role of foundations from traditional charity as an ameliorative use of resources to systematic study of the roots of social problems for long-term solutions.

Scientific philanthropy as it emerged in the United States generated an increasing chasm between the model of social economy that dominated in several European countries during the transition from the liberal state to the welfare state, on the one hand, and the American model, in which foundations acted as driving forces of social change in a corporate society, on the other. The logic of modern business corporation was linked simultaneously with the ascetic aim and human benevolence of philanthropy and with the social responsibility of the philanthropic entrepreneur and with the application of scientific methods.

Patterns of European resistance to this model are useful conceptual tools in analyzing the process of legitimization of foundations over the last century. Such analysis entails focusing on the different roles played by specific institutional actors, such as the church and the state, and on the relationship between them. It also means focusing on different conceptualizations of the public sector on each side of the Atlantic. It is accurate to say that U.S. foundations reflect the mirroring of philanthropic practices and the public sector to shape the direction of foundation giving. It is also clear that the definition is different in Europe, where it means instead state administration and related organizations.

Several questions arise from these considerations. How we can we deal with traditional Western philanthropy and the divide between it and the U.S. model of scientific philanthropy, and create a coherent framework for both? How are we to redefine philanthropy's variegated and often confusing terminology to embrace what is called a foundation in one country but could not be qualified as such in another?

Is this divide primarily related to basic differences in functions of foundations—that is, redistribution agents, as in the American tradition, or service delivery agents complementing the role of the state, as in most of Europe? How can we explain the fact that Christianity has been both a critical actor in spreading the aim and practice of charity as well as an obstacle to the development of philanthropy as scientific strategy of giving? And, finally, how can we explain the fact that resistance to modernizing and institutionalizing philanthropy through foundations has persisted in Europe despite the secularization of the state?

To frame the discussion I use *contrast of context* as an approach to compare the long-term legitimacy of foundations in two European countries, France and Italy. I do so by analyzing not only the roles of the state and the church but also the different effects in those two countries of the impact of American foundations in shaping international policies, particularly in the field of education and research.

The Italian Anomaly in the European Context

In the second half of the nineteenth century, as Germany and France were concerned with liberalizing associations, Italy was concerned with constraining them. The starting point came in 1848, after Italy's unification, with the Statuto Albertino, which created the legal framework to close down associations if they were suspected of being a threat to public order. The legislation was ambiguous and itself an authoritarian interpretation of the balance between state powers and

individual freedom of association. The final decision on an association's right to exist lay in the hands of the judges (the magistratura).

The idea behind this legislation was to inhibit by law what the law
was unable to stimulate in civil society. Intermediary entities between
the state and the private sector—that is, the enti morali as "amphibi-
ous" organizations—were relegated to a juridical no man's land, with
no status except that of being administered by the state through the
magistratura. The principle was simple: political control through a pre-
text of legal protection. In the Civil Code of 1942, during the Fascist
period, a legal form of foundations was introduced, but left the existence of an organization in the hands of the public authority that
might, or might not, choose to bestow legal status.

This framework was overwhelmed by the attitude of the Italian
state toward the church. Despite legislation oriented to contain the
expansion of church institutions (enti canonici), a new social set of
practices and institutions (beneficienza) generated a framework for the
bodies previously regulated by canonical legislation. These bodies (the
opere pie) fell under the same juridical framework of the enti morali
and were also placed under the control of the public authority. As
semi-public institutions, they were considered part of the state and
acted as bureaucratic entities, frequently dominated by either private
or political interests. They existed in Italy until the late 1980s, when
the opere pie began to be suppressed and the IPAB (Istituzioni pub-
bliche di assistenza e benevolenza) were privatized and rapidly—
I would say too rapidly—transformed into foundations. In most cases,
however, despite the privatization, they maintained the cultural and
political aims of the enti morali.

Over the last twenty years, the real effect of laws transforming public bodies into foundations has been to develop legislation designed to
downsize the public sector and reduce the financial burden of the state.
One might well wonder how moving institutions from a legal status to
another could effect a real change in cultural organization. The dictum
"le mort saisit le vif" (the living are in the grip of the dead) seems fairly
appropriate in this case when one considers that in Italy philanthropy
is still synonymous with beneficienza. Outstanding scholars credit that
philanthropy is just a modern substitute for charity as eleemosynary
(compassionate capitalism). This interpretation, which prevails, holds
that the legitimacy of foundations as institutions related to philanthropy cannot imply reciprocity, which is a relevant pattern in social
change (Melandri and Zamagni 2002, n1, 8–9).

The main difference between France and Italy is related to the fact that in Italy the opere pie and enti morali never gained full legal status as juridical bodies. In France, thanks to the Waldeck Rousseau's act of 1901 (la loi sur les associations reconnues d'utilité publique), intermediate bodies did achieve juridical autonomy and actively participated in building intermediate institutions as drivers of industrial democracy. Paradoxically, this legislation—which favored the acquisition of private donations and enhanced private initiative for public goals—reduced the need for institutions of the same nature, such as foundations, as private incorporated institutions. Corporate culture was not even part of the genetic code of French Republican society, which responded to the need for bridging private initiative and public goals by strengthening the role and legitimacy of associations. In France these are completely autonomous in defining their goals. The 1901 act was a driver of innovation in social legislation, institutional reforms, and cultural and scientific policies. It led, in fact, to rearticulating political power and civil society, and contributed to drive the social and intellectual capital produced by civil society in the direction of state administration through the role of intermediate institutions, such as associations. It reshaped patterns of communication between the central administration and the periphery by affirming the capacity of the state to act, in the words of Emile Durkheim, as the "thinking brain of society."

Contrast of Contexts: The Role of American Foundations in France and Italy

The problem of legitimacy in the last half of the twentieth century, however, cannot be reduced to the roles of the state and the church. It is also a problem of societal recognition, not only because of the social utility of foundations but also because of the process of institutionalization. The difference between the European and the U.S. models is significant. With their emphasis on exploring the causes rather than remedying the effects, U.S. foundations advanced to the center of the public policy debate and their actions began to change the national agenda. The ability of foundations to exert a substantial impact on society, however, remains under debate in the United States. Some expect an increase in influence based on the growth of new resources flowing into the foundation sector. Others dispute any "detectable dent" in the major social problems. What is not disputed, however, is that during the first part of the twentieth century, until the 1970s, the impact of U.S. foundations has been critical not only in the United States but in other areas of the world as well, including Europe, largely because of the nonexistence or limited existence of scientific philanthropy outside the United States. This impact has varied widely, not only as an effect of the quantity of grants, but in relation to the configurations of society.

To reinforce this argument it is enough to compare France and Italy during a period of institutional reforms, specifically, from the late 1950s to the late 1960s. This decade marks the peak of the role of U.S. foundations in shaping European scientific and social policies. That foundations have no clear-cut role in either France or Italy has been attributed to the pervasive importance of the welfare state and what amounts to state monopoly on education and research. My argument is that the expansion of state bureaucracy into areas where foundations were traditionally active does not entirely explain the complexity and the differentiated effects of foundations' policies in the two countries. Despite structural differences in their institutional and political systems, France and Italy present similarities that can be explored in relation to the United States. Since the late 1950s, the Rockefeller and Ford foundations tried to disseminate in both countries similar programs focused on developing empirical sociological research, management education, behavioral sciences, and applied psychology. U.S. foundations were confronted with two basic problems. First was how to adapt these patterns to different historical social and political contexts. Second was how to adapt international scientific strategies to strengthening European integration as a framework in which to consolidate Western alliances, bypassing not only the constraints of ideologies but also old-style bureaucracies. The Ford Foundation looked for the emergence in European countries of a powerful epistemic community, a network of professionals, with recognized expertise and competence and an authoritative claim to policy-relevant knowledge.

This was particularly the case for France and Italy in the mid-1960s, when institutional reforms in education and research topped the national agenda. This orientation fell in line with the Ford Foundation programs under McGeorge Bundy, which shifted from the Atlantic concern of the 1950s toward an international policy of large-scale cooperation among industrial countries under a strategic higher education and research framework. A key issue was concern about the weakness of social sciences and management studies in Europe. This shift occurred when international expansion of the social sciences became the new catalyst for liberal and antitotalitarian pragmatism. It implied a refocus of Ford Foundation policies, and its social impact was wider and deeper than the opposition to a Marxist philosophy of history and Leninist-Stalinist political aims. The dissemination of the empirical research patterns was directed not only to university programs but also to research centers, business schools, and training centers for professionals in private as well as public administration.

The process varied across Europe, depending on the number and activity of foundations dedicated to this aim and acting as catalysts in relations amongst government, universities, and the companies. Scandinavian countries, Belgium, and France were among the countries creating ad hoc foundations to channel this process. In Italy, and to some extent also in Germany, the same attempt failed. In France, paradoxically, U.S. programs had a significant impact during the de Gaulle era, a critical period in French-American relations marked by the strong expansion of state intervention in scientific research and educational policies. Analysis of U.S. foundations in France indicates that the theory of a strong state crowding out foundations should be reconsidered. This analysis also presents several interesting elements of comparison between France and Italy. Similar American programs had in fact different impacts in the two countries.

The first evidence reveals that France received a significant number of grants in applied social research. However, if one breaks down the data and looks only at grants to French national programs, the evidence indicates quantitative homogeneity in the two countries, in terms of both grant amounts and the type. Between 1958 and 1973, the largest grants went to the Maison des Sciences de l'Homme in Paris (MSH), the SVIMEZ (Association for the Development of Southern Italy), and the Bilateral Committee on Social and Political Sciences (CoSPoS) in Italy. The Maison project received grant of $1 million. The same amount went to the SVIMEZ in Italy, which had a relevant role in developing new methodologies in economic research, but its activity was gradually absorbed within the framework of economic planning with a strong intervention of state bureaucracy. The Bilateral Committee received $800,000 to support a program based on the cooperation of the U.S. Social Science Research Council and the Adriano Olivetti Foundation, created as a memorial to the Italian entrepreneur. Its goal was to professionalize social and political sciences by strengthening research in Italian universities. The institutions in both countries had similar strategic aims. They enhanced the role of institution builders, such as the French historian Fernand Braudel, the Italian economists Pasquale Saraceno and Giorgio Fuà, and the Italian political scientist Alberto Spreafico, and of leading scientific entrepreneurs, such as Gaston Berger, director of the French Ministry of Education, Vincenzo Caglioti, president of the Italian CNR, and Fabio Luca Cavazza, a leading personality in the il Mulino publishing house, which in 1959 received a Ford Foundation grant to study the reform of the Italian university system. These actors shared the idea that social research should be the framework of an increasing cooperation between public and private institutions as well as of the strengthening of international cooperation. They also shared the idea that research outcomes should be applied to concrete problems of advanced industrial societies.

The impact of these programs was significantly different in France and Italy. In France, a process of substitution of traditional elite by elites committed to change was at work, with "the setting-up of a transatlantic political and intellectual community" (Gremion 1998, 1). This process involved networks of change at the level of civil society, including higher education professors, state bureaucracy, and grands commis (administrators of science and brokers of ideas). In the framework of the Ministry of Education and of scientific agencies such as the Délégation Génerale de la Recherche Scientifique et Technique, an increasing cooperation with industries, private corporations, and international agencies developed. Rather paradoxically, this occurred in an institutional framework where, despite the total lack of philanthropic U.S.-style foundations, the same institutional patterns of interaction amongst government, private organization, and public utility associations that in the United States gave foundations their legitimacy were at work. The role of U.S. foundations was critical. Both the private and the public sector supported innovation and strengthened French performance in scientific research and educational strategies. The associations reconnues d'utilité publique were largely instrumental in this process, for several reasons, including the fact that they permitted the allocation of grants. The MSH created under the 1901 law was one of the primary and most successful results of the cooperation between the Ford Foundation, the French grand commis, and enlightened intellectuals such as Fernand Braudel, who acted as scientific entrepreneur and the Maison's institutional builder.

Italy, by contrast, despite the creation of a few U.S.-style foundations in the mid-1960s and their emerging role, suffered a systematic collapse of large-scale research programs in both the natural and the social sciences. At the same time, the few private research institutions were also facing a crisis, the very institutions that had tried to facilitate the dialogue among universities, private institutions, and the government and to enhance institutional competitiveness in the private and public sector. Experiments in innovation using foundations as catalysts were isolated rather than connected and led to a phenomenon that might be called an enclosure rather than a snowball effect.

The CoSPoS succeeded only partly in professionalizing the social sciences through research because it was not able to introduce postgraduate educational programs. And despite the impetus of a small group of men with vision in Italian government, inadequate commitment to long-range strategic planning and cooperation between state agencies and private institutions limited the potential for organizational development needed to accomplish social change in critical sectors. Avoiding reforms became a political practice for more than twenty years: another consequence was the almost complete retreat of private research institutions from cooperation with public agencies.

Nervus Societatis: Foundations as Agents of Change

The various effects of similar grant-making policies in Italy and France reveal a paradox beyond a state strong-arming foundations. The impact foundations have on scientific and institutional innovation does not depend either on the role of the state or on the cooperation between public institutions and private foundations, but instead on the complex articulation between the cultural and organizational patterns of both systems, the decision-making process, the role of national elites in strengthening institutional reflexivity and transparency, and evolutionary patterns. Legislation is also critical but, as the Hegelian metaphor suggests, should be introduced only at the "falling of dusk," when institutional policies are already consolidated and legislation becomes a concrete instrument to sustain social change and reform policies.

Comparing France to Italy supports the suggestion of differentiated isomorphism. In the mid-1960s, despite the growing expectation of foundations acting as drivers of scientific philanthropy, the effects of social change were consistently less in Italy than in France, where U.S.-style foundations did not exist. A possible interpretation is that a strategic vision of social change based on the existence of an institutional matrix combining state agencies, private institutions, research laboratories, and civil society associations and networks was at work. This matrix was to a large extent similar to that described by Oliver Zunz (1998) as the main feature of the American century—albeit certainly less structured.

These arguments lead us to further considerations. The first is that many of the studies on foundation roles and networking strategies in Europe are focused on legislation and particularly on the integration of European legislation on foundations, which is considered the driving force of change and the main vehicle for legitimacy. Legal issues and legislation are certainly relevant factors. Integrating legal issues and tax exemption regulation is critical if European context for foundations and their impact outside national and regional boundaries is to be enhanced. Foundation legitimacy, however, is the product of a more complex and long-term process. This was the case in the United States and it is the case also in Europe. The cycle is uneven, with phases of impact and retreat and of autonomy and defensiveness. In the United States pressures arose during congressional scrutiny, over concerns related to political activity, particularly but certainly not only during the Cold War. Foundations were subject to legislation and regulation, as in 1969 with the Tax Reform Act and more recently in relation to the uses of resources and payout. Despite the criticism and scrutinies, however, U.S. foundations became rooted in the structural configuration of American society and shared patterns at work in other institutions, in terms both of institutional culture and vision of social change.

The increasing concern over accountability, transparency, professionalizing foundations' staff, and expanding networks of competence are part of an evolutionary process in which foundations accept the challenges from society, government, and business as the framework on which to build legitimacy. The issue of legislation is important but should be integrated with others focusing on the relations between foundations and their external environment. To understand the legitimacy problem, in Europe as well as in the United States, we really do need to implement the study of foundations with research on their social and cultural history. Foundations are a modus of social action as well as of social interaction and of cultural representation of this interaction. They are a point of leverage in society only if they share society's vision of social change and act as independent bodies.

This leads to another consideration. To what extent is the legitimacy of foundations related to other entities within society, and to what extent is legitimacy consolidation limited or obstructed if other entities do not see the same degree of change? Because foundations are simply organizations within civil society, their role as drivers of innovation and social change can be enhanced only if other entities—communities, nonprofits, government, business—are oriented toward stimulating social and civic entrepreneurship rather than politics and economic profit.

New types of foundations that have developed in Europe over the last twenty years or so are relevant to this argument. One such example, in terms of both number (eighty-nine) and total endowment (36 billion euro), are bank-origin foundations, which came into being in Italy in 1990 on the heels of a law that broke up the old nonprofit banking institutions, the Casse di Risparmio, and gave banks the option to change their legal status. In 2004, after an exhausting controversy about their juridical status, the Constitutional Court held that bank-origin foundations are private bodies. This deliberation contradicted the order of Treasury Minister Giulio Tremonti that had placed them under the control of public entities, particularly local and regional governments. It also reaffirmed the historical identity of the Casse di Risparmio, which had been established in the past by entrepreneurial and civic groups as private and autonomous bodies supporting social, cultural, and economic values and community needs, though in a complementary role, not to substitute for public institutions. Italy is a country inherent with seeming self-contradictions. Despite the juridical ratification of the Constitutional Court's amendment, the identity of bank-origin foundations as private institutions is far from settled as far as institutional behavior, organizational culture, and the external pressure exerted by public bodies to be represented within their boards are concerned.[2] It should be no surprising that this issue is both political and historic. It will certainly take time to redirect foundation policies, to establish operational responsiveness, transparency, and accountability. It will also take time to develop proactivism and entrepreneurship, and to orient such policy toward resolving community needs rather than exclusively toward grant making. Last and certainly not least, it will take time for foundations to strengthen self-governance and private funding.

Conclusions

The legitimacy of foundations as proactive actors in high engagement philanthropy depends as much on a new model of partnerships within the nonprofit sector and between it, business, and governments as it does on foundation policy. Legitimacy implies a change of orientation and a consolidated strategic vision, the critical issue being social and civic entrepreneurship. That is, to establish legitimacy, a twofold process is needed: foundations should work for social investment beyond grant making, and nonprofit organizations need to abandon grant seeking as a priority. They should take the initiative to generate equal partnerships (Austin 2000) with private and corporate foundations, thus increasing their organizational capabilities and acting as social entrepreneurs rather than institutional beggars. The government could support this by facilitating growth of the sector, both by fostering another institutional dynamism and passing favorable legislation (such as fiscal exemption of donations).

In sum, strengthening legitimacy is certainly related to transparency and accountability practices but also to the ability of foundations to transform their grant-making policies into strategic philanthropy, by selecting those programs that are most promising in terms of organizational capabilities, social impact, and social change. Another avenue is to base funding cycles on a strategic long-term approach focused on the needs and aims of the organization they fund, rather than on short-term conveniences. The debate related to foundation type— operating or grant making—seems at risk of becoming both academic and a stumbling block to the roles that foundations might perform in the future.

Globally, foundations face a critical challenge. With seed grants, they may continue to fund programs they expect public agencies capable of carrying forward. They may differentiate even more and identify ever-narrower niches for their funding. They may also choose to work together to make strategic funding decisions and align their activities as never before (Bernholz 2000).

Notes

1. The concept of differentiated isomorphism has been defined and applied in mathematics as well as in cognitive sciences and sociological studies. It allows to better define the articulation between permanent functions and evolutionary patterns or configurations and to develop comparative issues. The seminal work of Lynne Zucker (1977) is a basic reference in the field of historical sociology of organizations.
2. "Foundations tend to adhere passively to the strategies, desires and orders of local administration, without developing their own vision of the 'public good' " (Barbetta and Demarie 2001, 176).

References

Austin, James. 2000. *The Collaboration Challenge. How Nonprofits and Business Succeed Through Strategic Alliance.* San Francisco: Jossey-Bass Publishers.

Barbetta, GianPaolo, and Marco Demarie. 2001. "Italy." In *Foundations in Europe, Society, Management and Law,* edited by Andreas Schlute, Volker Then, and Peter Walkenhorst. London. The Directory of Social Change.

Bernholz, Lucy. 2000. "Foundations for the Future: Emerging Trends in Foundations Philanthropy." The Center on Philanthropy and Public Policy, University of South California, Research Report (January 2000).

Cohen, Mark R. 2003. "Foundations and Charity. The Jewish Community of Medieval Egypt." Paper presented at the International conference Stiftungen in den grossen Kulturen des alten Europa. Humbolt–Universitat zu Berlin, Germany (June 13–14, 2003).

Gremion, Pierre. 1998. "The Partnership between the Ford Foundation and the Congress For Cultural Freedom." In *The Ford Foundation and Europe: Cross-Fertilization of Learning in Social Sciences and Management,* edited by Giuliana Gemelli. Brussels: P.I.E.

Melandri, Valerio, and Stefano Zamagni. 2002. "Il finanziamento del nonprofit in Italia fra intervento pubblico, filantropia e reciprocità, per una via italian al Fund-rising." In *Economia e management.* Milan: Bocconi University.

Wuthnow, Robert. 2003. "Lecture on Giving and Religion." The Center On Philanthropy. Indianapolis, Ind. (September 25, 2003).

Zucker, Lynne G. 1977. "The Role of Institutionalization in Cultural Persistence." *American Sociological Review* 42:726–43.

Zunz, Oliver, 1998. *Why the American Century.* Chicago: The University of Chicago Press.

Chapter 8

Roles of Foundations in Europe:
A Comparison

Helmut K. Anheier and Siobhan Daly

From a comparative, European perspective, few types of organizations have received less attention by researchers and policy analysts than foundations. Little is known in a systematic way about the current and future role and policy environment foundations are facing across Europe. Research on foundations has not been as forthcoming as that on other nonprofit organizations, where significant progress in data coverage and theoretical understanding has been achieved (for example, Salamon et al. 1999; Anheier and Ben-Ner 2003). Of course, countries such as the United Kingdom, Germany, Belgium, and Italy have been able to improve foundation statistics; yet most European Union member states have not. Significantly, and central to this chapter, we know little about the roles and contributions of foundations, and little understand the emerging policy environments.

Addressing the information gap in what we know of foundations in Europe is made all the more urgent by the fact that policy makers are calling for greater private, philanthropic involvement in fields as disparate as culture and the arts, social services, and research and education. What is more, not only politicians, but also representatives of corporate interests and civic leaders frequently stress the role foundations, along with other forms of philanthropy, could play in building and servicing civil society. As a result, in most European countries we face a growing gap between basic empirical knowledge about foundations on the one hand, and their policy relevance on the other.

In this context, we pose a number of questions. Are there challenges to the legitimacy of foundations in Europe? What do policy makers expect from foundations? Is there a potential legitimacy challenge in a mismatch between what policy makers would like and what foundations actually do? It is here that an examination of how European foundations perceive their own roles is an important step toward accessing the future legitimacy climate. Specifically, we present the results of a comparative European-wide project that involved approximately 300 interviews with representatives of foundations, policy makers, and other relevant stakeholders in the twenty countries that participated in the study (Austria, Belgium, Czech Republic, Denmark, Estonia, Finland, France, Germany, Greece, Hungary, Ireland, Italy, the Netherlands, Norway, Poland, Portugal, Spain, Sweden, Switzerland, and the United Kingdom).[1] Following a common set of conceptual guidelines, the field work was carried out by teams of local researchers in the various countries, many of whose work we refer to in the following discussion.

These in-depth, semistructured interviews, as well as the examination of foundation statistics and hundreds of annual reports that our colleagues collected in their respective countries, allowed us to probe more deeply into what are the common themes, debates, and challenges facing foundations in Europe today. By the same token, we sought to explore how European foundations view their role or roles in European societies, particularly vis-à-vis the state, the voluntary, and the business sectors, and how they perceive their roles as being affected by the opportunities and obstacles encountered in the prevalent policy environment. With very few exceptions, and in stark contrast to the United States, the European foundation literature and its broader political debates have rarely emphasized the question of roles explicitly, providing a limited starting point for our inquiry. As a result, European foundation representatives and other stakeholders are still less familiar with a number of potential foundation roles than their American counterparts. This lack of familiarity is reflected in the types, and levels of nuance, of reactions to certain roles, such as redistribution, that the research elucidated. Against this background, it is important at the outset to point out that the research we present here was not intended to determine whether—and if so how well—European foundations actually perform these roles. Rather, it was to establish which roles have resonance with foundation leaders and other stakeholders and which have none. Our basic argument, which we seek to examine with the data at hand, is that the legitimacy of foundations in

Europe will depend on a match between role performance and policy expectations.

Conceptual Challenge: Defining Foundations

The definition of foundations varies from one country to the next. Anheier (2001) underlines the "rich tapestry" of foundations in Europe that complicates our understanding of foundations because it produces a highly complex, sometimes confusing, terminology. Indeed, what is defined as a foundation in one country may not qualify as such in another. Moreover, not all organizations so labeled are in fact foundations. In central and eastern Europe, for example, many are either membership associations or corporations. The German political foundations such as the Friedrich-Ebert-Stiftung or the Konrad-Adenauer-Stiftung are registered associations with no significant assets of their own; their operating budgets are largely covered by annual subventions from the German Government (Beise 1998). In the Netherlands, the distinction between foundation (asset-based) and association (membership-based) has become largely indistinguishable in the field of education and social services. In Switzerland, some foundations are primarily investment trusts for families, pension schemes for corporations, or local sickness funds.

The definition of foundations varies from one country to another (Anheier 2001; Anheier and Toepler 1999), not along one primary axis, but frequently in several dimensions. Some legal definitions reflect either common law traditions with an emphasis on trusteeship (United States, the United Kingdom), or civil law traditions (for example, Switzerland and Germany), with an important distinction between legal personalities based on either membership or assets (Van der Ploegh 1999).[2] Other definitions bring in additional aspects, such as type of founder (private or public), purpose (charitable or other), activities (grant-making or operating), revenue structure (single or multiple funding sources), asset type (own endowment or regular allocations), and the degree of independence from the state, business or family interest. To cut across this terminological tangle, Helmut Anheier (2001) proposed a modification of the structural-operational definition that Lester Salamon and Anheier (1997) had developed for nonprofit organizations generally. Accordingly, a foundation has the following characteristics:

- It must be an asset-based entity, financial or otherwise. It must also rest on an original deed, typically a charter that gives the entity both intent of purpose and relative permanence as an organization.

- It must be a private entity. Foundations are institutionally separate from government, and are nongovernmental in the sense of being structurally separate from public agencies. Therefore, foundations do not exercise governmental authority and are outside direct majoritarian control.

- It must be a self-governing entity. Foundations are equipped to control their own activities. Some private foundations are tightly controlled either by governmental agencies or corporations, and function as parts of these other institutions, even though they are structurally separate.

- It must be a nonprofit-distributing entity. Foundations are not to return profits generated by either use of assets or commercial activities to their owners, members, trustees, or directors as income. In this sense, commercial goals neither principally nor primarily guide foundations.

- It must serve a public purpose. Foundations should do more than serve the needs of a narrowly defined social group or category, such as members of a family, or a closed circle of beneficiaries. Foundations are private assets that serve a public purpose.

Grant-making foundations are usually regarded as the prototype of the modern foundation, which is largely a reflection of the U.S. experience and its postwar dominance in the field of philanthropy (Toepler 1999). Whereas in the United States, over 90 percent of the more than 62,000 foundations are grant making, the majority of those in Europe are either operating, or pursue their objectives by combining grant-making activities with running their own institutions, programs, and projects. Historically, of course, foundations were operating institutions primarily, for example, hospitals, orphanages, schools, and universities, though many did distribute money (alms-giving) and contributions in kind (for example, food). By contrast, the sharp distinction between grant-making and operating foundations emerged much later, and is for both the United States and Europe largely a product of the nineteenth and early twentieth centuries (Karl and Katz

1987; Bulmer 1999). Behind the complexity of forms, there are nonetheless several basic categories:

- First are grant-making foundations, that is, endowed organizations that engage primarily in grant making for specified purposes. Examples include the Ford Foundation in the United States, the Leverhulme Trust in the United Kingdom, the Volkswagen Stiftung in Germany, the Bernard van Leer Foundation in the Netherlands, and the Carlsbergfondet in Denmark.

- Second are operating foundations, those that primarily operate their own programs and projects. Examples include the Institut Pasteur in France, the Pescatore Foundation in Luxembourg, which runs a home for senior citizens, and the Calouste Gulbenkian Foundation in Portugal (though this could also fall into the mixed category).

- Third are mixed foundations, those that operate their own programs and projects and engage in grant making on a significant scale. Examples include the Fundación BBV in Spain and the Robert Bosch Stiftung in Germany.

NGOs and nonprofit organizations would differ from a foundation in the sense that no asset base and original deed would be required. They would be either based on membership, that is, associations, or some other corporate form such as a limited liability corporation or a cooperative. Operating foundations and grant-seeking foundations are closer to the NGO form than they are to grant-making foundations. Of course, as with any comparative definition, some problems remain, specifically, in the four major areas where the definition proposed here encounters difficulties: first, where the label foundation disguises some other type of organization; second, where foundations engage with a market economy and change into primarily economic actors; third, where foundations become instruments of the state; and, fourth, where they become a dynastic means of asset protection and control (see Anheier 2001, 42–47).

Nevertheless, the definition gives us a benchmark against which we can conduct a comparative analysis of foundations in Europe. The three categories of foundations—grant making, operating, and mixed—capture the basic distinctions that can be made. Yet we remain mindful of the rich diversity of the landscape. What is more, it is clear that the different forms the foundation may take has the potential to impact on both the perception and performance of foundations and the types of roles they are able to perform in different countries.

Foundation Roles in the European Context

Given the variety and diversity of the foundation landscape in Europe, then, is there any one role or set of roles that might commonly apply? In contrast to the United States, where overall the foundation field is more homogeneous, at least in the sense of the predominance of the grant-making function, there has in Europe historically neither been much discussion of foundation roles nor a common understanding of what the dominant roles of foundations should be. Yet coming to terms with the question of foundation roles is important if not critical.

The various roles of foundations proposed in the international foundation literature are underpinned by fundamental questions of why foundations exist and what makes their presence publicly acceptable and legitimate (see chapter 2, this volume; Prewitt 1999; Anheier 2001). In response to these issues, various roles have been suggested in the literature, but by far the most common focus is on how foundations act as innovators, provide for redistributive giving and grant-making, push for policy change and act as an alternative to the state, by addressing the needs of those who are overlooked by the market or the state (Anheier and Leat 2002). These roles have been subject to debate. For example, Christine Letts et al. (1997) question just how innovative foundations are. One underlying issue is how relevant roles pertinent to explaining why foundations exist in the United States, such as the redistribution role associated with the (predominantly) grant-making foundations, are also applicable in the European context, where the delivery of services has been one of the principal reasons for the presence of foundations (see Anheier and Toepler 1999, 8; see also Toepler 2006).

From our reading of the relevant literature (chapter 2, this volume; Prewitt 1999; Anheier 2001), we propose six roles—complementarity, substitution, preservation of traditions and cultures, innovation, social and policy change, and redistribution—to serve as propositions for exploring what roles are consistent with the expectations of European foundations. Specifically, we sought to determine the extent to which foundation representatives and other relevant stakeholders are aware and have a clear understanding of different role; aim to meet the expectations they contain and prescribe and address gaps between role expectations and behavior.

Complementarity

The complementarity role suggests that foundations serve otherwise undersupplied groups under conditions of demand heterogeneity and public budget constraints. The idea of being involved in "doing what the state doesn't do" and "filling gaps" in areas that have been overlooked resonates clearly among foundations across Europe, with the majority of interviewed representatives and other stakeholders readily associating this role with their organizations. Foundations address gaps in state-led services or activities in one of three basic ways.

First, grant-making foundations may complement the government by providing financial resources for certain services. Second, they may address the needs of certain segments of society. The notion of foundations filling gaps is often prevalent here. For example, in Sweden the IRIS corporation, which is owned by the Foundation for the Visually Impaired, helps the Association for the Visually Impaired "act where society has not been able to live up to its responsibility" (Wijkström 2006). Third, foundations, whether normally operating or mixed foundations, may be engaged in providing services, such as running schools, hospitals, orphanages, and so on. Indeed, in the transition to democracy in central and eastern Europe and the Baltic States, foundations were earmarked by governments to provide such services. Hence, as one foundation in Estonia suggests, foundations played an important role in the deconstruction of the former communist state apparatus:

> The state got hold of many functions, which actually had no need of being governed by the state. At the same time it would have been very complicated to privatise them in the form of business enterprises. Take the hospitals. Health care services are not looked upon as business, but as a function guaranteed by the state. . . . There was one alternative—to turn the hospitals into foundations. It was the result of highly rational considerations. (Lagerspetz 2006)

Overall, the analysis of the role of foundations in complementing the state raises salient questions about their policy significance. Across the countries examined, complementarity is about cooperation through partnership, bargaining, and supporting the state through grant making, catering for specialist needs, and filling gaps where the state has failed to act or not acted in a sufficiently responsible way. Yet, terms such as bargaining, partnership, and supporting may put a "friendly gloss" on the relationships between foundations and governments, though, as Helmut Anheier and Diana Leat have noted (2006), they do little to clarify the precise nature of these relationships. In this regard, what is of particular interest is the degree to which the respective policy environment influences whether foundations proactively or reactively engage in the complementarity role.

Substitution

Substitution anticipates that foundations will take on functions that the state otherwise or previously supplied, that is, that foundations become providers of public and quasi-public goods. In general, as might be imagined, foundations do not appreciate the notion of being a substitute for the state. Avoiding such a role, however, is becoming more and more difficult. Foundations in western Europe are concerned about the implications that changing government roles and responsibilities in providing public services have for their autonomy: "We are legally required not to substitute but it's so grey now and government changes the rules so often, so now it's really hard to find a distinctive role" (Leat 2006).

In central and eastern Europe, although foundations were considered a lifeline by governments in the early years of the democratic transition (see Pinter 2001, 289), they are now beginning to call for the need for greater clarification of the division of responsibilities between foundations and the state. As a representative of the Partners Hungary Foundation explained,

> When the state does not wish [to] or cannot fulfill some of its own roles, these may be taken over on the basis of contracts by NGOs, but these roles must continue to be state roles by definition, and have to be covered from the central budget. (Wizner and Aszalos 2006)

Throughout Europe, similar challenges are facing foundations; the only difference being the context in which they have to be met. Where foundations in western Europe address the task of defining or redefining their roles in the context of broader reforms in public services, those in eastern Europe do so in the context of only recently democratized regimes. The nature of the relationship between foundations and the state dominates the analysis of the complementarity and substitution roles, and has serious implications for the roles, autonomy, and visions of foundations throughout Europe.

Preservation of Traditions and Cultures

We propose preservation as a role in which foundations oppose change and preserve past lessons and achievements likely to be swamped by larger social, cultural, and economic forces. However, such a role is often taken to be specific to an organization's objectives and activities, such as by foundations created to preserve the memory of prominent figures in arts and culture or to make a private art collection available to the public. Indeed, in the countries where this role is considered salient, such as Finland and Italy, culture and recreation account for a high concentration of foundation activity. The role also evokes negative connotations of foundations as backward-looking, as not at all progressive. This is contrary to the urgency that some respondents, in countries such as Switzerland and the United Kingdom, place on improving internal governance, transparency, and accountability among foundations. In this regard, the reluctance of interviewees to associate foundations with the preservation of traditions and cultures can be juxtaposed usefully against the prevalent climate of encouraging more strategic and transparent thinking among foundations (Breiteneicher and Marble 2001, 508–601). This, in turn, provides some explanation of why the interviewees are somewhat reluctant to associate with the preservationist role. Foundations want to be seen to be progressive, efficient, and forward-thinking institutions, as is particularly apparent in the analysis of the roles of innovation and social and policy change.

Redistribution

Redistribution suggests that the major role of foundations is to engage in and promote shifting primarily economic resources from higher to lower income groups. Redistribution is often taken to be "a convenient and comfortable answer to the puzzle of what legitimates foundations" (Prewitt 1999, 20). The role is rooted in early philanthropists' wishes, particularly in the nineteenth century, to give something back to society, which normally involved a focus on addressing symptoms of problems based on traditional notions of charity (see Anheier and Leat 2006). Hence many European foundations include alleviating poverty among their goals. As Wolpert notes in chapter 5 of this volume, however, claims about redistribution need to be taken with a grain of salt.

The preference of some foundations to treat redistribution as a de facto feature of foundation giving, rather than as a specific role, is explored in some of the interviews, notably in the Czech Republic and Sweden. A representative of a Swedish foundation argues the point:

> This [redistribution] might not be the primary purpose in establishing a foundation, that the intention of the donator is to redistribute his or her wealth. I do not believe so. . . .
>   If a very rich person makes a donation, a redistribution of wealth is in the nature of the transaction itself. And it is this redistribution that constitutes the basis for tax-exemption for foundations. This is the reason why they are tax-exempt; it is a way of paying your taxes. The law requires some kind of redistribution to grant the foundation tax-exemption. (Wijkström 2006)

This interviewee lends some credence to the claim that foundations seek to justify the tax exemptions they receive through redistribution—here by suggesting that the act of giving is redistributive in itself. There are problems with this line of argument, of course, such as the fact that it is not always evident that foundations' activity is really redistributive, that is, they may support the better-off as well as the less well-off sections of society, and that it is unclear whether funding by foundations is any more redistributive than had foundations been taxed in the first instance (Prewitt 1999, 21).

The feasibility of European foundations fulfilling a redistributive role is also fundamental to explaining why respondents overall are reluctant to identify with it. That the focus on the growth of American foundations in the early twentieth century underlines their financial and redistributive role, at the expense of adequately acknowledging the role of many European foundations in providing services has been acknowledged (Anheier and Toepler 1999, 8). Overall, our research suggests that redistribution is associated with the larger and wealthier foundations. Interviewees in countries with smaller foundation sectors, however, such as Austria and Hungary, questioned this role in the context of the limited financial resources of smaller and medium-sized foundations.

Social and Policy Change

The social and policy change role involves foundations in promoting structural change and a more just society, fostering recognition of new needs, and empowering the socially excluded. Whereas redistribution is associated with traditional notions of charity, the social and policy change role is linked with philanthropy, that is, addressing the root causes of problems (Prewitt 1999, 23). In the United States, the role of foundations in social and policy change has been a particular source of controversy. On the one hand, critics such as Joan Roelofs (2003, 121–35) argue that social change organizations funded by foundations are simply instruments of the broader agenda of the hegemonic elite. On the other, observers question the actual scale of the impact of foundations on social, economic, and political shifts in American society (Prewitt 1999, 25–27). The (potential) role of European foundations in social and policy change has not as yet proved as controversial as in the United States, though more recognition is being given to the political role of some foundations in the United Kingdom, for example (Davies 2004). What is more, in the early 1990s, foundations in eastern Europe who were seeking to promote social change were accused of social manipulation, with foreign funded foundations branded as agents of the "imperial West" (Pinter 2001, 284).

In our research, we found that this is a role that is specific to some (albeit few) foundations' objectives. In Poland, for instance, the Stefan Batory Foundation and the Helsinki Foundation have been engaged in the joint program Against Corruption, which has launched various initiatives such as the drafting of anticorruption legislative proposals, information and education campaigns, and legal aid for people who have encountered corrupt practices. The majority of foundations in each of the participating countries identified the potential for foundations to pursue this role, but many also questioned just how well-placed foundations are to fulfill such a role—as well as the types of difficulties it creates for foundations. This was particularly the case amongst the British foundations interviewed:

> We want to move towards influencing policy but the Board is still struggling with equating policy with politics. They say it will influence

by example rather than lobbying but we need to engage in a position to influence politics.

Why would anyone listen to us? We aren't service providers so we don't have that sort of knowledge and the knowledge we do have we don't really organise or use properly. What do we really have to say? (Leat 2006)

In Hungary, the interviewees strongly supported this role for foundations, but questioned the overall likely impact foundations can have in this area. Some argued that even powerful organizations, such as the Soros Foundation, for example, did not receive significant recognition of its role until the middle of the 1990s, when political actors began to recognize the importance of civil society actors: "Foundations have made a great effort in the past 10 years to achieve social and policy change. However, their overall impact is not significant" (Wizner and Aszalos 2006).

On the other hand, some respondents from the case of Portugal believe that foundations, by virtue of their independence, are ideally positioned to fulfill this role:

What primarily distinguishes a foundation from government and business is its high degree of freedom to take decisions and its particular timetable to implement the corresponding actions and programmes. As independent institutions, foundations do not depend on any political process, or on any past or future constituencies, on the market or publicity/propaganda. (Themudo 2004)

The notion of social change is itself contentious because it embraces various ideas ranging from changing how we think about and address social issues to the promotion of radical structural change (Anheier and Leat 2006). Although foundations identify with addressing what are essentially social issues in relation to other roles such as complementarity and innovation, with a foundation interviewed in Belgium being the only exception, they appear unaware of how to maximize their potential to fulfill a social change role via the functions they already serve. The key issue of how well-placed foundations are to effect social and policy change (the latter in particular) is not linked to the need for foundations to be more strategic in their operations. As Breiteneicher and Marble (2001, 581) argue, a foundation's operations are made strategic by its links to and understanding of the public policies that inform, influence, and perhaps even decide the outcomes and effect of grant making. The independence of the foundation's form may have little or no bearing on its ability to help bring about social and policy change without the strategic understanding of the environment in which foundations operate. This may, in part explain why this role is viewed as a potential, rather than a wholly realizable goal for many foundations.

Promotion of Pluralism

The promotion of pluralism can take a variety of forms. This role was presented as one where foundations are engaged in promoting experimentation and diversity in general, protecting dissenters and civil society liberties against the state, and challenging others in social, economic, cultural, and environmental policy. In some cases, the very presence of foundations is also considered a sign of pluralism (Toepler 2006).

For some foundations, in Austria, Denmark, and the Netherlands, for example, where foundations attach particular salience to this role, the promotion of experimentation and diversity is linked with the freedom and autonomy of foundations. In federalist countries such as Germany and Switzerland, this role is associated with foundations engaged in "bridge-building" activities between communities and areas. Differences in the importance attached to this role amongst foundations in the Czech Republic and Hungary reflect the gap between the ideal roles envisaged largely by foreign-funded foundations, on the one hand, and the issues of sustainability and survival that preoccupy other foundations, on the other.

In the Czech Republic, for instance, the larger foundations, funded by foreign resources, award particular importance to this role: "The importance of foundations lies in principle in pluralism and this presents a counterbalance to the one-sided bias in the support provided by the state. . . . A maximum plurality of democratic and stable institutions is always crucial" (Skovajsa 2006).

Smaller foundations, and particularly those of Czech origin, do not give the role as much weight. In some countries such a role is thought to be problematic: "Many of the Hungarian foundations are dependent on the state budget, since they receive very limited private money. This somewhat questions [their] independence and pluralism" (Wizner and Aszalos 2006).

As also emphasized by respondents in France and Portugal, the diversity of the foundation landscape across Europe means that we must recognize that foundations may neither be willing nor have the capacity to fund the "unusual or the unexpected" or the "diversity and differentiation" (Prewitt, 1999, 28–29) we might associate with the promotion of pluralism.

Innovation

Promoting innovation in social perceptions, values, relationships, and ways of doing things has long been ascribed to foundations. The majority of foundations in a majority of countries included in the study identify with it. This is consistent with the common expectation that foundations are ideally placed to facilitate innovation, take potentially controversial risks and act as philanthropic venture capital (Anheier and Toepler 1999, 15).

By itself, however, the consensus that innovation is a salient role for foundations does not tell us very much. In countries where the role is pronounced, interviewees question both the meaning of innovation and what it means to be innovative. Moreover, reflecting the different interpretations of the term innovation, different types of examples of innovative activities emerge across the countries included in the study. Using the four criteria that Kanter (1983) identified as common to successful innovation, we can explore the foundation representatives' interpretations of this role. These criteria include:

- a degree of uncertainty about both the process and outcome

- expertise in the situation, the process, and likely outcomes

- a demonstrated reach across established boundaries

- an element of controversy in deviating from established interests

UNCERTAINTY   Our research found that the ability of foundations to take risks (economic or otherwise) is associated with their ability to support projects in the longer term. Supporting new activities, particularly in research and development, features amongst the examples of foundations acting innovatively. Although the foundation representatives interviewed in Sweden struggled to give substantive examples of foundations acting innovatively, the emphasis fell on the ability of foundations to be more flexible and steadfast in their commitments rather than the public sector authorities in particular: "If the investment is not successful within [two to three] years, it will be discontinued . . . the example [of] the Wallenberg Foundation in their investments in science and research is an excellent example of endurance in the longer run" (Wijkström 2006).

EXPERTISE   Some stakeholders associated the innovative role with the ability of foundations to do a better job than the government in fulfilling roles such as complementarity and substitution. Applying existing ideas and expertise in new fields of practice is often considered more feasible for foundations than supporting completely new ideas, which is more typical of uncertain innovations (Gouwenberg et al. 2006).

In Belgium, Greece, France, and Sweden, for example, the innovation role appears intertwined with complementing state functions. For certain Belgian foundations that have developed close working relationships with the government, innovation involves identifying new social needs:

> One of the roles of the foundations is to find a niche that is not covered by the State, develop this niche and, at a certain point in time, tell the authorities that they can adopt this approach. We perform the work because we think it is an important niche, then we try to fit it into the state system. (Pirotte 2006)

CROSSING BOUNDARIES   Ideas about innovations are also linked to practices as well as activities. In this regard, crossing established boundaries in organizations, fields, and sectors is often viewed as key to foundations acting in an innovative way. In the UK, for instance, this is linked to the need for foundations to be more accessible and progressive in their outlook: "Foundations need to be more outward looking. . . . Awareness among the public and government is very, very low. We're just not maximizing our impact. We could be acting in a complementary fashion to think tanks and working with other foundations" (Leat 2006).

The four major examples of foundations engaged in innovative activities in Germany—Quandt, Freudenberg, Bertelsmann, and Bosch—share two characteristics: their openness to horizontal networking and collaboration with other civil society actors, and the emphasis they place on reviewing their goals and activities at regular intervals.

CONTROVERSY   The extent to which uncertain risks may also be controversial does not feature high on the stakeholders' agenda. Stakeholders are instead more concerned with how feasible fulfilling an innovation role is for the bulk of European foundations. Our interviews in Italy and Austria revealed that foundations are aware that they are often not up to the task of acting in an innovative way. A lack of professional governance and operational transparency, and sometimes the constraints posed by the founders, are also identified as obstacles to foundations acting innovatively. A Dutch respondent elaborates on this theme:

> All foundations feel that they are innovative, active, well-known and playing a major role in society. From the outside the image is quite different: 95% of the board members are male, over 55 years old, part of the "old boys" network, not granting any projects that might endanger the foundation. They are complaining that they do not receive any interesting project proposals or grants, but they do not want to go public because they are afraid to receive too many grant requests. How can they expect them if nobody knows of their existence? (Gouwenberg et al. 2006)

In all, the willingness of foundations to take risks is associated with funding research or activities that are deemed new, and with actions that are simply different from what the state does or from how public institutions choose to carry out certain responsibilities. Innovation for foundations also implies changes in prevalent practices. Although awareness of potential innovation is pronounced in this study, serious questions remain about the feasibility of the innovator role among European foundations. These questions are clearly linked to broader issues about transparency, economic resources, the need for greater professionalism, and the desire to be loyal to the wishes of the founder, on the one hand, versus the wish to change the vision of a foundation as circumstances dictate.

Findings

As illustrated in table 8.1, an analysis reveals different levels of awareness for different foundation roles. The high level for the complemen-

Table 8.1   Foundation Role Awareness, Acceptance, and Feasibility as Perceived by Foundation Leaders and Stakeholders

Role	Awareness	Acceptance by Foundation	Feasibility
Complementarity	High	Yes, but what is the role of government?	Medium, capacity of grant-making foundations in sustaining this role an issue
Substitution	Medium	No	Medium, capacity for grant-making foundations in sustaining this role an issue
Preservation of traditions and cultures	Medium	Specific to some foundations engaged as main activity	Foundation-specific
Redistribution	Low	No, range of factors motivate donors, among which redistribution is a minor one	Low
Social and policy change	Medium	Potentially, but need to address challenges	Medium
Promotion of pluralism	Medium	Not a guide, viewed more as a feature of foundations' existence	Medium
Innovation	High	Yes, but some inconsistency in interpretation of innovation and innovativeness	Medium to high, if a better understanding of innovation and implementation prevails

Source: Authors' compilations.

tarity role reflects ready identification with the role, which is reflected in the visions of foundations, though the language foundations use to articulate it vary widely. However, underlying issues about the blurring of boundaries between this and the substitution role are also prevalent across the countries examined. These issues raise questions about the extent to which the complementarity role guides foundations in their actions, or whether they are guided by the government, and whether they can sustain the role over the long term. It follows that stakeholders display less awareness and more disdain for the role foundations play in substituting the government. This is not one that foundations wish to guide the sector nor is it one they aspire to. Nonetheless, many policy makers and experts see the role as wholly feasible, despite the reservations foundations have.

Foundations are also acutely aware of the need for innovation and to be innovative. Stakeholders see this role as being reflected in the visions of foundations in different ways, varying from the risks foundations take with giving grants to certain projects, to "filling gaps" left by the government and being more efficient than the government in doing so. Context matters greatly to how innovative certain foundation activities are perceived to be. This is particularly evident in the central and eastern European cases, where innovation is often equated with adopting western practices. How foundations manage their operations is also key to strategic planning and carrying out foundation activities in an innovative way. Overall, the potential for foundations to be innovative exists, but stakeholders face the challenge of translating the role into practice.

As table 8.1 also demonstrates, foundations tend to be somewhat aware of other roles, notably preserving traditions and cultures, acting for social and policy change, and promoting pluralism. The first instance reflects the tendency to associate this role with foundations engaged in preservation as a primary activity. Thus, in terms of feasibility, it is linked to specific foundations. Similarly, promoting pluralism is associated with the bridge-building role certain foundations assume in Switzerland and Germany. This role functions less as a guide to foundation practices, as much as it is associated with the very presence of foundations as symbols of how "democratic" a society is. Stakeholders are clearly aware of the need to articulate a role in social and policy change. However, the extent to which this role is reflected in practice is somewhat curtailed by the obstacles and challenges foundations face. Although the role definitely has the potential to guide what foundations do, its feasibility is reduced by the concerns of foundations, such as the emphasis they place on being able to influence politics while not crossing the boundaries into active politics. These concerns are underpinned by questions as to how well positioned foundations are to influence policy. Does their existing role in complementing or substituting the state place them in an ideal position to influence change, or is it their autonomy that enhances this position? These are the types of questions that foundations need to consider in relation to their aspirations of affecting social and policy change. In this regard, it appears that foundations may be struggling to fully understand the context within which they operate and their role within it.

Emerging Themes

A key issue that emerges here is how foundations respond to a retreating welfare state. This issue is of course more pertinent to western Europe than to the former communist bloc but, as our research has shown, the issues facing all countries are remarkably similar. It is not our intention, however, to overstate either the centrality of foundations to the reform agendas of national governments, or the extent of the awareness of this broader scenario amongst foundations. Rather, foundations are, and despite their independence, affected by fluctuations in the policy environment. In this sense, they will have to react to changes in the role of the state as well as changes to the political architecture of Europe. This may well mean that they need to adjust their roles accordingly, and perhaps even find new ones, if they are to avoid future challenges to their legitimacy.

New Policies, New Roles?

Gaps between being aware of and understanding roles, on the one hand, and the feasibility of foundations to meet certain expectations or indeed the need for foundations to modify expectations, on the other, are influenced primarily by the nature of relations between foundations and the state. This involves rethinking the roles foundations have fulfilled in different countries and in the particular the near universally accepted complementarity role. The changing policy environments in which foundations operate have made it increasingly difficult for them to clarify where the boundaries between complementing and substituting the state begin and end. In countries such as the United Kingdom and Sweden, foundations have criticized governments for persistently changing the rules of the game, which often has the effect of forcing foundations to assume responsibilities that were previously the domain of the government. In central and eastern Europe, the principal concern of foundations is to clarify the division of responsibilities between governments and foundations in relation to activities and resources.

Research has shown that the foundation sectors of different European countries can be grouped as models (Anheier 2001), helping us articulate the roles of foundations in terms of their broader policy context.[3] However, in the prevalent policy environment, in which European governments are reassessing the role or roles of foundations in the light of proposed reforms to the traditional welfare state, foundations are faced with redefining the relationship between foundations and governments. Reflecting the concerns expressed earlier, one foundation representative in Sweden argued that the social democratic model, in which foundations exist in a coordinated role within a highly developed welfare state, is becoming less relevant. The withdrawal or retreat of the welfare state from certain responsibilities means that the role of foundations in substituting the state will become as, if not more, important than the role in complementing it (Wijkström 2006). Similarly, countries dominated by the corporate model, where foundations enjoy some form of subsidiary relationship with the state, have also encountered changes in recent years.

Overall, we have found that foundations like to see themselves as forward-thinking, innovative entities that exist parallel to the government, as an alternative to the mainstream—consistent with a liberal vision of society. As the distinction between mainstream and not mainstream responsibilities becomes more complex, signs of a shift toward the liberal model, where the complementarity and substitution roles are predominant, are evident, at least in the eyes of some foundations. This also suggests a shift in the liberal vision, from one in which foundations act not only in parallel to the state, but also in place of the state in terms of its traditional responsibilities. In this, foundations encounter significant internal and external obstacles—not least the fluctuating policy environment that is characteristic of European countries today. Above all, foundations face a significant challenge in defining and redefining their roles, whilst maintaining their objectives and autonomy in an ever-changing policy context.

Governance

Trends toward more public services contracted to nonprofit organizations has generated increased demands for enhanced transparency and accountability within the nonprofit sector. For some foundations in Germany, it is also about giving legitimacy to the initiatives and activities of foundations (Strachwitz et al. 2006). In practice, providing such transparency and accountability has involved entities such as the European Foundation Centre (EFC) developing codes of practice.

Spain's Fundación Lealtad's principles for Transparency and Good Practice are one example—an initiative that specifically aims to demystify the activities of foundations in the eyes of the public and, indeed, of politicians (Fraguas and Cabra de Luna 2006). Similarly, the Portuguese Centre for Foundations has played a key role in that country in lobbying for improvements to the legal framework in which foundations operate, and is seen as integral to improving governance and transparency (Themudo 2004). Yet, though these initiatives present a positive picture of efforts to improve governance amongst foundations, they are not representative. In the Netherlands, for example, our research found that some foundations remain reluctant to "go public" for fear of being unable to deal with the number of grant applications likely to follow the publicizing of their activities (Gouwenberg et al. 2006). Improving transparency and accountability, and increasing professionalism are high on the agendas of many foundations across Europe, but there is still some way to go before good governance is the norm.

The Challenge of Europe

We have focused so far only on the roles and visions of foundations in national contexts. But what of the role within a more integrated European Union? Developing a more European or international outlook is not without its challenges. The results of interviews conducted with foundation representatives across Europe reveal a sweeping lack of awareness of what the EU can offer foundations, and indeed of how and why foundations should be more engaged with the EU. Various reasons can be posited for this position, from limiting activities to a specific area, to prioritizing nationally oriented issues. Nonetheless, for some foundations, the influence of the European Union on their activities and strategies is becoming visible. In particular, increased interest and activity by some foundations in international grant making has encouraged greater cooperation between foundations and the EU, particularly with EUROPEAID. Foundations are also viewed as facilitators of information and dialogue on specific issues, and potentially as a means of disseminating information on EU policy, along with other civil society organizations (European Foundation Centre 2002). The key challenge is how to maximize this interest and motivation in a way that best benefits both foundations and the EU. For foundation leaders, this means engaging in what one interviewee termed the "hard bloody work" of building partnerships—learning about how you can do different things from what you can do in the national context as well as increasing awareness and monitoring European policy developments (Anheier and Daly 2006).

In conclusion, it is clear that the policy salience of foundations has increased in recent years. This is largely due to domestic reforms, but the growing influence of other factors, particularly membership in the European Union, is also evident. In the current policy environment, foundations have had to consider more deeply their roles and relationships, particularly with the state. Inwardly, they have sought to promote and implement governance reforms to be more transparent, accountable, and professional, thus also improving their image in the public eye. All of these themes are important because they have implications for what foundations do and how they operate. What is more, it is clear that the form of the foundation must be capable of meeting new challenges within and outside traditional domestic contexts.

Ultimately, as we have suggested, the legitimacy of foundations in Europe over the long term will depend on the match between role performance and policy expectations. Although there are no pronounced challenges at the moment, policy makers tend to expect much, perhaps too much, from foundations—a tendency fueled by Europe's somewhat complacent, passive, and at times even self-congratulatory, philanthropic culture. These expectations, however, rarely rest on a sound understanding of what foundations can and cannot do. They thus have the potential of giving rise to legitimacy challenges, and thus suggest the need for a realistic and proactive debate among Europe's philanthropic leaders.

We gratefully acknowledge the contributions and comments received from all participants in the project, including our country research teams and interviewees. The project has also been generously supported by a number of organizations: Bodosakki Foundation, Greece; Robert Bosh Stiftung; CAF (UK); Compagnia San Paolo, Italy; Levi Strauss Foundation; C. S. Mott Foundation; FIN, Netherlands; Finnish Cultural Foundation; Fondation de France; Foundation for Swedish Culture in Finland; Ford Foundation; Freudenberg Stiftung; Fritt Ord, Norway; Fundación ONCE; Haniel Stiftung; Riksbanken, Sweden; Swiss Foundations; and Wanger Advocatburo, Liechtenstein. We also thank the editors of this volume for their helpful comments and suggestions.

Notes

1. See Anheier and Daly (2006) for a more detailed description of approach, methodology and data.
2. For an overview of the legal framework and taxation treatments of foundations in European countries, see: European Foundation Centre (2002), Foundations in the European Union: Profiling Legal and Fiscal Environments. Brussels, European Foundation Centre.
3. Building on previous research, the *Visions and Roles of Foundations in Europe* project examined the following models: the social democratic model; the corporatist model; the liberal model; the business model; the state-controlled model and the peripheral model.

References

Anheier, Helmut K. 2001. "Foundations in Europe: A Comparative Perspective." In *Foundations in Europe,* edited by Andreas Schlüter, Volker Then, and Peter Walkenhorst. London: Directory of Social Change.

Anheier, Helmut K., and Avner Ben-Ner, eds. 2003. *The Study of the Nonprofit Enterprise: Theories and Approaches.* New York: Kluwer Academic/Plenum Publishers.

Anheier, Helmut K., and Siobhan Daly. 2004. "Philanthropic Foundations: A New Global Force?" In *Global Civil Society Yearbook 2004/05,* edited by Helmut K. Anheier, Marlies Glasius, and Mary Kaldor. London: Sage Publications.

———. 2006. "Foundations in Europe: A Comparative Analysis." In *The Politics of Foundations: Comparative Perspectives from Europe and Beyond,* edited by Helmut K. Anheier and Siobhan Daly. London: Routledge.

Anheier, Helmut K., and Diana Leat. 2002. *From Charity to Creativity: Philanthropic Foundations in the 21st Century.* Bournes Green, U.K.: Comedia.

———. 2006. *Creative Philanthropy.* London: Routledge.

Anheier, Helmut K., and Stefan Toepler, eds. 1999. *Private Funds and Public Purpose, Philanthropic Foundations in International Perspective.* New York: Plenum Publishers.

Beise, M. 1998. "Politische Stiftungen." In *Handbuch Stiftungen,* edited by Bertelsmann Stiftung. Wiesbaden: Gabler.

Breiteneicher, Joseph, and Melinda Marble. 2001. "Strategic Programme Management." In *Foundations in Europe: Society, Management, Law,* edited by Andreas Schlüter, Volker Then, and Peter Walkenhorst. London: Directory of Social Change.

Bulmer, Martin. 1999. "The History of Foundations in the United Kingdom and the United States. Philanthropic Foundations in Industrial Society." In *Private Funds and Public Purpose. Philanthropic Foundations in International Perspective,* edited by Helmut K. Anheier and Stefan Toepler. New York: Plenum.

Davies, J. S. 2004. "The Foundation as a Political Actor: The Case of the Joseph Rowntree Charitable Trust." *Political Quarterly* 75(3): 275–84.

European Foundation Centre. 2002. *EFC Communiqué: White Paper on European Governance.* http://www.efc.be.

Fraguas, Berta, and Miguel A. Cabra de Luna. 2006. "Spain." In *The Politics of Foundations: Comparative Perspectives from Europe and Beyond,* edited by Helmut K. Anheier and Siobhan Daly. London: Routledge.

Gouwenberg, Barbara, C. E. Van Der Jagt, and Th.N. M. Schuyt. 2006. "The Netherlands." In *The Politics of Foundations: Comparative Perspectives from Europe and Beyond,* edited by Helmut K. Anheier and Siobhan Daly. London: Routledge.

Kanter, R. M. 1983. *The Change Masters.* New York: Simon & Schuster.

Karl, Barry, and Stan Katz. 1987. "Foundations and the Ruling Class." *Daedalus* 116(1): 1–40.

Lagerspetz, Mikko (with Erle Rikmann). 2006. "Estonia." In *The Politics of Foundations: Comparative Perspectives from Europe and Beyond,* edited by Helmut K. Anheier and Siobhan Daly. London: Routledge.

Leat, Diana. 2006. "The United Kingdom." In *The Politics of Foundations: Comparative Perspectives from Europe and Beyond,* edited by Helmut K. Anheier and Siobhan Daly. London: Routledge.

Letts, Christine W. et al. 1997. "Virtuous Capital: What Foundations can Learn from Venture Capitalists." *Harvard Business Review* 2: 36–44.

Pinter, Francis 2001. "The Role of Foundations in the Transformation Process in Central and Eastern Europe." In *Foundations in Europe,* edited by Andreas Schlüter, Volker Then and Peter Walkenhorst. Directory of Social Change, London.

Pirotte, Gautier. 2006. "Belgium." In *The Politics of Foundations: Comparative Perspectives from Europe and Beyond,* edited by Helmut K. Anheier and Siobhan Daly. London: Routledge.

Prewitt, Kenneth. 1999. "The Importance of Foundations in an Open Society." In *The Future of Foundations in an Open Society,* edited by Bertelsmann Foundation. Gütersloh, Germany: Bertelsmann Foundation.

Roelofs, Joan. 2003. *Foundations and Public Policy: The Mask of Pluralism.* Albany: State University of New York Press.

Salamon, Lester M., and Helmut K. Anheier, eds. 1997. *Defining the Nonprofit Sector: A Cross National Analysis.* Manchester: Manchester University Press.

Salamon, Lester M., Helmut K. Anheier, Regina List, Stefan Toepler, S. Wojciech Sokolowski, and Associates. 1999. *Global Civil Society: Dimensions of the Nonprofit Sector.* Baltimore, Md.: Johns Hopkins Center for Civil Society Studies.

Skovajsa, Marek. 2006. "The Czech Republic." In *The Politics of Foundations: Comparative Perspectives from Europe and Beyond,* edited by Helmut K. Anheier and Siobhan Daly. London: Routledge.

Strachwitz, Rupert Graf, Frank Adloff, Philipp Schwertmann, and Rainer Sprengel. 2006. "Germany." In *Foundations in Europe: Comparative Perspectives from Europe and Beyond,* edited by Helmut Anheier and Siobhan Daly. London: Routledge.

Themudo, Nuno. 2004. "Portugal." *Visions and Roles of Foundations in Europe.* London: Centre for Civil Society. http://www.lse.ac.uk/collections/ visionsAndRolesOfFoundationsInEurope/documents.htm.

Toepler, Stefan. 1999. "Operating in a Grant-making World: Re-assessing the Role of Operating Foundations." In *Private Funds and Public Purpose: Philanthropic Foundations in International Perspective,* edited by Helmut Anheier and Stefan Toepler. New York: Plenum Publishers.

———. 2006. "Foundation Roles and Visions in the U.S.: A Comparative Note." In *The Politics of Foundations: Comparative Perspectives from Europe and Beyond,* edited by Helmut K. Anheier and Siobhan Daly. London: Routledge.

Van der Ploegh, Tymen. 1999. "A Comparative Legal Analysis of Foundations: Aspects of Supervision and Transparency." In *Private Funds and Public Purpose: Philanthropic Foundations in International Perspective,* edited by Helmut Anheier and Stefan Toepler. New York: Plenum Publishers.

Wijkström, Filip. 2006. "Sweden." In *The Politics of Foundations: Comparative Perspectives from Europe and Beyond,* edited by Helmut Anheier and Siobhan Daly. London: Routledge.

Wizner, Balasz, and Z. Aszalos. 2006. "Hungary." In *The Politics of Foundations: Comparative Perspectives from Europe and Beyond,* edited by Helmut Anheier and Siobhan Daly. London: Routledge.

Chapter 9

Supporting Culture and Higher Education: A German Perspective

Rupert Graf Strachwitz

One of the most difficult tasks in analyzing the role of foundations in supporting culture and science in the European context is to describe adequately the nature of a foundation and define what is meant by support—not to mention the futile attempt to define culture (Luhmann 1997, 93). With the rise of the U.S. grant-making foundation in the twentieth century and, perhaps even more forcefully, the wealth of American academic research on foundations (Toepler 1996, 157), comparative research has largely accepted the way in which foundations are understood and defined in the United States as a benchmark (Toepler 1999). Historically, however, foundations have been part of European culture since antiquity and have followed a much broader and much more diverse pattern of institutional development. In fact, the political, academic, and public debates on both sides of the Atlantic largely continue to overlook the fact that a German Stiftung or an Italian fondazione, to name just two examples, tend to have a wider meaning than the American-style modern grant-making foundation. Ever since the church became legally entitled to act as trustee in the fourth century, and individuals began to commit endowments to the purpose of erecting stone memorials to themselves (Bringmann and von Steuben 1995, 3), both cultural events of historical dimension, the concept of a foundation in Europe has developed in a complex way and in an unbroken tradition. As but one example, by far the largest subsector of the German foundation community exists solely to act as legal owners of historical buildings and safeguard their use as churches, many of them of particular importance in cultural terms.

Foundations in Europe today exist to protect ownership, to operate institutions and projects, and to grant financial and other aid to third parties, pursuing public as well as private purposes. Inevitably, and indeed more often than not intentionally, they exist also as living memorials to their creators, to whose will as laid down at creation they are bound for the length of their existence. Foundations are widely accepted as integral components of European, American, Islamic, Jewish, and other cultures to such an extent that an outright denial of their right to exist is seemingly not argued seriously either in the political arena or in academia anywhere. The famous French minister Turgot's proclamation in 1760 "Il faut les détruire" (they must be demolished) (Liermann 1963/2002, 173) and the French Republican model of public governance of 1791 explicitly forbidding any nongovernmental public purpose organization seems extraordinarily dated. Civil society organizations in general, created voluntarily and by private initiative, have become spearheads of new public governance models (Rifkin 2004, 255). Even France was induced to formally enable foundations again in 1983, and incidentally discovered then that its most prestigious scientific and cultural institution, the Institut de France, umbrella body to the Académie Française, among others, had always been a foundation in all but in name.

Given the significant historical range of foundation types and uses, I cannot simply address financial support by foundations to cultural and academic institutions and the rationale or theory behind the grant-making process. I will necessarily have to deal with a plethora of options. In current European thinking, the legitimacy issue arises from the question of the degree to which private initiative and action are acceptable in a society that believes in a democratically organized governance structure. Furthermore, this question has begun to take on new meaning with the new era of fiscal retrenchment and a general questioning of the limits of the traditional welfare state that has taken hold of Europe since the 1980s. Because of a growing realization that it may be undesirable for the government to have a virtual monopoly on funding public purposes, including arts, culture, science, and higher education, current debates about the role of private support and foundations have come to be not so much about the general acceptability of the principle of private philanthropy, but rather about the desirability of nongovernmental funding of public tasks as a means of compensation for empty public treasuries. Thus, the issue is not whether foundations are good or evil, but rather how much legitimate foundation action is tolerable in the context of civil society and society at large.

Culture and higher education, including the sciences, are two areas of public purposes that in the European cultural tradition provide very divergent answers. As I will show, higher education and promotion of the sciences have been regarded as a public task throughout continental Europe, as indeed has the whole area of education. State supervision of education is in fact a constitutional requirement in Germany. Culture, on the other hand, is a different matter. Although Europe's many sovereigns and rulers have in many ways and for many reasons contributed to the arts since at least the sixteenth century, culture certainly embraces more than the arts. Indeed, as has been mentioned, the concept of foundations, philanthropy, and private initiative is in itself strongly cultural (Rifkin 2004). Even artistic achievements in a narrow sense cannot possibly be restricted to organizational forms devised and supported by democratic institutions. For this reason alone, a comparative analysis of the role of foundations in these two areas may help shed some light on the legitimacy of foundations and the tolerable degree of their involvement in public affairs. Given that by their nature foundations are historically oriented bodies and that even today the vast majority of existing foundations predate the twentieth century (including the many church-related foundations whose main function it is to hold ownership of cathedrals, churches, and other church assets), the perspective needs to be historical. In other words, the history of foundations is all important in understanding and assessing their societal role and relevance today. Although I reference trends and cases across Europe where appropriate, I focus in this chapter on the evolution of the role of foundations in higher education and the arts in Germany.

Higher Education and Science: A Traditional Public Responsibility

Germany's first universities, like most in Europe, were established as foundations. Only in rare cases, such as Bologna, did they evolve as corporations based on membership. As a rule, a sovereign, or later in some cases a city government, would incorporate and endow an autonomous institution in perpetuity and commonly make particular provision for perpetual adherence to the original deed. Thus, the body had all elements that constitute a foundation in the European sense (Wagner 1999), and incurred all the problems that trouble this type of organization, most commonly the conflict between the original intent of the founder and the subsequent strategic directions developed by governors or trustees. One defining characteristic, however, was undoubted: their autonomy, supported by an endowment, by donations, and a steady influx of trusts. Medieval universities across Europe became increasingly wealthy, owning real estate, art collections, and liquid assets, as do U.S. and British universities and colleges to this day.

Over the centuries, quarrels with governmental authorities over infringements of status were notorious and, not without reason, universities were continually suspected by the authorities of harboring antigovernmental sentiments and thoughts as well as the authors thereof. Although the physiocrats in the period of the Enlightenment argued that privately managed educational institutions would be more efficient and save the government money (Mauvillon 1780/1979, 265), political objectives overruled such considerations and the prerogative of state control eventually gained supremacy over principles of academic independence and managerial effectiveness. By the end of the eighteenth century, France, Spain, Portugal, and, to some extent, Austria were not prepared to tolerate foundations at all, whether for cultural, educational, or other purposes (Smith and Borgmann 2001, 24). Germany developed a modified attitude. The lack of a unified state favored a variety of approaches. These tended to proliferate because of ongoing competition among the various political entities, which were comparatively small, and because their governments were comparatively quite poor. They could therefore not afford a total takeover of all public institutions, much as they aspired to do so.

In this climate, the late eighteenth and early nineteenth centuries also witnessed the emergence of educational societies, which, next to chapters of Freemasons, local clubs, and political associations, were a prominent part of the blossoming civil society driven by the emerging German bourgeoisie (Biedermann 2001). Research institutions outside the universities were established as civic, and quite regularly antigovernmental, organizations. After the 1815 restoration, however, German authorities grew increasingly circumspect and these private institutions were subjected to a slow process of either integration into a governmental structure or virtual extermination. Academia in particular was considered a potential danger, to such a high degree that only the strictest possible supervision was deemed safe enough.

Notwithstanding the academic ideals of Wilhelm von Humboldt, the early nineteenth-century Prussian educational reformer, the monarchs of Russia, Austria, and Prussia and their advisers, principally the Austrian chancellor Metternich, sought to suppress what was left of the revolutionary spirit that had spread from France all over Europe and remained alive particularly within the German academy. As a result, the Karlsbad Decrees of 1818 were intended to eliminate the political unrest among both faculty and students. Among the many items agreed upon by the ruling powers in Karlsbad were the placement of government supervisors in universities, the introduction of censorship of publications, and the requirement that university professors take an oath of allegiance to their sovereign. This was the spirit in which German educational institutions grew throughout the nineteenth and twentieth century.

The example of the Zeiss Foundation, founded toward the end of the nineteenth century, serves to illustrate the degree of public control of educational institutions. Ernst Abbe, an academic who had accumulated considerable wealth by becoming the partner of Carl Zeiss, inventor of modern optical instruments, decided to turn his entire fortune over to a foundation predominantly in support of Jena University, where he had continued to teach throughout his successful business career. This university, being a common undertaking of four tiny principalities, was notoriously underfunded and in urgent need of additional financial support. But although Abbe took great pains to remain anonymous and not to interfere with the governance of the university, his generosity was by no means universally welcomed, and clauses to secure complete government control were forced upon him in a long struggle to get his foundation, named after Carl Zeiss, recognized by the authorities (Strachwitz 1997).

The subjection to government supervision of legally autonomous foundations—determined to be ownerless and memberless legal entities—during the eighteenth and nineteenth centuries, particularly in the area of higher education, is thus largely the result of the government's firm will to police any politically dangerous centers of activity. Teaching, along with scientific research (pursuant to Humboldt's principle of unity of academic research and teaching), was considered the prerogative of government, and has predominantly remained so to this day. German universities evolved into governmental institutions with little autonomy, and with all the financial and managerial characteristics of the public bureaucracy. All faculty became and virtually still are civil servants. Of the 350 academic institutions in Germany today, only seventy-five are private and nongovernmental, of which forty are in turn operated by one of the established churches. However, only 2.6 percent of all students attend a nongovernmental institution.

The case of Frankfurt University illustrates these dynamics. Unlike other large cities in Germany, Frankfurt-am-Main did not have a university until the early twentieth century. It did, however, boast a strong sense of citizenship—documented by a well-above-average list of foundations—which had been dealt a severe blow when the city lost its political independence to Prussia (Kloetzer 1997). In an unheard-of move, the citizens of Frankfurt decided to set up and fund a nongovernmental university. Wealthy Jewish citizens from Frankfurt and elsewhere contributed particularly generously, to enable Jewish academics to gain full professorships, which where denied to them by the Prussian state. Against heavy opposition from the state authorities, the university was formally established as a foundation in 1911, only to lose its endowment in the 1923 hyperinflation, whereupon it had no option but to apply for government funding and gradually to become a "regular" state university.

The practice of complete state control was fully developed after World War I, when the welfare state became dominant in European political theory, and was in fact written into the first republican German constitution in 1919. Nongovernmental entities were brought into the public administrative system wherever possible, attracted to it by honors given in return for philanthropic deeds, or by government funding for nongovernmental activities. Supporting the national effort became the overruling rationale for philanthropy. This trend continued after World War II. That a foundation set up by government like the Volkswagen Stiftung, Germany's largest nominally nongovernmental research funder, should adopt a policy of closest cooperation with the state is not surprising. But that the Stifterverband fuer die Deutsche Wissenschaft (Association of Donors to German Science), set up in the early 1920s, should be such a typical example of this is only to be explained in the cultural context of early twentieth-century Germany. The purpose was not academic pluralism in the sense that non-governmental academic institutions should be supported, but rather a common fundraising effort of the business community in favor of the state universities and national research centers (compare Schulze 1995). Private initiative in support of research had largely become synonymous with financial support for the public university system. It was not until the late twentieth century that large funders such as the Stifterverband would assert their right to help shape the policies and that individual donors would scout around for alternative funding partners.

The Arts: A Cultural Conflict

In cultural matters, traditions are more complex. Whereas the arts—that is, the visual and performing arts, literature, architecture, and music—are often invoked as the essence of culture, culture in fact encompasses a much wider denominator of human life. Religion is undoubtedly an important cultural factor, as are cultural heritage and the plethora of rules, traditions, customs, and ways of life. Philanthropy in itself is a cultural phenomenon, and a comparative analysis can show that different cultures produce diverse notions and rationales of the existence, reasoning, and legitimacy of philanthropic action. It is only within a defined cultural context that a reasonable argument for philanthropy can be made. For example, the Fugger family, an important banking dynasty in sixteenth-century Augsburg, became philanthropists on a large scale both for needy citizens and for the arts. Their philanthropy was closely intertwined with religion, however, on the grounds that lending on interest, frowned upon by the church, was permissible, provided God received a substantial share of the interest earned for his purposes of caring and embellishing. The Fugger foundations were seen as God's interest, the family acting as God's representatives on the board to this day. In a more worldly sense, the Fuggers were social upstarts intent on showing their status as wealthy citizens, and, as Catholics in a predominantly Protestant community, they were eager to please their most important client, the Holy Roman emperor (compare Scheller 2004).

Rulers, aristocrats and citizens were patrons of the arts (Kocka 1998, 34), and of individual artists. The embellishment of a ruler's or aristocrat's seat, with works of both visual and the performing arts as a means of demonstrating wealth and power, remained an important motive. The arts served to underpin the attractiveness of any one place in an increasingly fiercely competitive Europe. Also, since the early 1500s, a spirit of scientific curiosity led to the establishment of public collections. But though admiration of beauty and artistic expression led men and women to collect artifacts not necessarily for their societal expedience, creative artists were generally supported in this wider context (Sauer 1993). In eighteenth-century Germany, the court theater, the national museum, and the new palace had become highly important assets to be appreciated by visitors, immigrants, businesses, and competing powers. They attracted a qualified workforce and boosted the reputation of the ruler in power, quite often far beyond his real political weight. Little wonder the city oligarchies aspired to do likewise. City burghers too collected art, and when it became fashionable to house collections in separate temple-like surroundings, cities, especially those that were constitutionally independent, competed with territorial rulers for the finest of these (Biedermann 2001). Art works were given in trust, and in some instances, separate museums were created as foundations to house them.

The Staedel Foundation, established by the will of Johann Friedrich Staedel, a citizen of Frankfurt who died in 1816, illustrates this point. His idea was to educate the general public by enabling anybody to come and admire the exhibited art works. The Staedel case became famous in German legal history by the fact that the foundation as a legal entity under state supervision was created on the basis of the Staedel will. That the Staedel Foundation is often hailed as Germany's first secular independent foundation is, however, a misinterpretation. Foundations with no apparent religious ties go back as far as the thirteenth century, and organizations stipulating a new and specific legal body of trustees rather than turning to existing legal or natural persons had been established for some time before Staedel (see Preiser 1991). It is interesting to note, however, that neither of these characteristics had drawn the attention of the public authorities before the nineteenth century. In a culture of overall state dominance, a totally independent foundation no longer seemed acceptable.

Another interesting aspect of this foundation is the coincidence that two other collectors created foundations during the same period, in different parts of Europe, with comparable aims—the preservation and public presentation of their art collections—and very different structures (Strachwitz 2003a, 9). Whereas Staedel, acting in Frankfurt, a city that had undergone a series of political reshuffles for twenty years, decided that only a truly independent and specific body of fellow citizens could possibly guarantee the autonomy of his foundation and thus incurred resistance by the government, his contemporary Baron Samuel von Brukenthal in Hermannstadt, a distant outpost of the Austrian empire (in today's Romania), deemed that given the political circumstances the Lutheran church alone would be a stable and yet nongovernmental trustee, despite the fact that neither he nor his collection nor his extensive library had a particular affiliation to the church. To this day, the church is involved in the management of the foundation. Sir Francis Bourgeois, who died in England in 1811, faced with the same situation—having to create an artificial heir to his important collection of pictures. In his will, equally estranged from traditional Christianity, he entrusted his collection to Dulwich College, an academic institution, which remains responsible for managing Dulwich Picture Gallery to this day. The Staedel Foundation, though independent in name, has long since become financially dependent on the state and city governments. In all three cases, the works of art have been kept together in keeping with the intentions of the original collectors.

In contrast to the burgeoning revolutionary sentiments in higher education, instances of revolutionary art became rare after 1815. With many artists ardently seeking the favor of the ruling classes, the patronage of rulers and governments and their social views prevailed. On the other hand, art clubs and art foundations were considered a safe haven for civic engagement, and, albeit not very frequently, art could and did openly or in camouflage become a signet of social change and antigovernmental sentiment. To be an engaged citizen and yet be patriotic, in the sense of recognizing complete government supremacy, was not always easy. Art was a field of activity where this worked best. Donations from private associations for works of art in public places are just one example of this corporatist attitude (Biedermann 2001, 49). On the other hand, though supporting higher education and business interests—such as the importance of the applied sciences to business particularly in a country with a scarcity of commodities—prevailed, and support of the arts was regularly coupled with social ambition. The emergence of newly rich industrial and commercial elites in the late nineteenth century saw a huge increase in private patronage, predominantly for traditional artistic expression.

One of the largest groups of philanthropists was the Jewish com-munity, which in the nineteenth century was going through a process of assimilation and recognition (Girardet 2000). Cities such as Berlin, Leipzig, Frankfurt, and Hamburg in particular boasted large numbers of foundations endowed with works of art on display in the public museums. Again, we increasingly find private initiative intertwined with public policy in a corporatist fashion. In the eyes of those in power, whether monarchical or republican, support was meant to read financial support, possibly support in kind, and certainly support of government policy and government institutions in a subservient way.

Foundation Support in Germany Today

The state's attempt to take over all matters of public interest in pursuit of a rationale that deemed all public activities to be its prerogative has been, in sum, near totally successful in higher education and the sci-ences, but less so in cultural matters. Admiration for beauty and for artistic expression led private citizens to collect artifacts for reasons other than their societal usefulness. Private patronage of the arts would cause theorists to wonder whether a foundation could be part of a system that depended entirely on the state. After all, this meant additional competition. Besides, from the beginning of the nineteenth century onwards, art was assuming a quasi-religious function in that intellectuals regarded it is a prime means of spiritual development. Culture had by this time not only become quite distinct from religion but in fact had also begun to supersede it in a way that made later com-mentators describe it as a secular religion in itself. It is not coinciden-tal that departmental responsibility within governments was regularly organized in a way that culture and religious affairs were grouped in one department.

New aspects of public benefit were put forward to justify the state's ever more dominating involvement. National identity, a high priority in the light of changing political affiliations, was just one of these (O'Hagan 1998, 40). Freedom of cultural development and disinter-ested pursuit of research were proclaimed best safeguarded by a sys-tem of state organized management. Prime works of art in private ownership now caused suspicion, as did research centers outside the government system of universities, academies, and other research institutions. Private initiative intending to oppose rather than support the state system fell under this category, a difficult proposition, the state having assumed the role of inventor, creator, and manager of all things public (with the notable exception of the social welfare provision), and most particularly of all aspects of education. Throughout the twentieth century, this role was accepted by the great majority of citizens. It was part of continental Europe's culture to believe in the supremacy of the state. In this context, private foundations were relegated to a grant-making role. And whereas in the area of associative bodies, the sharp increase in numbers in the 1970s and 1980s was instrumental in bringing about a change of outlook, a similar increase in new foundations did not. Foundations did not yet believe themselves an active part of civil society, and with few exceptions did not claim a distinct influential role. By their own belief and in public opinion, philanthropic action meant—until well into the 1990s—supporting causes the government deemed appropriate.

Despite these odds, the level of qualitative contributions of foundations to the cultural and scientific life today is substantial. In both Denmark and Portugal, it is said, for some years the arts budgets of the Karlsberg and Gulbenkian foundations respectively were larger than those of the national governments. The Gulbenkian Museum in Lisbon certainly ranks among the finest in the country and belongs to Europe's top class of visual arts institutions, as do the historic houses operated by the British National Trust, the Berlin museums operated by the Stiftung Preussischer Kulturbesitz (albeit a public sector foundation), and countless others all over Europe. Other forms of artistic expression receive financial support from grant-making foundations, whether by scholarships or awards or by selling works of art to them. The list is endless, and yet, with few exceptions, the quantitative contribution that foundations make in form of grants to arts organizations and institutions of science and higher education in general is, compared with public sector expenditures, not that important.

Available data are scarce. Of the sources of funding for the arts in Germany, 67 percent are estimated as coming from box office and other forms of earned income, 15 percent from public broadcasting fees, 13 percent from government, and 5 percent from private sources. Within the private bracket, 50 percent each are estimated as coming from business sponsorship and philanthropic giving, with foundation grants accounting for a maximum of 20 percent of the latter, that is, 0.5 percent of the total. For the support of the sciences, which in

Germany is still largely synonymous with support for universities, no similar data are available. But in view of the budgetary requirements in the natural sciences, it is certainly safe to say that the percentage of foundation funding is even lower than for the arts.

Obviously, in quantitative terms, foundation support of the arts and sciences is minimal and irrelevant. But because it is increasingly sought by public clamor, political statements, and the institutions and personalities concerned, a qualitative component that gives relevance and meaning to this support, as well as the legalistic one derived from history, must exist. Indeed, the number of foundations active in these particular fields has risen in the wake of a general influx of new creations since World War II. In 2001, 21.2 percent of German foundations supported culture, and 21.7 percent supported the sciences (Sprengel 2004, 30–31). But with the dividing line between science and general higher education funding not very precise, probably a good share of the 35.2 percent of foundations that support education in general do so at the university level. The data on total giving are too scant to be comparable. The budgets of operating foundations are even more difficult to analyze, because most include government funding or earned income at a high level, or both. Finally, foundations, whose purpose consists in the ownership of, say, a church, a historical monument, or works of art, quite frequently do not even have a budget, because all maintenance costs are borne by a third party (Strachwitz 1989, 24). It should also be remembered that European foundations are under no obligation to publish annual reports or financial statements, or both, so that all statistics depend entirely on the information foundations are willing to share.

Bearing in mind the deficiencies in quantitative evidence, it seems more relevant to look at defining commonalities that indicate a quality of support discernible from that others provide, an approach supported by Frank Adloff's findings for Germany (2002, 73). The dividing lines between operating and grant-making foundations are becoming increasingly blurred, with grant-makers developing into more proactive partners, indeed even project partners, project managers, and possibly institutional managers, even as they stress that it is not their mission to replace public funding or action.

This gradual change of attitude has been noticeable throughout Europe since the 1990s. The rise of the concept of civil society as a societal actor in its own right, prompted not least by the successful experiences of a decidedly antigovernmental civil society in central and eastern Europe beginning about 1989, the increasing failure of government to perform the duties it had so ardently aspired and sought to perform, and—last but not least—the growing financial difficulties of the state were both separately and in combination making citizens and decision makers alike rethink the role of nongovernmental noncommercial institutions. In this context, foundations gained specific attention. They were considered at the same time to be powerful funders and allies in structural conservativism, which indeed they usually were, both by their obligation to adhere to the original founder's intentions and by the conservative outlook of their present-day managers. Thus they were not viewed with as much suspicion as were independent membership organizations, whose decision-making processes were apt to produce unwelcome results. Founders were also more easily coopted by chances to meet powerful leaders, whether by honorary professorships or other measures of public recognition. It is not coincidental that the legal framework for foundations in Germany was reformed in 2000 and 2002, making it easier and fiscally more advantageous to set up a foundation, and that the much more important step of reforming the general fiscal framework for all civil society organizations has so far not been taken. Today, foundations are popular. Although the number of new creations is soaring, their performance is only rarely evaluated professionally and is generally viewed with all too little public criticism. Furthermore, the divide between private philanthropy and the public and business sectors is quite often unclear.

A number of private universities in Germany are either organized as foundations (the Otto-Beisheim-Stiftung, for example) or are looking for a private foundation to take them under their wing, while a number of large private foundations (the Hertie Stiftung and the Zeit Stiftung, for example) have created and manage their own teaching and research centers as well as museums as part of their regular programs. The state itself has used the foundation model to reorganize governmental institutions (compare Strachwitz and Then 2004): all seven Hamburg state museums, all three Berlin opera houses, and four of the Lower Saxony universities have been restructured as foundations, despite a number of unresolved legal issues raised by the fact that the state itself created these bodies by act of parliament, thus automatically reserving the right to change or abolish them by the same procedure (Kilian 2003, 99). Larger German governmental arts and research institutions are actively advocating that foundations be set up in their favor and if possible under their management, and are thus fierce competitors with those nongovernmental institutions seeking private philanthropic funding, whether set up as foundations themselves or not. It is not the legitimacy issue that is raised at this point, but the marketing issue of more private funding for public purpose enterprises.

The increasing number of foundations created by business companies shows the attraction of the foundation model as an instrument not of philanthropy, but instead to pursue corporate interests in corporate communications, corporate citizenship, and sponsorship. France, to this end, created a specific legal form of foundation, the fondation d'entreprise, that expressly obliges them to use the name of the company as part of their own. Used nearly exclusively in the arts, these bodies, such as the Fondation Cartier, have developed into powerful patrons (compare Rigaud 1995).

Conclusions

As a result of their undisputed popularity, serious issues about foundations are in danger of being overlooked. First, foundations are widely perceived as contributing to the support of the arts and sciences in a quantitative way. This is in no way supported by evidence. On the contrary, the contribution foundations can make, is, and always has been, entirely qualitative. Second, it is of course debatable whether and to what extent certain public tasks may be or should be entrusted to autonomous bodies governed by their own regulations put in force generations, possibly centuries, ago, or destined to remain unchanged for centuries to come. Clearly, on this point, it is a matter of discussion whether all societal tasks merit the same answer. The examples of culture, the evolution of which is a highly complex procedure with fewer short-term but immense long-term implications, on the one hand, and higher education with a more clear-cut role, on the other, demonstrate the difficulties in forming a uniform policy. Third, the diversity of founders (compare Timmer 2005)—private citizens, business companies, and governmental bodies—has tended to blur the essential commonalities and consequently the arguments for their role in society. Fourth, including the foundation subsector into the overall civil society sector merits particular attention, given the attention awarded to the redistribution of public benefit tasks in contemporary society.

To provide a valid answer to these questions, it seems appropriate to revisit the definition of foundations. What emerges from their long and complex history is that they have one thing in common that distinguishes them from other instruments of action: they are bound to follow the will of their founders in perpetuity. This is clearly the intention of the founders, be they natural or legal persons, and the basis of all legal frameworks. Foundation administrators are thus obliged to follow the founder's orders and may take decisions only within the limits of the original deed of establishment. Consequently, they are less susceptible to pressure and influence from a broader membership and outside than other types of organizations, and are potentially less prone to abruptly change their policies, rendering them more reliable. On the other hand, they also risk becoming complacent and potentially autistic. Their individualistic approach and their resource-based autonomy make them view limitations to personal civic liberties with suspicion. It is therefore not surprising that foundations have always been anathema to totalitarian regimes. At the same time, their historical anchorage renders them susceptible to an innate conservatism.

These observations lead to suggesting a theory of foundations. Whereas in modern societal culture the rule of democracy is considered the overriding principle, it cannot be overlooked that the rule of law is of near-equal importance. Long-term protection offered to the outcome of legitimate action, be it a building or a foundation, is as much a pillar of society as the ongoing chance offered to all citizens to take and review decisions relevant to and binding for all. Indeed, the rule of law may in some instances supersede democratic procedures, if a society is to function and develop in an organized fashion as appreciated by most citizens. Of the organizational options offered to civil society in a twenty-first century societal framework, foundations connect to the rule of law rather than to democratic principles, whereas membership organizations clearly connect primarily to the principles. There seems to be little reason to assume that civil society should not be able to embrace both priorities, so the legitimacy of voluntary private initiative exercised in a manner that eventually evolves into a foundation must be seen as legitimate as any other civil society initiative.

Having thus, albeit sketchingly, established the legitimacy of foundations in contemporary society as such, we may now turn to the particular legitimacy of the existing ones. If we accept the legitimacy of a principle under which an organization may consider itself and be considered bound by its own history, it seems clear that older foundation models retain their legitimacy even if a new concept has in fact superseded it (Strachwitz 2003b, 58–60). Organizations obviously cannot diverge from the terms under which they were established. And because longevity is one of their characteristics, arguably not a defining one, we have to accept the fact that a great number of foundations exist that do not correspond to a recently defined model. Moreover, newly established foundations all over Europe have tended to adopt models representing the full range of options that traditional foundations offer them, and increasingly so. And, finally, twentieth-century foundations are scrutinizing their own deeds of establishment to see whether they might legitimately expand their range of activities. The political and cultural battle cry for sustainability adds a new reasoning for bodies shaped to give a future to an idea.

The historical overview of European foundations supporting the arts and sciences has shown the broad range of ways in which they have attempted to do so. It is hardly surprising that the outspoken civil society approach is not a phenomenon shared by all. Recent findings by Adloff and Schwertmann (2004), in the context of a pan-European research project on the visions and roles for foundations in Europe, have shown very clearly that the German foundation sector is divided into two distinct subsectors, not as might be expected by their size or the way they function (operating versus grant making), but by their attitude. The majority adopt a corporatist model, either as prescribed by the founder or as defined by the administrators, but an increasing minority embrace a liberal philosophy in seeing foundations firmly rooted in civil society and thus as part of a group of societal agents distinct from the state. Given the state's traditional position in two areas devoted to creativity, communication, and debate to such a degree as are the arts and sciences, and the increasing role of civil society as a whole, it will be of particular interest to see whether and to what extent foundations will join this effort. Whether their innate autonomy and their increasingly liberal attitude will position at least some of them in a watchdog role remains to be seen.

Civil society depends on watchdogs of this type, and the infinitely larger associative side of it depends to some degree on foundations, not simply to fund institutions and projects, but to demonstrate that the other dimension of society, the one operating predominantly in time, is included in the overall approach. Societal support of foundations will certainly derive increasingly from this insight and role, and it will be the task of foundations to take it on. Both culture and sciences are such critical elements of societal life that a uniform approach driven by considerations of political expedience or worse, fiscal restraints, cannot succeed. Pluralistic individuality remains the only guarantor of a nonconformist, pluralist, and future-oriented model. If foundations live up to this expectation, the support they can offer, whether as grant makers or managers of science and culture or in any other form, will increase in importance.

Whether foundations can live up to these expectations remains unclear. The chance to act individually has in the past attracted institutional and private founders with no notion of this particular role. Social climbers (compare Gregory 1993), and business sponsors are but two of many groups of founders whose motives do not aspire to this normative approach, albeit implicitly. But with the development of foundation theory (Anheier and Toepler 1999), it seems possible to underpin foundation activity with this normative argument. In this context, the nature of the founder, the mechanisms of support, the financial resources, and even the governance system, let alone the immediate success of the operations, though important in themselves, lose priority to the fulfillment of the societal role. This societal expectation is matched by that of the individual philanthropist that in a society in which the rule of law prevails his law-abiding action will not later be legally questioned by public authorities.

References

Adloff, Frank. 2002. *Untersuchungen zum deutschen Stiftungswesen 2000–2002, vier Forschungsberichte.* Berlin: Maecenata.

Adloff, Frank, and Philipp Schwertmann. 2004. "Visions and Roles of Foundations in Germany." In *Visions and Roles of Foundations in Europe, The German Report,* edited by Frank Adloff, Philipp Schwertmann, Rainer Sprengel, and Rupert Graf Strachwitz. Berlin: Maecenata.

Anheier, Helmut, and Stefan Toepler, eds. 1999. *Private Funds, Public Purpose, Philanthropic Foundations in International Perspective.* New York: Kluwer.

Biedermann, Birgit. 2001. *Bürgerliches Mäzenatentum im 19. Jahrhundert. Die Förderung öffentlicher Kunstwerke durch den Kunstverein für die Rheinlande und Westfalen.* Petersberg, Germany: Imhof.

Bringmann, Klaus, and Hans von Steuben. 1995. *Schenkungen hellenistischer Herrscher an griechische Städte und Heiligtümer,* vol. I. Berlin: Akademie.

Girardet, Cella Margaretha. 2000. *Jüdische Mäzene für die Preussischen Museen zu Berlin : Eine Studie zum Mäzenatentum im Deutschen Kaiserreich und in der*

Weimarer Republik. Frankfurt-am-Main: Frankfurter Verlagsgruppe Holding AG August von Goethe.

Gregory, Alexis. 1993. *Families of Fortune. Life in the Gilded Age.* New York: The Vendome Press.

Kilian, Michael. 2003. "Der Staat als Stifter." In *Der Staat als Stifter,* edited by Enrico Bellezza, Michael Kilian, and Klaus Vogel. Gütersloh, Germany: Bertelsmann Stiftung.

Kloetzer, Wolfgang. 1997. "Über das Stiften—zum Beispiel Frankfurt-am-Main." In *Stadt und Mäzenatentum,* edited by Bernhard Kirchgässner and Hans-Peter Becht. Sigmaringen, Germany: Thorbecke.

Kocka, Jürgen. 1998. "Bürger als Mäzene." In *Mäzenatisches Handeln, Studien zur Kultur des Bürgersinns in der Gesellschaft,* edited by Thomas Gaehtgens and Martin Schieder. Berlin: Fannei und Walz.

Laum, B. 1914. *Stiftungen in der griechischen und römischen Antike,* vol II. Leipzig, Germany.

Liermann, Hans. 1963/2002. *Geschichte des Stiftungsrechts.* Tübingen, Germany: Mohr Siebeck.

Luhmann, Niklas 1997. "Die Kunst der Gesellschaft." In *Unternehmen Kultur—Kultur Unternehmen,* edited by Kulturbrauerei Berlin. München: Maecenata.

Mauvillon, Jakob. 1780/1979. *Physiokratische Briefe an den Herrn Professor Dohm. Oder Verteidigung und Erläuterungen der wahren staatswirtschaftlichen Gesetze, die unter dem Namen des physiokratischen Systems bekannt sind.* Braunschweig Koenigstein, Germany: Scriptor.

O'Hagan, John. 1998. *The State and the Arts.* Northampton, Mass.: Edward Elgar.

Preiser, Gert. 1991. "Johann Christian Senckenberg und seine Stiftung." In *Dr. Senckenbergische Stiftung. Frankfurter Beitraege zur Geschichte, Theorie und Ethik der Medizin,* vol. 10, edited by Naujoks / Preiser. Hildesheim, Germany: Olms.

Rassem, Mohammed. 1979. *Stiftung und Leistung. Essais zur Kultursoziologie.* Mittenwald, Germany: Maeander.

Rifkin, Jeremy. 2004. *The European Dream.* New York: Jeremy P. Tarcher–Penguin.

Rigaud, Jacques. 1995. "Le mécénat cultural d'entreprise en France." In *Kultursponsoring in der Diskussion. Deutschland und Europa,* edited by Kulturstiftung Haus Europa. München: Maecenata.

Sauer, Christine. 1993. *Fundation und Memoria, Stifter und Klostergründer im Bild, 1100–1350.* Göttingen, Germany: Vandenhoeck und Ruprecht.

Scheller, Benjamin. 2004. *Memoria an der Zeitenwende, Die Stiftungen Jakob Fuggers des Reichen vor und während der Reformation 1505–1555.* Berlin: Akademie Verlag.

Schulze, Winfried. 1995. *Der Stifterverband für die deutsche Wissenschaft 1920–1995.* Berlin: Akademie Verlag.

Smith, James Allen, and Karsten Borgmann. 2001. "Foundations in Europe: the Historical Context." In *Foundations in Europe—Society, Management, and Law,* edited by Andreas Schlüter, Volker Then, and Peter Walkenhorst. London: The Directory of Social Change.

Sprengel, Rainer. 2001. *Statistiken zum deutschen Stiftungswesen 2001, ein Forschungsbericht.* Berlin: Maecenata.

———. 2004. "An Empirical Profile of the German Foundation Sector." In *Visions and Roles of Foundations in Europe. The German Report,* edited by Frank Adloff, Philipp Schwertmann, Rainer Sprengel, and Rupert Graf Strachwitz. Berlin: Maecenata.

Strachwitz, Rupert Graf. 1989. "Mäzenatentum und Kunst, zur Förderung der Kunst durch Stiftungen." *Kunst und Antiquitäten* 1: 22–26.

———. 1997. "Ernst Abbe." In *Die grossen Stifter,* edited by Joachim Fest. Berlin: Siedler.

———. 2003a. "Die Stiftung des Barons von Brukenthal." *Maecenata Actuell* 40: 9–13.

———. 2003b. *Philanthropy and Civil Society.* Berlin: Maecenata.

Strachwitz, Rupert Graf, and Florian Mercker. 2005. *Stiftungen in Theorie, Recht und Praxis, Handbuch fuer ein modernes Stiftungswesen.* Berlin: Duncker & Humblot.

Strachwitz, Rupert Graf, and Volker Then. 2004. *Kultureinrichtungen in Stiftungsform.* Gütersloh, Germany: Bertelsmann Stiftung.

Timmer, Karsten. 2005. *Stiften in Deutschland. Die Ergebnisse der Stifter-Studie.* Gütersloh, Germany: Bertelsmann Stiftung.

Toepler, Stefan. 1996. *Das gemeinnützige Stiftungswesen in der modernen demokratischen Gesellschaft.* München: Maecenata.

———. 1999. "On the Problem of Defining Foundations in a Comparative Perspective." *Nonprofit Management & Leadership* 10(2): 215–25.

Volkswagen Stiftung. 2003. *Jahresbericht 2002.* Hannover, Germany: Volkswagen Stiftung.

Wagner, Wolfgang Eric. 1999. *Universitätsstift und Kollegium in Prag, Wien und Heidelberg, eine vergleichende Untersuchung spätmittelalterlicher Stiftungen im Spannungsfeld von Herrschaft und Genossenschaft.* Berlin: Akademie.

Chapter 10

Industrial Foundations: Foundation Ownership of Business Companies

Steen Thomsen

In addition to serving as donors, foundations can own business companies. This was not uncommon in the United States until passage of the 1969 Tax Reform Act, which effectively prevented U.S. foundations from owning more than 20 percent of a corporate entity (Fleishman 2001). But in northern Europe, foundations continue to own and operate world-class companies such as Bertelsmann, Heineken, Robert Bosch, Carlsberg, and Ikea. In Denmark, particularly, foundations own and operate some 25 percent of the 100 largest Danish corporations and control close to 50 percent of the major Danish stock index (KFX).

The question in this context is whether ownership of a business company is a legitimate role for a foundation. Apparently, U.S. regulators answer this question in the negative and European regulators in the affirmative.

Legitimacy can be defined as the generalized perception that the actions and existence of an entity are desirable, proper or appropriate within a given social system of norms, values and beliefs (Suchman 1995). It therefore involves both normative (that is, moral) pragmatic and cognitive issues. The normative issues concern whether foundation ownership of business companies in and of itself is consistent with the values and norms of the society, in which the foundation operates. Pragmatic issues concern whether foundation ownership is regarded as a satisfactory institution by the actors involved (founders, governments, company managers, potential beneficiaries). Finally, cognitive issues concern whether foundation ownership is justified by its social performance (see chapter 1, this volume).

Here I discuss the normative, pragmatic and cognitive legitimacy of foundation ownership comparing U.S. and European perspectives on the subject, particularly why the structure was not adopted in the United States and how it performs in Europe. In Europe, legislators and managers stand to benefit from recognizing that like other ownership structures there are disadvantages and advantages to foundation ownership. The advantages can be guarded by maintaining existing regulation allowing foundation ownership to coexist with other ownership structures. Disadvantages in terms of funding, conservatism, and entrepreneurial drive mean that a change of ownership structure may sometimes be called for. Flexible and pragmatic regulation of ownership changes seems likely to benefit the foundations, their companies and society in general.

What Is Foundation Ownership?

Formally, an industrial foundation is an organization created to administer a large ownership stake in a particular company, very often donated to the foundation by the company's founder. The foundation itself is a nonprofit entity. It has no owners. Its board of directors is often self-elected, constrained only by the law and its charter, which frequently stipulate that the foundation should serve some broadly defined social purpose, for example, to act in the company's "best interest" and use excess revenue for charitable purposes. Often, but not always, the founder's family continues to play a role in the management of the company. The institutional set up resembles what would have been the case if the Ford Foundation had maintained majority control of Ford Motor Company.

As an example consider William Demant, a listed Danish company, one of the world's largest producers of hearing aids and European company of the year in 2003. The company is majority-owned by the Oticon Foundation.

Following Kronke (1988) an industrial foundation can be defined by:

- creation by donation ("Endgültige Trennung von ausgesetzten Gütern")

- independence

Figure 10.1   Foundation Ownership: An Example

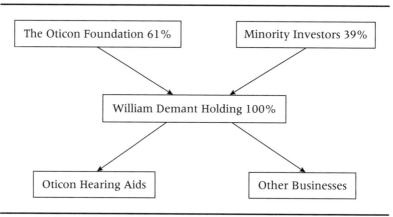

Source: Author's compilation.

- an altruistic purpose ("Stiftungszweck")

- a foundation endowment (Stiftungsvermögen)

- a foundation organization and charter (Stiftungsorganisation und Stiftungsverfassung)

- ownership of a majority of the shares or votes in a business company

CREATION BY DONATION   An industrial foundation is created when someone (the founder) entrusts the foundation with an endowment consisting of ownership rights to a business company. The existence of foundations therefore presupposes a gift, a renunciation on part of the donor or founder. This transaction is irreversible.

INDEPENDENCE   The foundation is a private (nongovernment) institution. It has no owners and no members. Industrial foundations are therefore sometimes referred to as self-owning institutions. The irreversibility of the decision to found a foundation is underlined by its legal personality. The decisive factor is a clear separation between the personal economic affairs of the founder and those of the foundation. The separation transforms the foundation into a nonprofit entity which as emphasized by Hansmann (1980, 1987) may earn profits but cannot redistribute them except for charity.

A CHARITABLE PURPOSE   Running a business for the good of society is considered an acceptable charitable aim. The foundation may or may not have other philanthropic goals, but most industrial foundations typically support other worthy causes. The foundation cannot, or can only to a limited extent, redistribute income to the founder or the founder's family.

ENDOWMENT   Independence presupposes a certain initial wealth, an endowment or at least privileged access to a source of future income (such as the right to future profits from a company owned by the foundation). Once created, however, foundations are in principle self-perpetuating bodies provided that they are financially viable. In principle, they will continue to carry out the will of the founder in perpetuity.

GOVERNANCE BY CHARTER   Like other foundations the industrial foundation is formally governed by a charter that defines its purpose and organization. The foundation is obliged to own and manage the company according to the charter, which represents the will of the founder (although behavioral rules are often informal rather than formal). For example, the charter may prescribe that certain worthy causes (such as research, art or charity) should be supported by revenues beyond what is considered necessary to reinvest in the business. The foundation charter may also specify that the foundation should act for the benefit of the company, the employees, or the national interest. Moreover, the charter may oblige the foundation to maintain majority ownership of the company. It may furthermore include specific rules on the composition of the foundation board, for example, whether it is self-elective or whether the founder's descendants are entitled to a seat. It also sets the constraints, subject to government approval and supervision, that limit the board's discretion.

BUSINESS ACTIVITIES   Industrial foundations are defined here by majority ownership of a business company. If the foundation is the sole owner, that is, there are no minority shareholders, the company and foundation board members may be identical and even (in a few cases) use the foundation structure to conduct business without incorporating a separate company. If a minority of the company's shares are held by other shareholders—for example, if they are listed on the stock exchange—the company will in principle act as any other joint stock company. The company is legally responsible to (all of) its shareholders and at an annual general meeting they will elect a board to represent their interests. However, as a majority owner, the foundation possesses a controlling influence, which it may (or may not) choose to exercise. European industrial foundations often retain a voting majority by having the company issue shares with limited voting rights (B shares) to the public while the foundation maintains shares with full voting rights (A shares) only to the foundation.

Normative Legitimacy: The Political Theory of Corporate Governance

Over the past two decades, business ownership has mainly been discussed as a pragmatic, economic question of establishing structures, which maximize value creation or competitiveness of the business sector (for example, Jensen and Meckling 1976; Putterman 1993; Hart 1995; Hansmann 1996; Williamson 1996; Shleifer and Vishny 1997). In contrast to this "economic model" an alternative line of research argues that ideological or political differences play a major role in determining international differences in corporate governance. This view has been clearly articulated in Mark Roe's political theory of corporate ownership (1991, 1994, 2003) and receives widespread empirical support (for example, Pedersen and Thomsen 1997).

The economic model tends to predict international similarities in corporate governance.

> The economic model says many corporate structures arise due to economies of scale, wide capital-gathering and the resulting divergence of managerial goals from stockholder goals. . . . But if the economic model were universal it would predict that other nations with similar economies would have similar structures. There is a best way to make steel and presumably there is a best way to organize large steel firms. (Roe 1994, 28)

The obvious implication is that firms in similar industries and size classes will have similar ownership structures across the world. But Roe's point is that this is not so. He finds that ownership structures in for example, the United States, Germany, and Japan are very different even for firms of the same size in the same industry. He therefore argues that " there is more than one way to deal with these economic problems. And, the differences suggest that differing histories, cultures and paths of economic development better explain the differing structures than economic theory alone" (Roe 1994, 28). Different laws with regard to foundation ownership of business enterprise would seem to be a case in point.

Roe's main argument is that American political life is founded on a distrust of centralized authority and concentration of power. For example, he argues that distrust of economic power has led to a protection of small investors, suppression of the U.S. banking sector, and the 5 percent upper ceilings for financial investor stockholdings. Effectively, this regulation has promoted ownership diversification and discouraged large owners from exercising control over large U.S. companies and thus—like many other institutions—supported the market-based model of corporate governance. In fact, dispersed ownership (weak investors and strong managers) appears to have become institutionalized to the extent of acquiring the status of a social fact (Goodrick and Salancik 1996). Preventing foundations from exercising ownership control thus fits into the general pattern known as the market model of corporate governance.

Fleishman (2001) summarizes and criticizes the arguments put forward for the U.S. excess business holding provisions in 1969 laws.

1. The unfair competition argument, according to which foundation-ownership would subsidize foundation-owned companies by lowering required rates of return, thus giving them an unfair advantage against investor-owned companies. However, subsidies of this kind, Fleishman argues, are already effectively prevented by other parts of foundation law.

2. The diversion of attention argument, according to which the foundation would be unable to simultaneously perform the two roles as corporate owner and donor in an effective way. This argument, Fleishman maintains, is not persuasive for large foundations, which can afford to set up separate offices for the two functions.

3. The personal material benefit argument, according to which founders may receive benefits from tax-sheltered wealth and income in the foundations. This kind of abuse, Fleishman observes, is not unique to foundations and it is anyhow addressed as offence in other parts of foundation law.

4. Inadequate dividend income argument, that foundation-ownership would lead to a preference for retained earnings in the company. Because foundations may require continuous financing of their expenses, it is not clear that foundations will be less inclined to require dividends from the company.

Altogether, Fleischman concludes, "we arrive at what seems to be an inescapable conclusion therefore, that the US excess business holding provision in its present form was, simply put, a wrong-headed idea, unevenly applied. In other words, it probably shouldn't have been enacted at all" (Fleishman 2001, 394).

Moreover, given that a significant share of the largest U.S. foundations were actually established by donations of shares, the 1969 laws appear to have impeded the creation of new, large foundations. One can wonder why, therefore, in a country with a strong tradition for liberalism and freedom of contract, the rule was enacted anyway. Using a term from the legitimacy literature, one reason may be isomorphism with other elements of the market-based governance system, in particular the distrust of concentrated power and the inclination to reproduce democratic governance structures in corporate governance.

Pragmatic Legitimacy: Foundation Ownership and Economic Performance

Foundation ownership is something of an enigma to economic theory (Thomsen 1996). Since the 1970s a large body of literature has emerged emphasizing that risk diversification and incentives play a key role in the efficient operation of business companies (for example, Jensen and Meckling 1976; Putterman 1993; Hart 1995; Hansmann 1996; Williamson 1996; Shleifer and Vishny 1997). A possible exception is nonprofit organizations, which are clearly not monitored by owners, but rather by donors or users (Hansmann 1980; Fama and Jensen 1983a). But a nonprofit organization is generally believed to be competitive only in certain industries (hospitals, universities, charities, and the like) and not, in the absence of tax subsidies, to be a viable business model for commercial enterprises (Fama and Jensen 1983b). The theoretical implication is that nonprofit entities—companies without owners—should be a rare phenomenon outside of these special industries, and in other industries their performance—in terms of profitability, growth, cost efficiency, or other measures—would be expected to be below average. Nonprofit enterprises lack a personal profit motive to monitor managers, and their ability to attract capital from outside investors is also limited. Altogether, agency theory would predict that foundation-owned companies would perform badly compared to investor-owned companies on criteria such as profitability, growth, and shareholder value.

But this is inconsistent with anecdotal evidence. Some foundation-owned companies are among the best-managed in the world. How, for example, could foundation-owned William Demant become European company of the year—an award that honors a European firm consistently producing outstanding financial and business results among more than 6,200 others? How could foundation-owned A. P. Moeller–Maersk be one of the leading shipping companies in the world? And how could German SAP be the world's leading producer of enterprise management systems?

Moreover, empirical studies—three studies on Danish data over the period from 1982 to 1999 (Thomsen 1996, 1999; Thomsen and Rose 2004) and a study on German data (Herrmann and Franke 2002)—found the economic performance of foundation-owned companies to be no worse or even slightly better than that of companies with more common ownership structures—measured on accounting profitability, growth, and even stock market returns. Table 10.1 summarizes

Table 10.1   Corporate Ownership and Performance of the Largest Danish Companies

	Investor	Family	Foundation
Return on equity percentage			
1982 to 1992	10.9	11.3	11.4
1995 to 2002	9.1	12.4	14.5
Growth (sales) percentage			
1982 to 1992	8.9	11.6	10.2
1995 to 2002	7	2.1	9.3
Survival frequency percentage			
1982 to 1992	71	76	77
1992 to 1999	66	84	87
Equity/assets ratio percentage			
1982 to 1992	36	38	47
1995 to 2002	50	56	54
Number of companies			
1982 to 1992	47	62	48
1995 to 2002	58	63	50

Source: Author's compilations.

and updates the Danish evidence, which now covers a twenty-year period.

It appears that foundation-owned companies had rates of return on equity that consistently exceeded those of other ownership categories. Moreover, they also had faster sales growth than the other ownership categories over the period, growing a little slower than family-owned companies in the first decade, but much faster in the last seven-year period. Moreover the survival frequency and equity base (equity–assets ratio) of the foundation-owned companies were higher than the same ratios for investor-owned companies. This indicates that the foundation-owned companies obtained their results with less financial risk.

Given high standard deviations, most of these differences are not statistically significant. But altogether the empirical evidence indicates that the performance of Danish foundation-owned companies has been at least as good or even slightly better than that of other ownership categories.

Further research (Thomsen 2005) indicates that foundation-owned companies have a significantly better corporate reputation than investor-owned companies when rated by image-surveys. Danish foundation-owned companies are believed to have better employee relations and to be more socially responsible as well as being financially stronger and better managed than investor-owned companies. This can be regarded as a test of pragmatic legitimacy in the sense that the foundation-owned companies are regarded as good social citizens.

Table 10.2 summarizes the German evidence over the period from 1990 to 1992 based on Markus Herrmann and Gunter Franke (2002).

The profitability of the foundation-owned firms is found to be higher than that of other corporations, sometimes significantly so. Over the three years, foundation-owned companies made on average 14.2 percent on their equity, whereas other German corporations made only 10.5 percent. The tendency is therefore the same as in the Danish figures.

However, unlike the Danish figures, the equity-assets ratio for foundation-owned companies is no different from that of other companies. There is some indication, though, that foundation-owned enterprises tend to reinvest more of their earnings because the payout ratio is significantly lower than that for other companies. The differ-

Table 10.2   Foundation Ownership and Performance
of German Companies

	Foundation-Owned Firms	Other Corporations
Return on equity percentage (before taxes)		
1990	16.7	15.9
1991	15.9	11.2
1992	10.2	4.5
Equity/assets (percentage)		
1990	30.3	32.8
1991	30.1	31.7
1992	28.7	31.1
Pay out ratio percentage (dividends/earnings)		
1990	42.7	56.5
1991	38.6	52.2
1992	36.5	59.0
Number of firms	178	846

Source: Herrmann and Franke (2002).

ences are robust to controls for size and industry effects. As in the Danish data, foundation-owned companies are generally more labor intensive than the control group because they have more employees per DM of turnover. They also pay lower salaries. Both board income and personnel expenses are lower per individual than in other companies.

Altogether, the German and Danish evidence on this issue points in the same direction: foundation-owned companies appear to be slightly more efficient than other companies in terms of the available performance measures. Their good performance is something of a paradox to standard economic theories of the firm, which tend to emphasize the advantages of profit-based incentives and diversification of risk.

Cognitive Legitimacy: Explaining the Performance of Foundation-Owned Firms

Foundation ownership is found mainly in northern Europe—Denmark, Germany, Sweden, Norway, the Netherlands, and Switzerland. Examples include world-class companies such as Ikea from Sweden, Carlsberg from Denmark, or Krupp, Carl Zeiss, and Robert Bosch from Germany. There are a few examples from the United States and the United Kingdom (Hershey Foods, the Welcome Foundation up to the Glaxo-Welcome merger), but these are clearly the exception to the rule. This is probably not a coincidence.

Taxation   High taxation of wealth, capital gains, and inheritance have historically made the foundation an attractive alternative for family owners wanting to maintain control. However, once the foundation structure has been established, foundation-owned companies are taxed similarly to other joint stock companies. Moreover, the foundations themselves are taxed by the same rates as corporations.

Monopoly   There is no indication that the performance of foundation-owned companies is based on market power or protectionism. Steen Thomsen (1999) finds that the Danish foundation-owned companies are more international (measured in terms of international sales or total sales). However, relatively high profit margins (profit to sales ratios) indicate that they may have competitive advantages within their markets.

Other Control Mechanisms   In principle, the absence of control by ownership might be corrected by other control mechanisms—creditor monitoring, bankruptcy risk, managerial labor markets, product market competition, or other measures. However, none of these explanations appear convincing. For example, relatively strong balance sheets indicates financial independence and low creditor pressure. And managers of foundation-owned companies tend to have long terms of office—though there is some evidence that replacement risk is more sensitive to performance than for other ownership categories. In other words, the impact of the other governance mechanisms appear to increase rather than to resolve the theoretical paradox.

Family Control   The best bid so far for an explanation appears to be that foundation-owned companies are often managed by the founding families, who continue to take a strong personal interest in the firm. Several recent studies have emphasized the strong performance (for example, Anderson and Reeb 2003) and it is possible that foundation-owned firms can benefit from this type of long-term commitment. Thomsen (1999) finds that foundation-owned companies that retain a tie to the founding family do better in terms of profitability. However, even foundations without ties to the founding family do as well as investor-owned companies in terms of profitability and other performance measures.

Cognitive Legitimacy: Disadvantages of Foundation Ownership

Despite their apparent success it would be foolhardy to overlook potential weaknesses of foundation ownership. Some of these have already been mentioned. There appears to be a risk that foundation-owned companies can in some cases be capital rationed because of their inability to tap the stock market for funds. Another concern is that a lack of personal incentives will reduce entrepreneurship in the foundation-owned companies. After all, the people who manage them will not (or only to a small extent) benefit from successful business ventures. The obligation to carry on in the founder's spirit—for example, to operate in the same industry or geographic location and to plow back profits to the company as retained earnings—could also involve considerable conservatism. Finally, because the foundations value the survival of their company as an independent business, foundation-ownership could in some cases function as a barrier to restructuring.

An added concern is that the families that operate industrial foundations must suffer from the same succession problems as other families. Although founders of business dynasties in many cases possess unquestionable business talent, it is less clear that their offspring will inherit that talent. Thus one could hypothesize that the relative success of foundation-owned companies would tend to deteriorate over time. Statistical support for this hypothesis is found in Thomsen (1999): the profitability of the foundation-owned companies tends to decline with company age compared to the investor-owned companies. The effect, however, is not strong enough to indicate that even old (three-generation) foundation-owned companies underperform significantly compared to investor-owned firms.

All of this implies that foundation-ownership can under certain circumstances be a disadvantage for a company, which in turn implies that the ability to change ownership is an important topic. Many industrial foundations have no formal limitations on their ability to sell or transfer ownership of the company to other parties and so are in a way obligated to do so if they consider this in the best interest of the company. Others have clauses in their charter that obligate them to maintain majority ownership, but it is questionable to what extent such clauses would be considered binding in case of a perceived conflict with the best interests of the company. Two recent Danish cases, Novo-Nordisk and Carlsberg, have indicated that the authorities are flexible in interpreting the statutes and allow the foundations to accept less than complete control, should this be considered desirable from the company's viewpoint (for example, in case of a merger). Moreover, hybrid solutions—such as spinning off a part of the company in a subsidiary, which is then sold to a third party—could make it very difficult to enforce formal limitations against the wish of the foundation board.

Discussion

Altogether, foundation ownership of business companies appears to pass what could be termed the pragmatic legitimacy test: it meets all reasonable expectations of company performance. In fact, given the weight of the empirical evidence, it is perhaps time to turn the tables and question the legitimacy of breaching the freedom of contracts with regard to foundation ownership (the 1969 U.S. laws).

The competitive advantage of industrial foundations appears to involve the ability to support long-term corporate strategies independently of stock market fluctuations and the temptations of short-term financial gain. Patient foundation ownership can support research-based companies, which invest in the very long term. R&D intensive German companies such as Robert Bosch or Carl Zeiss are world-class examples of this. Eli Lilly would have been, had U.S. law allowed it.

The foundation structure can also support contrarian strategies— sell when the prices are high, buy when they are low—which can make a difference in cyclical industries. The foundation-owned A. P. Møller Maersk—the largest container-shipping company in the world—is well-known for relying on this strategy in a highly cyclical shipping industry.

Finally foundation ownership can support implicit contracts with employees and customers and thereby benefit companies that invest in human capital and reputation. The foundation-owned Novo group, a pharmaceutical company, emphasizes the triple bottom line— environmental and social goals as well as profits. A counterfactual

British example could be the Welcome Foundation, which invented the anti-AIDS drug Retrovir, one of the most successful drugs of all time, but whose business is now part of Glaxo Welcome. Welcome had a large research program in tropical medicine, an area which is now widely regarded as underresearched because of the poor purchasing power of Third World countries.

On the negative side, some companies may be less suited for foundation ownership. Potential disadvantages of the foundation structure include capital scarcity, conservatism, and inadequate control of managers. Because foundation-owned companies must rely mainly on financing by retained earnings and bank loans, the foundation structure is less suited for businesses that require substantial lump sum investments in company specific assets with little collateral value. However, to the extent that foundation boards respect the overall aim of the company interest, which is written into most foundation charters, selling out is actually required if this is needed to ensure the future survival of the company.

In conclusion, there is a strong case for pragmatic and cognitive legitimacy of foundation ownership. It can be argued that this was phased out in the United States mainly because of a lack of normative legitimacy (isomorphism) with the "market model" of corporate governance, that is, dispersed ownership, arm's-length distance between owners and companies, formal adherence to profit maximization objective, and so on. Thus the increase in internal consistency gained by removing foundation ownership most likely came at the cost of reduced economic efficiency.

With regard to the balance between charity and business, industrial foundations call into question public inconstancy with regard to these two goals. Why are donations to widows and orphans more to the public good than running a company in a socially responsible way?

Suspicions that business goals come to override charity find some support in a tendency among the industrial foundations to consolidate rather than to pay out dividends (Thomsen 1999). However, the excesses business holding rule may have reduced the number of new foundations created in the United States. It is not obvious, therefore, that donations would have been smaller had the rule not been adopted. Moreover, it is possible that there may be positive synergies between business and charity. For example, management expertise generated by a competitive world-class business could be useful to the efficient management of the activities of the foundation itself. This seems to be a belief cherished by the German Bertelsmann Foundation.[1]

In Europe, legislators and managers stand to benefit from recognizing that, as with other ownership structures, there are disadvantages and advantages to foundation ownership. The advantages can be guarded by maintaining existing regulation allowing foundation ownership to coexist with other ownership forms. Disadvantages in terms of funding, conservatism, and entrepreneurial drive mean that a change of ownership structure may sometimes be called for. Flexible and pragmatic regulation of ownership change seems likely to benefit the foundations, their companies, and society in general.

Note

1. Confirmed by private correspondence with Volker Then of the Bertelsmann Foundation.

References

Anderson, R. C., and D. Reeb. 2003. "Founding-Family Ownership and Firm Performance: Evidence from the S&P 500." *The Journal of Finance* 58(3): 1301–28.

Fama, Eugene F., and Michael C. Jensen. 1983a. "Separation of Ownership and Control." *Journal of Law and Economics* 26(2): 301–25.

———. 1983b. "Agency Problems and Residual Claims." *Journal of Law and Economics* 26(2): 327–49.

Fleishman, Joel. 2001. "Public Policy and Philanthropic Purpose—Foundation Ownership and Control of Corporations in Germany and the United States." In *Foundations in Europe: Society, Management and Law,* edited by Andreas Schlüter, Volker Then, and Peter Walkenhorst. London: Directory for Social Change.

Goodrick, Elizabeth, and Gerald R. Salancik. 1996. "Organizational Discretion in Responding to Institutional Practices: Hospitals and Cesarean Births." *Administrative Science Quarterly* 41(1): 1.

Hansmann, Henry. 1980. "The Role of Nonprofit Enterprise." *The Yale Law Review* 89(5): 835–901.

———. 1987. "Economic Theories of Nonprofit Organization." In *The Nonprofit Sector—A Research Handbook,* edited by Walter W. Powell. New Haven, Conn.: Yale University Press.

———. 1996. *The Ownership of Enterprise.* Cambridge Mass.: The Belknap Press of Harvard University Press.

Hart, Oliver. 1995. *Firms, Contracts and Financial Structure.* New York: Oxford University Press.

Herrmann, Markus, and Gunter Franke. 2002. "Performance and Policy of Foundation-Owned Firms in Germany." *European Financial Management* 8(3): 261–79.

Jensen, Michael C., and William H. Meckling. 1976. "Managerial Behavior: Agency Costs and Ownership Structure." *Journal of Financial Economics* 3(4): 305–60.

Kronke, Herbert. 1988. *Stiftungstypus und Unternehmensträgerstiftung.* Tübingen, Germany: J. C. B. Mohr.

Pedersen, T., and S. Thomsen. 1997. "European Patterns of Corporate Ownership." *Journal of International Business Studies* 28(4): 759–78.

Putterman, Louis. 1993. "Ownership and the Nature of the Firm." *Journal of Comparative Economics* 17(2): 243–63.

Roe, Mark J. 1991. "Political Theory of Corporate Finance." *Columbia Law Review* 1: 10–67.

———. 1994. *Strong Managers, Weak Owners—the Political Roots of American Corporate Finance.* Princeton: Princeton University Press.

———. 2003. *Political Determinants of Corporate Governance.* New York: Oxford University Press.

Shleifer, Andrei, and Robert W. Vishny. 1997. "A Survey of Corporate Governance." *Journal of Finance* 52(2): 737–83.

Suchman, Mark C. 1995. "Managing Legitimacy: Strategic and Institutional Approaches." *Academy of Management. The Academy of Management Review* 20(3): 571–610.

Thomsen, Steen. 1996. "Foundation Ownership and Economic Performance." *Corporate Governance* 4(4): 212–21.

———. 1999. "Corporate Ownership by Industrial Foundations." *The European Journal of Law and Economics* 7(2): 103–17.

———. 2005. "Foundation Ownership, Corporate Reputation and Economic Performance." Paper presented at the Conference on Corporate Governance of Closely Held Firms, Copenhagen Business School (June 16–18, 2005).

Thomsen, Steen, and Caspar Rose. 2004. "Foundation Ownership and Financial Performance." *The European Journal of Law and Economics* 18(3): 343–64.

Williamson, Oliver E. 1996. *The Mechanisms of Governance.* New York: Oxford University Press.

Chapter 11

Foundation Legitimacy at the Community Level in the United Kingdom

Diana Leat

Community foundations claim to be the fastest-growing form of philanthropy (Walkenhorst 2001), yet in most countries they are also the newest. This raises a number of questions concerning the diffusion of philanthropic innovations, including how novel foundation forms carve out distinctive roles and build legitimacy and trust in their roles, capacity, and viability. The story of community foundation development in the United Kingdom also highlights issues about legitimacy and accountability in an era of third-party government (Salamon 2002).

For the purposes of this discussion, a community foundation is defined as "an independent philanthropy organization working in a specific geographic area which, over time, builds up a collection of endowed funds from many donors, provides services to those donors, and makes grants and undertakes community leadership and partnership activities to address a wide variety of needs in its service area" (Feurt 1999, 10). Compared with the United States, community foundations in other countries are fewer and less established, although similar structures have existed for some time. During the 1990s the number of community foundations worldwide began to grow and are now found in thirty-seven countries, with an estimated global total of near 1,100 (Sacks 2000; Feurt and Sacks 2001; WINGS-CF 2003). In the United Kingdom in 2003 there were said to be sixty-five at various stages of development. Here I discuss the development of community foundations in the United Kingdom, focusing in particular on the factors that contributed to the development of their roles and the generation of both legitimacy and trust in their capacities as institutions new to the U.K. context.

Foundations in the United Kingdom

Although the nonprofit sector in general is relatively well-developed in the United Kingdom, the foundation sector is not. Estimates for 2003 and 2004 put the number of foundations giving grants of around £2 billion at about 3,500. Assets and income are very unevenly distributed, with a very small number of relatively wealthy foundations and a very large number of very small ones (see http://www.acf.org/uk).

Whereas in the United States the legitimacy of foundations has been periodically challenged (Troyer 2000; Brilliant 2000), it has not been in the United Kingdom, at least, not for several hundred years. Only two have been the subject of popular critical media attention in recent years—the National Lottery Charities Board, now The Big Lottery Fund, and the Diana, Princess of Wales Memorial Fund. In both cases, the challenge related not so much to foundations in general but to the fact that these were organizations spending the "people's" money. (There was no link to the notion that other foundations also spend public money in the form of tax expenditures.) In general, foundations bask in the halo of sedimented, but limited, legal legitimacy enjoyed by all charities and confirmed in Charity Commission endorsement. Foundations, like charities, are broadly accepted as legitimate because they "do good."

Having rarely been challenged, then, foundations do not provide any detailed articulation of their legitimacy and roles. They have traditionally seen their role as complementing rather than substituting for the responsibilities of government, and have not typically used words such as redistribution, preservation, or pluralism in their self-definitions. Nor, with a few notable exceptions, have they presented themselves as agents of policy and practice change. They have traditionally seen themselves primarily as risk-takers and innovators, giving short-term gifts that others (primarily government) would then pick up and sustain. These roles went hand in hand with traditional practices that stressed being responsive rather than proactive, making smaller short-term grants, giving grants for specific projects rather than for core funds, and often for capital rather than revenue purposes (Leat 1992). Although U.K. foundations have now changed in many respects, this was the dominant prevailing philosophy and practice when community foundations were first promoted.

Context

Understanding the social and political context into which community foundations were introduced is important, not least because legitimacy is socially constructed and situated. The U.K. context of the late 1980s and later presented a number of both opportunities and challenges in establishing the legitimacy of community foundations as new and unknown institutions. These challenges and opportunities were in several respects both similar to and different from those that confront and have confronted U.S. community foundations.

Opportunities

First, community foundations enjoyed the advantage of widespread acceptance of the legitimacy of charities and charitable giving. Second, the foundation sector in the United Kingdom was widely regarded as underdeveloped relative to the United States, presenting an opportunity to legitimize their introduction in terms of potential capacity to exploit hitherto unexploited means of capturing private wealth for public good. Third, in developing this role, community foundations did not face competition from United Way or Community Chests, neither of which were significant players in the United Kingdom. Fourth, community foundations also did not face significant competition from private foundations—the culture of privacy and the lack of media and public-policy questioning of foundations had kept the profile of private foundations so low as to be almost invisible. The low rate of foundation formation at the time suggested that this was not on the menu of activities for potential wealthy donors. Fifth, there was a growing perception that charitable (and government) funds were increasingly concentrated at national level, providing an opportunity for community foundations to legitimize their introduction in terms of building on local allegiances and feelings of disempowerment.

Sixth, as I will discuss in more detail later, the changing policy context provided a major opportunity for development of the legitimacy of community foundations. As is well known, in the U.K., attitudes to the roles of business, nonprofits, and government are very different from those in the United States. In the twentieth century the British typically looked first to the state to provide, and nonprofits were allocated the role of supplement and innovator; the role of business was, first and foremost, to be a good employer. From the early 1980s, with the administrations of Margaret Thatcher and John Major, government policy began to change. The role of the state was to be reduced and charities were expected to take up the slack. Larger charities and other nonprofit organizations increasingly worked on contract to both central and local government. Charitable giving was encouraged and businesses were later exhorted to become "socially responsible" and "good corporate citizens"—which included but went beyond charitable giving. Changing government policy thus provided a space and basis on which to develop the legitimacy of community foundations.

Challenges

Community foundations also faced several challenges in establishing their legitimacy, some of which were the opposite sides of the coin of their opportunities. Some of the challenges were those faced by all new community foundations, some were more specific to the United Kingdom.

The common challenges included, first, the fact that, unlike traditional endowed foundations, community foundations have no "ready-made" corpus and must fundraise.

Second, unlike many service organizations, they seek funding not to meet immediate needs but to build a reserve for the future. While community foundations are building their endowment they give very few, if any, grants. They solicit donations, and substantial ones at that, with nothing to show for it. In effect, they say, "I haven't done anything and I'm not going to do anything for a long time, but give me your money anyway." Building this level of legitimacy and trust without a track record is difficult in itself. It is especially difficult in a culture in which nonprofit organizations are judged on what they spend on the immediate and direct relief of "the needy." Once the community foundation is established, the presence of respected community leaders on the board usually signals trustworthiness of sorts, but at the outset getting high-profile community leaders to lend their reputations and legitimacy to new, untried institutions may be extremely difficult.

Third, in countries where community foundations are not established, they face the "liability of newness" (DiMaggio 1992). Fourth,
in many countries, community foundations are not merely unknown
but are also entrants in a highly competitive and, in some cases, over-
crowded fundraising market.

Challenges specific to the United Kingdom included the fact that
although charities were accepted as a good thing, reliance on charitable giving was not necessarily seen as a legitimate way of providing for
public good. Another was that the treasured privacy of foundations
rendered them almost invisible. That foundations had not been the
subject of public enquiries and debate, as in the United States, has been
an advantage to foundations in the United Kingdom in that their
established formal legitimacy has not been openly challenged, but a
disadvantage in terms of public awareness and understanding of the
concept of endowed foundations. Endowment was, and is, not a concept that is widely understood. Furthermore, when it has been in the
limelight, it has attracted criticism as unnecessary hoarding of money
for the sake of continuity, and the interests of trustees and staff, rather
than for the immediate public good. It is also important to note here
that in the United Kingdom, unlike in the United States, there is no tax
advantage in giving to a community foundation rather than setting up
a private foundation.

Another important factor in the U.K. environment of the 1980s was
that large national nonprofit organizations increasingly dominated the
ever more competitive fundraising and contracting scene, partly as
a result of Thatcher's concentration on efficiency and effectiveness.
Community foundations were country cousins on a very crowded
fundraising block dominated by the national big boys. On the other
hand, as noted, this could also be seen as an advantage in demonstrating the legitimacy of the community foundation form as a vehicle
for encouraging local giving for local benefit.

Thus, in establishing their legitimacy in the United Kingdom, community foundations faced a number of challenges. On the one hand,
as charities they enjoyed the formal legitimacy—and privileges—
accorded to all charities. On the other, they had to overcome wariness
about the role of charities vis-à-vis that of the state, lack of a tradition
of widespread corporate giving, lack of awareness of foundations and
of the concept and practice of endowment, lack of any very clear definition of the distinct societal roles of foundations beyond that of

"doing what the state doesn't do" and innovation, and the national bias in both the voluntary and statutory sector. If community foundations were to attract donors, they needed to present a convincing case regarding their distinctive functions and roles, and their credibility as effective and efficient vehicles for giving. But, as Gaynor Humphreys (2002) notes, community foundations were, initially at least, swimming against the tide on several counts: a strong belief in the value and importance of state services, endowment trusts had largely gone out of fashion, and in their emphasis on supporting small or local rather than large or national organizations.

Advantages

In building their case, community foundations could draw on potential advantages over traditional foundations in responding to current social and political themes. By providing a vehicle for donors without enough wealth to create an independent foundation, community foundations had the potential to play a role in capturing more private wealth for public good. Their geographic focus enabled them to raise the profile of philanthropic giving, generating new money based on regional or local allegiances from both private individuals and businesses. They could add to the innovative and complementary capacity of foundations at a local, rather than national level, balance the perceived London–Southeast bias of traditional private foundations, and perform a geographically redistributive role. Working at local level and with a more participative structure, they could open foundations to wider community representation, inclusion, and pluralism. By acting as convenors and brokers, they could build bridges between nonprofit organizations, local government, and business at local level and play a civic leadership role. With a geographic focus, they could adopt a more holistic approach than the more piecemeal, special-interest style of national foundations. By developing on the ground local knowledge of needs, capacities, and gaps in funding and provision, they could play a role in getting money to small, underfunded local groups and act as informers and agents of national, London-based foundations. By building endowments, they could provide for sustainability, balancing the wider foundation tendency to give small, short-term project specific grants.

The Story

Community foundations in several countries—including the United States, Italy, and Australia—were originally established with the support and imprimatur of major banking institutions from whom they, in a sense, borrowed a degree of legitimacy. This was not the case in the United Kingdom.

The first community foundation in the United Kingdom was the Northern Ireland Voluntary Trust (NIVT), established in 1979 with an initial challenge grant of £500,000 from central government. In an important sense NIVT was seen as a one-off creation in that its geographical remit was too large for it to provide a model for other community foundations, and its role was specifically to provide non-sectarian, apolitical support to voluntary and community groups in tackling Northern Ireland's peculiar, complex, and tragic problems.

The first systematic attempt to introduce community foundations to the United Kingdom came in the late 1980s. Michael Brophy, then director of Charities Aid Foundation (CAF), with financial support from the C. S. Mott Foundation, had visited community foundations in the United States and returned home convinced that community foundations could work and had a role to play in the United Kingdom as well.

The support and championing that such an influential figure as Brophy provided was an important first step in generating understanding of the potential roles of community foundations. To build the legitimacy of community foundations' potentially distinctive roles and their credibility as viable and effective institutions, Brophy drew on the successes of community foundations in the United States, citing their huge assets, their decades of experience, and the spread of the movement across that country. These might be virtually unknown organizations in the United Kingdom, but they had a long pedigree on the west side of the Atlantic and were enormously successful there. The clear message was that the same thing could happen in the United Kingdom.

But Brophy was aware that simply talking about the success of community foundations in the United States would not be enough to establish trust and legitimacy in the United Kingdom. Some indigenous, and preferably quick, wins were necessary to demonstrate the roles, viability, and effectiveness of community foundations. By the mid 1980s Brophy had persuaded the central government to put resources into promoting community foundations. CAF and the government set up the Community Trust Development Unit to support community foundation development. Among other things, the unit advised the Home Office on grants to emerging community foundations and £300,000 over three years was given to emerging community foundations for set up and administrative costs (Humphreys 2002).

In establishing legitimacy, community foundations had to convince potential board members, donors, and others, of their distinctive roles, viability, probity, and effectiveness. Establishing understanding of the potential roles and viability of community foundations was difficult with no examples to point to, other than those in the United States. Observable examples of the roles community foundations could play required money, but endowment building is almost by its very nature a slow process; and it is a particularly difficult process when the notion and advantages of endowment building are not widely understood. How could the process of establishing legitimacy, demonstrating the roles, viability and effectiveness of community foundations be speeded up?

Two important steps were taken in 1991. First, the Association of Community Trusts and Foundations (ACTAF), was formed with a brief to promote and support the roles and development of community foundations. Second, in 1991 the CAF-Mott Endowment Challenge Grant Program was launched with £1 million from each organization (C. S. Mott Foundation 2001). Three embryonic community foundations were each offered a grant of £666,666 on the condition that they raised funds on a two to one basis, thus providing an endowment of £2 million. To qualify for the grant, each foundation had to raise at least £1.33 million by a set deadline. Each met the challenge. Despite these successes, development of community foundations remained relatively slow throughout the 1990s (see table 11.1). In 1991 and 1992 fifteen community foundations with a total endowment of £9 million were formed, making grants of £1.5 million. These figures did not change significantly until the end of the decade.

By 2002, thirty-one community foundations had been established, and another thirty-three were in the planning stages. Total endowment came to £90 million, and grants of £28.1 million were dispersed (Community Foundation Network 2002; see also Humphreys 1999).

Table 11.1   Average Endowment and Grant Making, 1992 to 2000

Year	Number of CFs	Average Assets	Average Grant Making (£)
1992 to 1993	15	865,636	90,251
1993 to 1994	15	1,122,200	109,254
1994 to 1995	15	1,295,262	146,012
1995 to 1996	17	1,819,388	220,537
1996 to 1997	18	1,993,598	544,638
1997 to 1998	22	2,962,361	580,854
1998 to 1999	24	3,052,044	790,250
1999 to 2000	29	3,165,600	758,161

Source: Community Foundation Network (2001).

By 2004, fifty-seven had been formed—thirty-seven fully established and another twenty at varying stages of development—with total endowment at more than £90 million, and more than £52 million in grants dispersed (see http://www.communityfoundation.org.uk).

Building Roles and Establishing Legitimacy: Drivers and Facilitating Factors

Development of community foundations in the United Kingdom falls into two broad phases. In the first, from the early 1980s to the mid- to late 1990s, understanding of and trust in the roles and potential capacities of community foundations was slowly, and painfully, developed. Community foundations remained few in number and generally small in size. In the second phase, from the late 1990s onward, understanding and trust increased and the numbers and size of community foundations grew more quickly. Was this simply a function of the time it takes to establish understanding of roles and build legitimacy of a new institution? Or were there other factors at work providing a more conducive environment for acceptance of community foundation roles and legitimacy?

Fundamental to the first phase was the U.S. example. To gain support, community foundations had to effectively demonstrate their potential role in action to be seen as viable and effective vehicles. A selective picture of the growth and roles of community foundations in the United States—the American Dream—provided that credibility. The strategic use of international visitors to publicize, advocate, and gain access to government circles ensured that this was communicated. If the spectacular results achieved by the small proportion of asset-rich U.S. community foundations could happen there, then surely they would also occur in the United Kingdom.

Closer examination of the history of U.S. community foundations, however, reveals slow and uneven growth over time (rapid growth in only three of eight decades between 1921 and 2001), uneven geographical coverage, and uneven distribution of assets (Hall 1989; Hammack 1989; Seeley et al. 1957/1988). Community foundations took decades to develop and went through low times and good times. They still do not exist in many places and were much slower to develop in some places than others. Very few have the huge assets of the leaders in the field: indeed, those often presented as representatives tend to be notably unrepresentative. They show greater success in areas with an established nonprofit culture and infrastructure, and in both metropolitan (populations of more than 1 million) and wealthy areas. Significantly, in the light of developments in the United Kingdom, they are related to desires for and faith in the efficacy of local self-determination in the context of perceptions of centralizing state and federal government (Hall 1989).

The history of community foundations in the United States suggests that they grow fastest when they have champions, favorable economic and financial market conditions, and favorable tax and legal conditions relative to the alternatives. Running through the U.S. history are two deeper themes. One theme is that of oscillating perceptions of the proper roles and responsibilities of the state and local philanthropy in ensuring the public good. When trust in government is high, and low in nonprofits, growth of community foundations tends to slow, and vice versa (Hall 1989). The second and related theme concerns perceptions of the nature and source of key problems and their solution. Community foundation legitimacy depends on a belief that at least some key problems can be solved at local level (Leat 2004). These conditions shed some light on the two phases of community foundation development in the United Kingdom.

The First Phase: Champions and Challenge Grants

As mentioned earlier, Michael Brophy and Charities Aid Foundation (CAF) first introduced and promoted understanding of the potential roles of community foundations in the United Kingdom, providing initial trust and legitimacy for the concept and encouraging financial support from the government. These factors further increased formal legitimacy and set community foundation start-ups in motion to demonstrate roles. CAF and government support also led to support from other U.K. foundations such as the Baring and the Esmee Fairbairn foundations, thus further demonstrating that community foundations had potentially important roles and were institutions that respected and experienced funders were prepared to trust with their money. CAF and others, including government, were also instrumental in the events leading up to the creation of ACTAF, thus providing community foundations with a dedicated body not only to promote their roles, viability, probity, effectiveness, and legitimacy, but also to provide practical support.

Challenge grants, primarily from the C. S. Mott Foundation, were another important factor in establishing and demonstrating roles and legitimacy building in this phase. Challenge grants have been widely used throughout Europe to stimulate community foundation growth, and some see such grants as a powerful tool to that end. Apart from the obvious attractions of making a donor's money go further, challenge grants also demonstrate the role of community foundations in generating new money, building legitimacy for the community foundation concept, and establishing trust in a particular entity: "If x thinks this organization can be trusted with $1 million then it must be right." In the United Kingdom, challenge grants acted as a spur to local initiatives and a means of ensuring quick wins, further demonstrating the viability of the community foundation role in both local fundraising and grant making. Insofar as challenge grants raised the profile of the notion of community foundations, created tangible demonstrations of roles and viability, and provided reflected trust and legitimacy from those who gave them, they helped not only those who received them but also the wider movement.

The Second Phase: National Branding and Open Policy Windows

The second phase was characterized by much faster growth. This may in part have been simply a function of the time it takes to build understanding of, trust in, and legitimacy for a new institution. In part, it may also have been related to national promotion of community foundations' potential roles and capacities. As community foundations grew slowly during the 1990s, the Association of Community Trusts and Foundations (ACTAF) realized that more promotion was needed.

In 1998, Sir John Weston—recently retired British ambassador to the United Nations and board member of leading companies—was appointed as honorary president. Weston immediately saw that though community foundations were developing public recognition of them was still low. This was related to the variety of names community foundations adopted and to the lack of attention to developing visibility of a national brand, profile, roles, and objectives. A new national promotion campaign was launched in which Weston played a major part, and ACTAF changed its name to Community Foundation Network.

But the suggestion here, drawing on the discussion related to the United States, is that the perceived legitimacy of community foundations also grew because wider environmental factors provided a more favorable policy context that community foundations adroitly exploited.

The history of community foundations in the United States illustrates the way in which community foundation growth was related to, among other things, the political and cultural climate of the day, as well as the diverse and changing purposes of community foundations enabling them to adapt to new issues. That relationship is also apparent in the United Kingdom. The development of community foundations in both countries highlights the way in which presentations of roles and legitimations have to be fit for context—they need to express claims to provide solutions to perceived gaps or problems. Also, policy contexts obviously differ between and within societies, and change over time.

From the early 1980s the Conservative governments emphasized the need to "roll back the state," "encourage responsibility," and so on. There was also emphasis on encouraging more private and corporate giving, but this was largely more exhortatory than practical. Although this policy climate was favorable to more charitable giving and thus broadly helpful, community foundations remained largely unknown bit players in a drama with some very wealthy, marketing skilled stars, that is, the large national nonprofits. The Conservative government policies did, however, indirectly set the scene for demonstrating distinctive roles for community foundations by "actively reducing the powers and financing of local government, as deliberate policy, and while some new streams of funding were being created at national level, local organizations were facing increasing difficulty in obtaining grants from local government" (Humphreys 1999, 40).

At the same time, community foundations began to play into other agendas: the much-vaunted and long-awaited intergenerational transfer of wealth, a desire to capture the wealth of the new, young rich, increasing loss of trust in some large charities due to publicity around misuse of funds and fundraising expenditures, and fears that large charities were too far removed from local concerns and that smaller, more cost-effective local charities were being overlooked. Thus, as in the early years of community foundations in the United States, interest in community foundations came from diverse constituencies for a variety of not necessarily related reasons.

By 2000 the policy climate was more specifically favorable in several respects to recognition of the roles of community foundations. The New Labour government's policies were peppered with notions such as "the Third Way," "social capital," and "civil society." In particular, building social capital and civil society were seen as the new approach to regenerating disadvantaged neighborhoods that had not fully responded to financial investment in physical and economic infrastructure. In this context, revival of local voluntary organizations and activities acquired a new significance, further underlined by New Labour's commitment to devolution and regional government.

Given these definitions of the problems and the solutions, community foundations were able to exploit open policy windows (Kingdon 1995) and present themselves as one means of marrying problems and solutions. Community foundations would not only support local voluntary organizations, build local capacity, increase social capital, encourage local involvement (especially of wealthy donors), but might also be a potential vehicle through which national government might channel its funding into local areas. Community foundations married these various interests in their claim that:

> The special attractions of community foundations in the United Kingdom is seen to be their local focus, at a time when most resources are available for national and international charities and the tradition among better off people to give to those. Another attraction of community foundations is their ability to make grants to very small and new groups. . . . Finally, community foundations' ability to offer a business-like service to donors is seen as a significant advantage. (Humphreys 2002, 20)

From the turn of the new century, community foundations agreed to manage an increasing array of local grant-making programs on behalf of the central government. These included Health Action Zone and Education Action Zone programs, the Children's Fund, a Community Chest initiative (£50 million over three years), and the Big Lottery Fund Fair Share Trust programme (£50 million over ten years).

From the central government viewpoint, community foundations offered a widespread network with access to other financial resources, political impartiality, local knowledge and contact with grassroots organizations, skills in grant assessment and monitoring, and mechanisms for grant making and financial management (Unwin 2000). From the community foundation viewpoint, managing government grant-making programs was consistent with their missions of local benefit and increased their incomes and local and national profiles; it associated them with the distribution of money and, significantly, seats at influential and respected tables. The extent to which community foundations controlled the allocation of resources varied from program to program, each of which had its own accountability structures, priorities, and constraints. In general, however, community foundations were constrained in the size of grants they could give, the geographical area, purposes of grants, and the types of organizations they could give to, as well as by the terms and conditions attached to grants. They were more than post boxes through which government money was challenged, but they were generally not entirely free to allocate resources as they chose. Furthermore, for many, the grants they gave from government monies exceeded those they gave from their private resources.

Community foundations were trusted by government and were seen as playing important roles in their local areas, thus significantly increasing trust in their viability, probity, and effectiveness, as well as increasing their legitimacy as institutions. As Weston said: "When people saw the British government supporting community foundations as vehicles to disburse funds to nonprofit groups it implied safety and transparency. It is a measure of their confidence in us" (quoted in C. S. Mott Foundation 2001, 51).

The potential, at least in terms of raising money, of community foundations was also increased by new tax advantages introduced by the New Labour government. Although these new tax measures benefited all charities, the provision for shares to be given free of capital gains tax and benefiting the donor through income tax relief on their current value was of particular advantage to asset-building community foundations.

Thus 2000 provided a very different environment for the growth of community foundations in the United Kingdom than the early 1980s had. Community foundation development was no longer the project of one organization, but rather a meeting of many minds, for different reasons, with resources, interrelated influential champions, skilled, knowledgeable operators, and a conducive policy environment. Building understanding and acceptance of the distinctive roles of community foundations, however, is still a work in progress.

Future Issues

Community foundations in the United Kingdom face a set of complex interrelated issues.

Donors and Endowment Building

The greatest overall growth in community foundations income has come not from private and individual donors giving to endowment but from government flow-through funds managed on contract. Community foundations in general in the United Kingdom still face significant challenges in communicating to wealthy potential donors the value of endowment building in a context in which foundation formation is not a widespread practice.

The major growth phases of U.S. community foundations have tended to be related to favorable economic and financial market conditions. Community foundations were first introduced into the United Kingdom in buoyant market conditions. But the legitimacy and attractions of contributing to a corpus are not so easily explained when under less buoyant market conditions community foundations themselves admit that their main aim is not to lose money. Even in the United States, where endowment building and the notion of a community foundation are better established, the *Chronicle of Philanthropy* reported in its October 16, 2003, issue that community foundations were showing downward trends in both donations and investment returns.

Donor Control and Public Benefit

One major way in which U.S. community foundations have sought to establish a distinctive niche and encourage giving by wealthy donors is to stress that the community foundation exists to serve donors, giving them a high degree of control over the direction of their funds. By allowing control over grant making to remain in the hands of the donor, emphasis on "advised funds" has the advantage of reducing the community foundation's need for trust and appears to increase donations (Monroe 2001). But too much emphasis on donor-advised funds has disadvantages. They may raise legal issues. They are also relatively expensive to administer, may lead to the community foundation being seen as little more than a club for the wealthy, and, most significant, may conflict with the pursuit of community benefit. They may serve the interests of the wealthy, but whether they serve the full spread of interests of the community comes into question (see, for example, Covington 1994; Ocejo 2001; Carson 2002). Interestingly, in an important sense, community foundations in the United Kingdom now serve central government as donor but it remains to be seen what effect, if any, this will have on other donors.

Colonization by the Central Government

Working as an agent of central government has, as discussed above, raised the profile and income of community foundations, and increased perceptions of their probity, and the viability and effectiveness of their roles. Working on contract to government has raised difficult issues to do with covering the costs of grant making and complying with performance and accountability requirements areas (Community Foundation Network 2002; Leat 2002). But working on contract to government on the current scale may entail other, more significant, risks. Insofar as community foundations become too dependent or simply too closely identified with government, they may be seen more as an offshoot than an alternative to government. If this deters donors from giving, the foundations' relationship with government could become a self-fulfilling prophecy. In this situation, community foundations may gain in legitimacy (as agents of government) but lose both trust and legitimacy in their roles as independent institutions.

Relationships with Local Government

The legitimacy of community foundation roles depends, in important ways, on perceptions of roles and responsibilities of alternative vehicles for pursuit of the public good. Although in many respects trust in the role and capacity of government is low in the United Kingdom today, arguably there still is a deeply rooted reluctance to let go of the idea that it is government's role to provide. Furthermore, though central government broadly supports the development of community foundations, the reactions of local governments are more variable.

In theory, community foundations and local governments share the same mission and roles: the pursuit of local public good. In the largely U.S.-dominated literature, relationships between community foundations and local governments are rarely discussed (Berresford 1989). In the United Kingdom, local government may be represented on the community foundation board, and community foundation literature talks about working across all sectors. In reality, however, many community foundations admit that relationships with local government range from nonexistent to friendly. The use of community foundations as central government's preferred distribution vehicle into local areas has clearly not escaped the notice of local governments. Addressing the relationship between community foundations and local government remains a significant challenge, raising important issues about the legitimacy and role of "private legislatures" in a democracy, as well as practical issues about how to relate.

References

Berresford, Susan. 1989. "Collaboration: Models, Benefits and Tensions." In *An Agile Servant: Community Leadership by Community Foundations,* edited by Richard Magat. Washington, D.C.: The Council on Foundations.

Brilliant, Eleanor. 2000. *Private Charity and Public Inquiry: A History of the Filer and Peterson Commissions.* Bloomington: Indiana University Press.

Carson, Emmett. 2002. "A Crisis of Identity for Community Foundations." In *The State of Philanthropy 2002,* edited by Richard Cohen. Washington, D.C.: National Committee for Responsive Philanthropy.

Community Foundation Network. 2001. "U.K. Community Foundation Network Facts and Figures: 1992–2000." Available at: http://www.communityfoundations.org.uk.

———. 2002. *Annual Report 2002.* London: Community Foundation Network.

Covington, Sally. 1994. *Community Foundations and Citizen Empowerment: Limited Support for Democratic Renewal.* Washington, D.C.: National Committee for Responsive Philanthropy.

DiMaggio, Paul. 1992. "Nadel's Paradox revisited: Relational and cultural aspects of organizational structure." In *Networks and Organizations: Structure, Form and Action,* edited by N. Nohria and R. G. Eccles. Boston, Mass.: Harvard Business School Press.

Feurt, Suzanne. 1999. "International Perspective: Models, Experience and Best Practice." In *Community Foundations in Civil Society,* edited by Bertelsmann Foundation. Gütersloh, Germany: Bertelsmann Foundation Publishers.

Feurt, Suzanne, and Elinor Sacks. 2001. "An International Perspective on the History, Development and Characteristics of Community Foundations." In *Building Philanthropic and Social Capital: The Work of Community Foundations,* edited by Peter Walkenhorst. Gütersloh, Germany: Bertelsmann Foundation Publishers.

Hall, Peter Dobkin. 1989. "The Community Foundation in America 1914–1987." In *Philanthropic Giving Studies in Varieties and Goals,* edited by R. Magat. Oxford: Oxford University Press.

Hammack, David, C. 1989. "Community Foundations: The Delicate Question of Purpose." In *Making the Nonprofit Sector in the United States,* edited by David C. Hammack. Bloomington: Indiana University Press.

Humphreys, Gaynor. 1999. "The Development of Community Foundations in the United Kingdom." In *Community Foundations in Civil Society,* edited by the Bertelsmann Foundation. Gütersloh, Germany: Bertelsmann Foundation Publishers.

———. 2002. "Community Foundation Network." In *Philanthropy in a Global Community,* vol. 2: *Case Studies of Organizations Supporting Community Foundations,* edited by Diana Leat. Brussels: WINGS, Council on Foundations and Community Foundations of Canada.

Kingdon, John W. 1995. *Agendas Alternatives and Public Policies.* New York: HarperCollins.

Leat, Diana. 1992. *Trusts in Transition: The Policy and Practice of Grant-Giving Trusts.* York: Joseph Rowntree Foundation.

———. 2002. *The Price of Giving,* London: Community Foundation Network.

———. 2004. *The Development of Community Foundations in Australia, Recreating the American Dream.* Brisbane: Queensland University of Technology.

Monroe, Helen. 2001. "Community Foundation Asset Development." In *Building Philanthropic and Social Capital: The Work of Community Foundations,* edited by Peter Walkenhorst. Gütersloh, Germany: Bertelsmann Foundation Publishers.

C. S. Mott Foundation. 2001. *Sowing the Seeds of Local Philanthropy. Two Decades in the Field of Community Foundations.* Flint, Michigan: Charles Stewart Mott Foundation.

Ocejo, Almudena. 2001. "Catalyzing Community Based Philanthropy." *Community Foundation Research.* Washington, D.C.: National Committee for Responsible Philanthropy.

Sacks, Elinor. 2000. *The Growth of Community Foundations Around the World: An Examination of the Vitality of the Community Foundation Movement.* Washington, D.C.: Council on Foundations.

Salamon, Lester M., ed. 2002. *The Tools of Government. A Guide to the New Governance.* New York: Oxford University Press.

Seeley, John R., et al. 1957/1988. "Community Chest." In *Making the Nonprofit Sector in the United States,* edited by David C. Hammack. Bloomington: Indiana University Press.

Troyer, Thomas A. 2000. *The 1969 Private Foundation Law: Historical Perspectives on Its Origins and Underpinnings.* Washington, D.C.: Council on Foundations.

Unwin, Julia. 2000. *Tackling Multiple Disadvantage: The Role of Community Foundations.* London: Community Foundation Network.

Walkenhorst, Peter. 2001. "Introduction." In *Building Philanthropic and Social Capital: The Work of Community Foundations,* edited by Peter Walkenhorst. Gütersloh, Germany: Bertelsmann Foundation Publishers.

WINGS-CF. 2003. *Global Status Report.* Brussels: Worldwide Initiatives for Grantmaker Support. Available at: http://www.wingsweb.org.

Part IV

Conclusion

In Search of Legitimacy: Similarities and Differences Between the Continents

Mattei Dogan

Legitimacy is a belief, not a legal prescription that can be implemented by a ruler's decree. Foundations flourish only in democratic regimes, where they are expressions of the civil society. The legitimacy of philanthropic foundations involves the belief that they are the most appropriate institutions to fill certain social functions in the sense that they are considered more efficient and more sensitive to the needs of the society than the state bureaucracy or the liberal market.

Comparing the functions of foundations on both sides of the Atlantic is not an easy task. The difficulties come from the fact that we have on one side only one country under study, and on the other thirty extremely diverse countries differing in size, standard of living, historical heritages, and national legislations. We are facing, in fact, two kinds of comparisons: one, within Europe, the other across the Atlantic.

It is possible, however, to underline significant analogies between the two continents. On both we notice a process of secularization over the last century. In the more distant past, most foundations were built on religious foundations because some believed that by stripping themselves of their wealth they would earn or deserve divine mercy and pardon. Such a philosophical conception had enormous beneficial consequences for the underprivileged because it alleviated their suffering. In Europe this religious motivation generated numerous institutions such as hospices, orphanages, and hospitals that received all kinds of people regardless of confessional affiliation, such as those forgotten by the state and the market. One example among many is that, of the twenty most important hospitals in Paris today, nineteen were created long ago as private religious foundations, some of them by wealthy and pious widows. Today all are financed by the government.

A proof that contemporary pluralist democracies cannot function properly without multiple intermediary private organizations is the fact that in almost all European democracies the state directly subventions philanthropic associations, and even foundations. In France, for example, it was noticed on the occasion of the centenary anniversary of the 1901 law concerning the freedom of associations that the state had, in the previous year, furnished about 60 percent of the total budget of the 800,000 recognized associations—from taxpayer revenue. These associations ensure public service missions for the state and in place of the state. In this massive subvention is irrefutable proof that the state needs intermediate organizations, particularly the philanthropic sector. Certainly the state prefers to help associations rather than foundations, which have their own endowments and thus do not depend on the state. At the same time, the state helps both by allowing tax reductions.

The number of foundations is an indispensable dimension in evaluating their role. It is not a complete one, however, even if the calculation is made by millions of inhabitants (ignoring the size of the countries). The number of foundations and their sizes and scopes vary enormously within Europe. To explain this a variety of factors must be taken into account, two of which being fiscal legislation and, particularly, the threshold for building a foundation. The minimal capital, to take one example, is much higher in France than in most other European countries and the United States. To take another, there is at least one fiscal foundation paradise. The smallest country in Europe, Liechtenstein has as many family foundations—30,000—as it does families. Helmut Anheier and Siobhan Daly have explored this statistical European universe and offer meaningful explanations (see chapter 8 in this volume).

Why do foundations play a more important role in the United States than in Europe? The first explanation that comes to mind is the space that the state allots to the civil society, the place of the so-called welfare state. A basic difference between the United States and Europe is in the amount of the gross national product collected and redistributed by the state. Excluding the military budget, which, for geopolitical reasons, is devolved to the "inadvertent empire" the proportion of the GNP controlled by the state is, in Europe, twice as high as it is in the

United States. Within Europe it varies from more than half in the Scandinavian countries and France to about one-third in Ireland and Greece. The stronger role of the state in Europe can be explained by the fact that all European countries (with the exception of Switzerland and Luxembourg, which are fiscal shelters, even for American citizens) have a strong socialist party. The United States, in fact, is the only advanced democracy without one. "Why is there no socialism in the United States?" is a question first asked in 1906 by the German sociologist Werner Sombart. Dozens of historians and sociologists have since tried to answer the question, but none has investigated the relationship between such an absence and the simultaneous presence of a strong third sector. Clearly, socialist leaders and their followers are not enthusiastic to see "pieces of the state" falling into private hands, but do not oppose the current legislation and practice. Such a hostility would be a serious mistake because it would alienate the modal voter.

The second important explanation arises from the tortured twentieth century in Europe. We should not forget that during the interbellum period, Europe was the cemetery of seventeen democracies: Italy in 1922, Portugal in 1926, eleven others between 1926 and 1938, and four more between 1939 and 1941. The dictatorial or totalitarian regimes had suppressed most foundations or forced them into inactivity, therefore impoverishing them. Confiscation, loss of propriety, capital depletion, and war damages destroyed most existing foundations.

A third explanation is the troubled rivalry between the church and the state, particularly in the Catholic countries. At a certain époque, most foundations were tied to ecclesiastical institutions. Long before the 1789 revolution, Turgot condemned what he called la main morte, the wealth accumulated by the church. In 1789, revolutionary extremists confiscated ecclesiastical propriety. In 1905, the French Republic, in one of its most important laws, proclaimed the strict separation of the church from the state. In most Catholic countries, one of society's main cleavages separates, the traditionalists, on one side, from the anticlericals, on the other. In Spain after the reign of Franco and the cardinal Segura, anticlericalism became virulent. In Italy, the political cleavages are deeply embedded in religious attitudes. In Austria, a country divided into the Catholic and the Social Democrat camps, private foundations mean Catholic foundations, which created Catholic schools, hospitals, libraries, cemeteries, and banks; this situation is unacceptable to the other half of the population, which for this reason, has been reluctant to favor philanthropic foundations.

A fourth explanation is outdated legislation. France, a country that pretends to be a model of democracy, maintains an anachronic civil code elaborated two centuries ago by Napoleon. This code inhibits foundations by forbidding a potential donor to freely dispose of his or her patrimony on the basis of the réserve héréditaire (a significant part of the proprieties of any French citizen, which is reserved for biological heirs, legitimate or illegitimate). The Napoleonic code has been exported to several European countries. In Britain, the dust of some legislation is proverbial, with unfavorable consequences on foundations. In Belgium foundations were legally recognized only in 1921. In Spain, the wait was longer, not until 1978 did its constitution explicitly acknowledge the right to create foundations.

A fifth explanation is the educational system, a centralized and uniform institution in Europe and diversified into hierarchical strata in the United States. The mission of foundations cannot be the same in a country where mass education, scientific research, and the promotion of the arts are financed almost entirely by the state, and in one where a significant part of these domains are financed privately. In many European countries, the entire educational system, at the three levels (primary, secondary and college), is financed by the state, which allocates about a fifth of its national budget to the ministry of education, the largest bureaucracy in many European countries. In most of Europe, teachers and professors are civil servants with tenure, with the exception of a small minority teaching in private religious schools.

In advanced democracies, there are no homogenous majorities, only pluralities of minorities of various sizes and nature in terms of social stratification and of ethnic, religious, racial, and generational cleavages. A law adopted in democracies is theoretically a decision taken by a majority, but the majority often neglects certain segments of the population, and consequently its action may be unfair to specific groups. Because the state makes laws for and by majorities, foundations tend to see the possibility of protecting certain minority groups. This aspect is also discussed in this volume, particularly by Kenneth Prewitt in chapter 2, who calls it pluralism. When we consider vertical redistribution of wealth by foundations, we in fact describe a bird's-eye view. In reality, most foundations, the small more so than the large, target specific domains: orphans, the blind, the deaf, protection of young girls, the elderly, children, minorities, and hundreds of others. The motivation to donate funds arises from the fact the state does not and cannot take care of such groups. Here we have a deep source of legitimacy because it is the natural role of the civil society, not the state or the market, to protect the vulnerable. Together they represent a significant proportion of the society. Once again, advanced democracy flourishes in a pluralist society made up of such minorities. Because foundations enjoy a great deal of latitude they can easily focus their activities on helping groups passed over, for whatever reason, by the political process. All contributors to this volume refer, in some way or another, to these groups. Foundations may even be able, in this respect, to exercise a kind of reverse discrimination. This source of legitimacy is important on both continents, even if foundations have to function in different contexts.

The legitimacy of foundations can also be demonstrated by a deliberate absurd hypothesis as it is played in game theory: suppose that a revolutionary movement takes the power in an imaginary country and confiscates the endowments of all foundations. In the first year, the new leaders turn the funds over to the bottom third of the population, offering the equivalent of one month of average income. In the second year, however, there would be nothing left to redistribute, and the new leaders would realize that they had killed the goose that laid the golden egg. Fictitious scenario? It has already happened several times: in France in the 1790s, in Russia in 1918, in Nazi Germany in the 1930s, and in the eastern European countries in the mid-1940s. Golden eggs can be laid only by perennial philanthropic foundations thanks to their endowments.

In discussing legitimacy, one needs to look at what foundations have effectively achieved rather than at what they have not been able to accomplish. As Mark Dowie argued, "those empowered to make grants should not assume that they have the wisdom to solve serious problems simply because they control the money" (2001). The history of American and European foundations shows that many of them have indeed had not only the money, but also the wisdom, the perspicacity, and the will to solve problems, or at least to correct dysfunctions. On the American side, a long series of examples has been given, many of them in this volume. On the European side, Rupert Graf Strachwitz gives in chapter 9 numerous illustrative examples. Dozens more could be given.

Vertical Generosity and Horizontal Redistribution

A distinction is needed, however, between what might be called vertical and horizontal redistributions of the national income. By such a distinction we put our finger on one of the most significant differences between the role foundations play on the two continents. From a sociological retrospective view, the horizontal elitist redistribution of wealth may appear, in a sense, as important as the vertical.

To grasp the importance of this, let us look at the history of scientific progress over the last century. The Carnegie, Rockefeller, and Ford period is well known, thanks to a variety of testimonies, in particular those drafted by Warren Weaver and Raymond Fosdick, both competent experts and long-time officers of those foundations. We do not, unfortunately, have an equivalent work for foundations in Europe, for the very simple reason that nothing similar has happened on that side of the Atlantic. Only in earlier centuries can we find any seemingly horizontal redistribution in Europe, in the Renaissance, in the courts of Empress Catherine of Russia and of Queen Christina of Sweden, but in these cases the move was directed more toward the arts than the sciences.

Weaver asked noteworthy scientists to evaluate, each in his own specialty, the achievements and impacts that foundations have had in scientific research in the United States. Contributors include Nobel prize winners in biology, physics, chemistry, biochemistry, medicine, public health, demography, economics, and education. In reading these testimonies, one is amazed by the premonitory feeling, by the wise and courageous decisions some grand foundations took to develop science in all domains. What is astonishing, retrospectively, is the capacity of these foundations to invest money in strategic places and at the right moments. Neither the state nor the market would have been capable of investing money for projects that were not sure to succeed. The amount of money given by these endowed foundations appears minimal in relation to that awarded by the entire philanthropic sector. We are taken aback today at how it was possible, with so little money to engender so much scientific growth. If the United States is today the most powerful nation in the world in so many domains, it is in part attributable to a few visionary owners of capital, eminent managers who invested adequate funding in the right domains at the right times. The United States has built monuments to celebrate some of its founding fathers, but has not done so to celebrate these few visionary entrepreneurs who contributed to American preeminence. The amounts invested a half a century ago in science are today drops in the bucket of America's economic power today. This achievement is, in my opinion as an outsider, the greatest justification for the tax deductions granted to U.S. foundations. In the gallery of the greatest men in American history, Andrew Carnegie has an honorable place for having helped the development of science and for modernizing the educational system. The corresponding figure in Germany would be Wilhelm von Humboldt, a remarkable scholar who succeeded in modernizing the German university and educational system. Without his reforms there would perhaps not have been, two generations later, a powerful Bismarck Empire. Of course, these foundations have at the same time helped the underprivileged strata of American society. But the long-term merit stems mostly from the horizontal, even elitist, redistribution.

The concept of horizontal redistribution implies a long causal chain: the investment in science has favored technological development, with decisive impacts on economic growth, and finally improved the standard of living of the underprivileged. Horizontal redistribution, in the case of foundations, was based on a premonitory intuition that sciences were the resources for tomorrow's growth. The choices that owners of capital and perspicacious trustees and officers of foundations made stemmed from this. It is unlikely that the federal government could have done the same. One could even say, without exaggeration, that without the help from its great private foundations, the United States would not be where it is today.

At the height of the Cold War, in the 1970s, the federal government in Washington began increasing grants for scientific research and technological development and is now the primary financer of scientific and technological progress, even though the major American foundations continue to invest.

In the domain of the arts, Europe has of course accumulated a vast store of priceless treasures over the centuries. But these are inherited, not the result of any philanthropic generosity. If we consider the contemporary situation, we find again, in the arts as in the sciences, that the philanthropic horizontal transfer really occurs only on the west side of the Atlantic. All museums in the United States, save the National Gallery and similar institutions in Washington, have been built and are financed by private foundations. In Europe, on the contrary and with very few exceptions, museums function only with the taxpayer's money. The same is true for most libraries, old palaces, castles, and historic archives. The management of such cultural institutions is very costly. Take, for example, the opera in Vienna and in Moscow, both of which are a heavy financial burden for those respective citizens. It is a well-known phenomenon that these cultural institutions are frequented far less frequently by the masses than by the well-to-do, even if they are source of pride for everyone. In financial terms, then, this is largely a down-up transfer of taxpayer money. The alternative to this paradoxical vertical transfer upward is either recourse to endowed philanthropic foundations or national decadence.

Kenneth Prewitt, in his analysis of the reasons why foundations are accepted by a large majority of the American public in his chapter, emphasizes the liberal economy much more than the four other arguments legitimizing foundations—grants to the poor and the powerless, pluralism, efficiency, and promoting social change. His arguments could, with some adaptations, be transplanted to Europe, except that many Europeans would prefer to replace the word liberal with the word capitalist in describing the contemporary economy. In fact, most founders of great foundations were, in the literal sense of the word, capitalists, that is, the owners of means of production. The problem is perhaps largely semantic: liberal sounds better to some social scientists, but most Europeans are not afraid to use the word capitalist in their daily.

What is clearly legitimate today in both Europe and the United States is the free market because, contrary to earlier belief, it is considered as more efficient than a statist economy. In a free market, however, it is unavoidable that some, not many, accumulate enormous capital. If this is returned wisely through private foundations to society, philanthropic foundations can achieve legitimacy by recycling private fortunes in service of the public good.

That most founders of foundations were not inheritors but instead builders is an additional reason to legitimize the institutions. Such builders have served the society twice: first by creating enterprises, thus creating employment for many, and second by building foundations devoted to the public interest. Capitalists do not, after all, take their accumulated wealth with them. Across Europe, the palaces and castles built by kings and princes are today the proprieties of the public. Rather than leaving their wealth to their children, some capitalists build philanthropic foundations, and such a generosity contributes to nourish the legitimacy of foundations.

Today, in almost all democracies, except perhaps the Scandinavian, political institutions are mistrusted by a large segment of the population (see Dogan 2005; Lipset and Schneider 1987; Nye, Zelikov, and King 1997; Sztompka 1998). One of the main preoccupations in the political literature is this lack of confidence in government institutions, and particularly in a certain kind of politician who, in Weberian vocabulary, lives more from politics than for politics. Who searches for legitimacy more eagerly today, philanthropic foundations or government institutions?

I would go so far as to advocate that it would be difficult today to conceive of postindustrial democracy—which, as we all know very well, is full of dysfunctions—without these foundations. They play, after all, several critical roles in responding to the needs of the pluralist society, in taking care of various groups neglected by the market, and in supporting meritocracy in a society that prides itself on equality.

The moment has arrived for a new inventory of achievements accomplished by foundations, in the line of the inventories made half a century ago by Raymond Fosdick (1952), George Corner (1964), and Warren Weaver (1967) and to include this time the European experience. Such a volume would demonstrate that the philanthropic foundation is an integral component of any advanced postindustrial democracy.

References

Dogan, Mattei, ed. 2005. *Political Mistrust and the Discrediting of Politicians.* Boston: Leiden, Brill.

Dowie, Mark 2001. *American Foundations: An Investigative History.* Cambridge, Mass.: MIT Press.

Fosdick, Raymond B. 1952. *The Story of the Rockefeller Foundation.* New York: Harper and Brothers.

Lipset, Seymour M., and William Schneider. 1987. *The Confidence Gap.* Baltimore, Md.: Johns Hopkins University Press.

Nye, Joseph S., Philip D. Zelikov, and David C. King, eds. 1997. *Why People don't Trust Government.* Cambridge, Mass.: Harvard University Press.

Sztompka, Piotr. 1998. *Trust, Distrust and the Paradox of Democracy.* Berlin: Wissenschaftszentrum Berlin für Sozialforschung gGmbH.

Weaver, Warren. 1967. *U.S. Philanthropic Foundations: Their History, Structure, Management and Record.* New York: Harper and Row.

Index

Boldface numbers refer to figures and tables.

A. P. Moeller-Maersk, 243, 248
Aaron Diamond Foundation, 36
Abbe, E., 221
abortion, 16
academia, 50–51
Academy for the Advancement of Science, 85
accountability: of community foundations, 156–58; current practices, 104–10; definition of, 17; in Europe, 211–12; future of, 110; justifications for, 17–18, 41, 99–101; and legitimacy, 4, 110–13; and relationship with government, 113–18; scope of, 42–44; types of, 102–4
accrediting system, 110
ACTAF (Association of Community Trusts and Foundations), 259, 262–63
Adloff, F., 228, 232
administrative expenses, 108–9
Adriano Olivetti Foundation, 185
adversarial relationship, with government, 116–17
advised funds, 267
advocacy, 115, 129
African Americans, 63, 71, 85n18
Agard, K., 157
The Agile Servant (Magat), 158
Ahn, C., 119n5
alternative funds, 104
American Education Society, 84n14
American Federation of Labor, 68–69
American Foundations and Their Fields (American Foundations Information Service), 88n39
American Foundations (Harrison and Andrews), 60
American Foundations Information Service, 83n6, 88n39
American Missionary Association, 84n15

Anderson, E., 71
Andrews, F., **55,** 60, 74–75, 83n6, 84n15, 87n32, 88n36
Anheier, H., 8, 11, 194, 274
Anna Jeanes Fund, 85n18
Annenberg, W., 138
Annenberg Foundation, 35, 141
annual reports, 87n31, 159
anti-apartheid movement, 16
anticlericalism, 275
arrogance, 138–39
the arts: in Germany, 223–26, 227, 228, 229; grants to (in U.S.), 126, **127, 128**; in U.S. vs. Europe, 279–80
assets: community foundations, 154–55; of European foundations, 9, 10; of U.S. foundations, 9, 10, 54–58, **61, 62,** 154–55
Association of Community Trusts and Foundations (ACTAF), 259, 262–63
associations, 9, 179, 194
Austrian foundations: innovation of, 207; religious issues, 275; role of, 204
autonomy, 45, 117–18, 133

Baker, N., 87n30
banking foundations, in Italy, 14, 189
banking industry, 241, 258
Baptist Foundation of Texas, 76, 77–78, 82n1
Baptists, 76–78, 84n15
Baring Foundation, 262
Baylor University, 64, 77
Belgian foundations, **8,** 203, 206
beneficiary designations, 170n6
bequests, 63, 170n6
Berger, G., 186
Bertelsmann Foundation, 119n1, 250
Big Lottery Fund, 253, 265
Bilateral Committee on Social and Political Sciences (CoSPoS), 185, 187

Bill and Melinda Gates Foundation, 28, 30, 38, 129, 141
blacks, 63, 71, 85*n*18
boards of directors, 159, 239–40
Bork, R., 119*n*4
Bourgeois, F., 225
Boy Scouts, 68
Braudel, F., 186, 187
Breitneicher, J., 203–4
Britain. *See* United Kingdom, foundations in
British National Trust, 227
Brophy, M., 258–59, 261
Brown Foundation, 60
Brown University, 64
Brukenthal, S. von, 225
Buhl Foundation, 59
Bundy, M., 184

C. S. Mott Foundation, 22, 78, 155, 258, 259, 262
CAF (Charities Aid Foundation), 258, 259, 261
Caglioti, V., 186
California foundations, 59–60, 77, 78
Callaway Foundation, 78
Cal Tech, 86*n*26
capital, 247, 249
capitalism, 51
capitalists, 280
Carlsberg, 245, 248
Carl Zeiss, 221, 245, 248
Carnegie, A., 65–66, 76
Carnegie Corporation of New York, 66
Carnegie Endowment for International Peace, 66
Carnegie Foundation: causes supported by, 58, 70; Foundation Center support, 74; historical background, 65–66; libraries, 35, 86*n*24; NY headquarters, 76; research contributions, 72–73; on top twenty-five list, 28
Carnegie Foundation for the Advancement of Teaching, 66, 68, 71
Carnegie Institution of Pittsburgh, 66, 70
Carnegie Institution of Washington D.C., 66, 68
Carnegie Tech, 86*n*26
Carrie J. Loose Fund, 77

Casse di Risparmio, 189
Castle Foundation, 59
Catholic Church, 64, 77, 78, 179, 275
Cavazza, F., 186
CCT (Chicago Community Trust), 59, 154, 164–65, 172*n*28
Census, **61, 62**
Centre College, 86*n*25
certification standards, community foundations, 156
challenge grants, 262
change, social, 35–39, 187–90, 202–4, **208,** 253
charitable contributions, by individuals vs. foundations, 125. *See also* individual donors and gifts
charitable tax deduction, 28, 131–32, 151
charitable trusts, 63, 75–76, 170*n*6
charities, public. *See* community foundations
Charities Aid Foundation (CAF), 258, 259, 261
charity, Rockefeller on, 29
charters, 68, 79, 85*n*20, 239
Chicago, study of philanthropic and public human service funders, 159, 163–65
Chicago Community Trust (CCT), 59, 154, 164–65, 172*n*28
Children's Fund of Michigan, 59
Children's Fund (U.K.), 265
Christian Education and Ministerial Relief of the Presbyterian Church, 76
Christian Education Handbook (Wickey and Anderson), 77
Christian Foundation, 77
Chronicle of Philanthropy, 266
civic organizations, 52
civil law, 194
civil society, 228, 232–33, 273
Clark, E., 83*n*6
Clark University, 65
Cleveland Foundation, 59, 73, 87*n*32, 153–54
Cleveland Trust Company, 73
Clontz, B., 152
Clotfelter, C., 33
cognitive legitimacy, 245–47, 249
Cohen, M., 178
collectivism, 50

colleges and universities. *See* higher education

Colombo, J., 6

Colorado, foundations in, 77

Columbia University, 64, 65, 67, 86*n*26

Columbus Foundation, 170*n*11

common law, 9, 194

Commonwealth Fund, 66, 73, 87*n*29

Communities Foundation of Texas, 88*n*37

Community Chest, 265

community colleges, 35

Community Foundation Network, 263

community foundations: accountability, 156–58; assets of, 154–55; boards of directors, 159; challenges, 255–56; in Chicago, 165; and community needs, 162–63; and DAFs, 169; definition of, 150, 252; donations, 160; donor control, 266–67; features of, **152**; fundraising efforts, 165; and government spending cuts, 169; grant-making process, 166–68; grant sources, 160, **161**; growth of, 154–55, 252, 261; history of, 73, 153–55; legitimacy of, 155–61, 165, 168–69; models of, 154; operational issues, 166; vs. private foundations, 151, **152**; private label gift funds, 153; public information, 158–59; and public policy awareness, 163–65; resources, 160–61; role of, 73, 155; staff, 159; tax advantages, 151; turnover in funded agencies, 167

community foundations, in United Kingdom: advantages of vs. traditional foundations, 257; challenge grants, 262; endowment and grant-making, 256, **260,** 265, 266; future issues, 266–68; number of (2002–04), 252, 259–60; origins of, 258–60; phases of development, 260–66; policy issues, 263, 264; social and political context, 252–57; U.S. influence over, 258–59, 260

Community Trust Development Unit, 259

complementary relationship, with government, 115–16, 198–99, **208,** 209

compliance, 143

Comstock, A., 85*n*20

Congregationalists, 77, 84*n*14

Congress: accountability, 42, 108–9; charters, 68, 79, 85*n*20; hearings on tax-exempt status of nonprofits, 6

Conservative Party (U.K.), 263

conservatives: criticisms of foundations, 50, 119*n*4, 139; NCRP's analysis of grants by, 140; redistribution, 37; on role of government, 137; Scaife Foundation, 16

Cooper Union, 70

Cornell University, 63, 86*n*26

Corner, G., 281

corporate foundations: boards of directors, 159; in Chicago, 165; and community needs, 162–63; in France, 230; in Germany, 230; grant-making process, 167–68; grant sources, 160, **161**; growth in U.S., 155; public information, 158–59; and public policy awareness, 163–65; resources, 160–61; staff, 159; turnover in funded agencies, 167. *See also* industrial foundations

corporate model, of welfare state, 211

corporations: German universities, 219; governance, 240–42, 246; as legal form for foundations, 9; performance measures, 242–45; role in U.K., 255

corporatist model, of German foundations, 232

corrupt practices, 202

CoSPoS (Bilateral Committee on Social and Political Sciences), 185, 187

cost-effectiveness, 34–35

Council on Foundations, 42, 81, 153

Cox Committee, 42

cross-national comparisons, 7–12

crowding-out hypothesis, 114

culture: definition of, 223; preservation of, 200, **208**

Curti, M., 88*n*35

Czech Republic, role of foundations in, 201, 204

DAFs (donor advised funds), 150, 153, 169

Dallas Foundation, 78

Daly, S., 274

dance companies, 52

Danforth Foundation, 59, 77, 87*n*29
Daniels Foundation, 88*n*37
data sources and limitations: bias in,
    58–59; cross-national comparison
    issues, 7; early, 58–59; European
    countries, 192, 193; redistribution,
    124, 125–26, 145, 147
democracy, 231, 273, 275, 276,
    280–81
democratic theory, of accountability,
    102
Denmark: industrial foundations in,
    236, 237–38, 243–45, 246, 248; role
    of foundations in, 204
de Rance Foundation, 78
devolution, 155
Diamond Foundation, 36
Diana, Princess of Wales Memorial
    Fund, 253
disclaimers, 72
discrimination, 24
diversification, 241, 242
diversity, 24, 50, 204–5, **208,** 209,
    276–77
Doheny Foundation, 78
donor advised funds (DAFs), 150, 153,
    169
donors: control of, 266–67; intent of,
    20–21, 119*n*4; motivations of, 134,
    138; paternalism and arrogance of,
    138–39
donors' forums, 142
Dowie, M., 138, 277
Drury College, 86*n*25
Duke, J., 76
Duke Endowment for the Carolinas, 59,
    60, 76
Duke University, 67, 86*n*26
Dulwich College, 225
Durkheim, E., 183
Dutch foundations: associations vs.,
    194; fear of "going public," 212;
    industrial foundations, 245; number
    of, **8**; role of, 204

eastern Europe, 199, 202
economic theory, 82–83*n*4, 240–41, 242
education: for African Americans, 63,
    71; Carnegie Foundation's support of,
    70; early U.S. foundations' support of,

63; in Europe, 276; grants (U.S.), 126,
    127, 128. *See also* higher education
Education Action Zone, 265
EFC (European Foundation Centre), 211
effectiveness, 119*n*7, 137–38
Eisenberg, P., 119*n*5
El Pomar Foundation, 59, 77
Emory University, 64
employees, 159
Encyclopédie, 51, 180
endowments: community foundations,
    151, 255, 256, **260,** 266; industrial
    foundations, 238, 239; and legiti-
    macy, 4; in U.K., 256, **260,** 266
England. *See* United Kingdom, founda-
    tions in
Enlightenment, 180
entrepreneurship, 274
environmental issues, 37, **127, 128**
equity-assets ratio, 244–45
Esmee Fairbairn Foundation, 262
estate taxes, 100, 111, 136
Estonia, foundations in, 198
EUROPEAID, 212
European Foundation Centre (EFC), 211
European foundations: accountability,
    211–12; asset requirements, 9, 10;
    churches' role in, 178; data sources,
    192, 193; definition of, 194–97, 217;
    within EU, 212–13; history of, 51,
    179–87; legitimacy of, 6, 14–15,
    188–90, 213, 218–19, 231–32; vs.
    NGOs, 196; vs. nonprofits, 196; num-
    ber of, **8**; research issues, 192–93;
    roles of, 197–211, 217–18, 274–76;
    and social change, 187–90; trans-
    parency, 211–12; types of, 195–96; vs.
    U.S., 7–12, 273–77. *See also* industrial
    foundations
European nonprofits, 9, 196
European Union (EU), 212–13
evaluation, of grantees, 168
excess business holding provisions,
    241–42, 249
expertise, and innovation, 206

fairness, 112
Falk Foundation, 59
family foundations, 160. *See also* founda-
    tions, private

fellowships, 72
Fidelity Investments, 153, 170*n*8
Filer Commission, 81
Finland, foundations in, 200
Fleishman, J., 241–42
flexibility, 50
Flexner, A., 72
Ford, H., 76
Ford Foundation: causes supported by,
29; European programs, 184–85, 186;
Foundation Center support, 75;
founder's intentions, 20–21; Green
Revolution, 29–30; international
studies, 35; NY headquarters, 76;
size of, 29; targeted groups for grant
making, 126, 129; on top twenty-five
list, 28
Fosdick, R., 278, 281
Foundation Center: assets of foundations, 56, **61, 62**; establishment of,
74–75, 87*n*32; expansion of, 81; foundation categories, 171*n*15; number of
foundations, **55**; redistribution analysis, 125, 126; tax return data, 7
Foundation Directory, 59, 60, 75, 76, 83*n*7
foundation-owned companies. *See*
industrial foundations
foundations, private: achievements,
42–43, 50, 281; assets, 9, 10, 54–58,
61, 62, 154–55; boards of directors,
159; causes, 31–33, 49–50, 58, 60;
characteristics of, 30, 194–95; in
Chicago, 165; vs. community foundations, 151, **152**; and community
needs, 162–63; cost-effectiveness,
34–35; criticisms, 44–45, 50–51,
68–73, 80, 85*n*22, 138–40; cross-
national comparisons, 7–12, 273–77;
data sources, 58; definitions of, 10,
49, 194–97, 217, 231; donors' motivations, 134; effectiveness of, 119*n*7,
137–38; features of, **152**; future
research, 281; growth in U.S., 54–62,
155; issues, 230; legacy issues, 177–78;
legal forms for, 9–10; lists of, 73–75;
number in U.S. vs. Europe, 8–9; professional networks of, 103–4; public
information, 158–59; and public policy awareness, 163–65; regional distribution analysis, 58–62, 75–79;

relationship with government,
113–18; resources, 160–61; roles of,
21–24, 31–39, 113–18, 274–76; short
term vs. long term impact, 135–37;
staff, 159; turnover in funded agencies, 167. *See also* European foundations; *specific entries*
France: corporate foundations, 230;
GNP controlled by state, 275; government funding of foundations, 274;
history of foundations, 179, 183; hospital foundations, 10; innovation of
foundations, 206; legislation, 276;
number of foundations in, **8**; regulation, 11; role of foundations, 184,
205; separation of church and state,
273–74, 275; U.S. foundations in,
184–86
Franke, G., 244
Frankfurt University, 222
Franklin Fund, 70
free market economies, 280
Fremont-Smith, M., 119*n*6
Frumkin, P., 17, 43, 89*n*43
Fuà, G., 186
Fugger family, 223
Fundación Lealtad, 212
funding, by government, 266, 274, 276.
See also grants

game theory, 277
Gates Foundation, 28, 30, 38, 129, 141
General Education Board, 68, 84–85*n*18
general purpose foundations, 66, 70–72
George Pepperdine Foundation, 77
Georgia, foundations in, 76, 78
German foundations: the arts, 223–26,
227, 228, 229; corporate ownership,
230; current situation, 226–30; higher
education, 219–23, 226, 228, 229;
historical building ownership,
217–18; industrial foundations,
243–45; innovation of, 206–7; legal
formation, 229; legitimacy of, 211;
number of, **8**; operating vs. grant-
making foundations, 228; political
associations, 194; regulation, 11; role
of, 204; scientific research, 222–23,
226, 227–28; state control over, 14,
179; subsectors of, 232–33

Germany: higher education in, 219–23; role of government, 226–27, 229. *See also* German foundations

GIFT (Giving Indiana Funds for Tomorrow), 157

Glaxo-Welcome, 246, 249

Goff, F., 73, 153–54

Gompers, S., 68

government, foundations' relationships with: and accountability, 113; adversarial relationships, 116–17; autonomous relationships, 117–18; complementary relationships, 115–16, 198–99, **208,** 209; supplementary relationships, 114–15; types of, 113–18; in U.K., 264–65, 267–68

government, role of: in Europe vs. U.S., 274–75; in Germany, 226–27, 229; and legitimacy, 111; in U.K., 255, 267–68; in U.S., 39, 137, 274–75

government funding: of education in Europe, 276; in France, 274; in U.K., 266

government spending: crowding out hypothesis, 114; cutbacks in, 139, 169; social services, 101, 125

grant applicants and recipients: power asymmetry with foundations, 101; surveys of, 105

grant-making foundations: causes, 28–29; complementary role, 198; definition of, 196; in Germany, 228; history of, 70–71; number of in U.S., 7, 28; role and impact of, 28; time frame of, 29–30; in U.S. vs. Europe, 195–96

grants: challenge grants, 262; by geographic region, 58; for new program initiatives, 101; process, 111–12, 166–68; by sector, 126–29; sources of, 160, **161;** strategic grant making, 29, 112–13, 190; total number (2001–02), 58, 123, 124

Grassley, C., 108

Great Britain. *See* United Kingdom, foundations in

Greece: GNP controlled by state, 275; innovation of foundations, 206

Green, A., 84*n*12

Green Revolution, 29–30, 31

Grønbjerg, K., 171*n*17

Guggenheim Fellowships, 87*n*29

GuideStar, 81, 88*n*36

Gulbenkian Foundation, 227

Hall, P. Dobkin, 82*n*3, 83*n*12

Hampton Institute, 70

Hansmann, H., 238

Harlan, L., 71

Harrison, S., 60, 83*n*6, 84*n*15

Hartford Foundation, 60

Harvard University, 25*n*2, 64, 65, 67, 86*n*26

Haynes Foundation, 59

Health Action Zone, 265

health sector, grants to, 126, **127, 128**

Hearst, W., 76

Hearst Foundation, 60, 76

Helsinki Foundation, 202

Herrmann, M., 244

Hershey Foods, 245

Hewlett Foundation, 28

higher education: community colleges, 35; endowments (1890s), 84*n*14; in Germany, 219–23, 226, 228, 229; gifts to (late nineteenth century), 67; grants to, 126; low-end career preparation, 31; nonprofit entities, 52; religious support, 64, 71, 77, 84*n*14; science-based initiatives, 65

Hill, D., 83–84*n*12

Hill Foundation, 59

HIV-AIDS, 16, 30, 36

Holland, foundations in, **8,** 194, 204, 212, 245

Hollis, E., 82*n*2, 86*n*26, 87*n*31

Homeland Security Act, 170*n*9

homelessness, 129

horizontal redistribution, 278–79

hospital foundations, 10

House of Representatives, mandated payout bill, 108–9

Houston Endowment, 60, 78, 83*n*7

Howard, D., 85*n*21

human services: foundation grants, 124–25, 126, **127, 128,** 129; funders' response to community's needs, 161–63; government programs and spending, 101, 125, 130–31; policy issues, 163–65

Humboldt, W. von, 221, 279
Humphreys, G., 257
Hungary, role of foundations in, 203, 204

Ikea, 245
income redistribution. *See* redistribution
income tax, 7, 64, 67, 79
Independent Sector, Incorporated, 81
Indiana, community foundations, 157
Indianapolis, Christian Foundation, 77
individual donors and gifts: charitable tax deduction, 28, 131–32, 151; as percentage of total charitable contributions, 125; privacy protection, 111; vs. professional grant makers, 106–7; to religious organizations, 129
individual sovereignty, 20–21
industrial foundations: advantages and disadvantages of, 237, 248–50; definition of, 237–40; family control, 246; financial performance of, 15, 242–45; in Germany, 12; governance, 240–42, 246; legitimacy of, 14–15, 240–49; monopolistic tendency, 246; taxation, 246; U.S. limitations, 236. *See also* corporate foundations
inequality, 50. *See also* redistribution
in-kind services, 131
innovation: in Europe, 197, 205–7, **208**, 209; and government involvement, 117–18; types of, 50
Institut de France, 218
Institute for Medical Research, 84*n*18
intellectuals, 62, 65, 84*n*16
Internal Revenue Code, 10, 150–51
Internal Revenue Service (IRS), 7, 58, 60, 74, 75
international foundations, 16, 184–85
international giving, **127, 128,** 129
internationalism, 50
investment income, taxation of, 100
Ireland: GNP controlled by state, 275; role of foundations in, 200
IRIS corporation, 198
IRS (Internal Revenue Service), 7, 58, 60, 74, 75
Irvine Foundation, 60, 108
Islamic foundations, 177
isomorphism, 178, 188

Italy: banking foundations, 14, 189; history of foundations, 181–83; innovation of foundations, 207; number of foundations in, **8**; religious issues, 275; role of foundations, 184, 200; U.S. foundations in, 184–87

J. Bulow Campbell Foundation, 76
J. E. and L. E. Mabee Foundation, 77
James Irvine Foundation, 60, 108
Jena University, 221
Jesup, M., 85*n*20
Jewish organizations, 77, 78, 177
Jews, 222, 226
Johns Hopkins University, 65, 67, 86*n*26
Jones, E., 171*n*7
Jones, J., 78
Julius Rosenwald Fund, 66

Kansas City, Carrie J. Loose Fund, 77
Kanter, R., 205
Karlsbad Decrees, 221
Karlsberg Foundation, 227
Kellogg (W. K.) Foundation, 59, 60, 78–79, 155
Kellog (W. W.) Foundation, 35
Kentucky, foundations in, 76
Khamvongsa, C., 119*n*5
Kramer, M., 119*n*7
Kresge Foundation, 60, 77
Krupp, 245

Labour Party, 264, 265
Lagemann, E., 70, 71
legacy, 177–78
legislation, 63–67, 188, 276. *See also* regulation
legitimacy: and accountability, 4, 110–13; and achievement, 277; and autonomy, 45; challenges, 4–7, 12–19, 113; of community foundations, 155–61, 165, 168–69; definitions of, 19–21, 236, 273; establishment of, 190; in Europe, 6, 14–15, 188–90, 213, 218–19, 231–32; of industrial foundations, 240–49; of nonprofits, 52–53; and nonprofit ties, 79–82; public goods provision, 40–41; reasons for, 45; and

legitimacy (*cont.*)
  relationship with government,
  113–18; and social roles, 21–24; social
  vs. legal aspects, 19–20; sources of, 4,
  111–12; in U.S., 4–6, 15–16, 52–53,
  62–67
Leonard, J., 154, 170*n*10
LeTourneau Foundation, 76
Lettie Pate Evans Foundation, 76
Letts, C., 197
liberals and liberalism, 16, 37, 40–41
Liechtenstein, 274
life insurance, 170*n*6
Lilly Foundation: causes supported by,
  36, 60, 77; community foundation
  initiatives, 155; in 1930s, 59; on top
  twenty-five list, 28
Lily Endowment (LIE), 157
lists, of foundations, 73–75, 83*n*6
lobbying, 115
local government, community foundations and, 267–68
Lutherans, 77, 225

MacArthur Foundation: fellowships,
  87*n*29; founder's intentions, 20–21;
  security studies, 36; targeting of spe-
  cific groups, 126, 129; on top twenty-
  five list, 28
Machen, J., 85*n*21
Magat, R., 158
Magdalen Society, 63
Maison des Sciences de l'Homme
  (MSH), 185, 186–87
Major, J., 255
Marble, M., 203–4
Margo, R., 126
market indifference or failure, 31–33
market model, of corporate governance,
  241–42
Marshall, J., 82*n*3
Mary A. Crocker Trust, 78
M.D. Anderson Foundation, 59
media, 137
median voter, 82*n*4
medical centers, 52
membership associations, 194
Mercury News, 108
Merrill Lynch, 153
Methodists, 76, 77, 84*n*15, 86*n*25
Metternich, 221

Michigan, foundations in, 78
microfinance, 102–3
Milbank Memorial Fund, 72, 73, 85*n*18
Minnesota, tax on railroad property,
  84*n*13
minority groups, 276–77
mission statements, 42
mixed foundations, 196, 198
monitoring, of foundations, 140–44
monopolies, 246
Moody Foundation, 60
moral rights, 20
Mott Foundation, 22, 78, 155, 258, 259,
  262
MSH (Maison des Sciences de
  l'Homme), 185, 186–87
museums, 52, 224, 229, 279
mutual accountability, 102–4
mutual companies, 179
mutual funds, donor advised funds
  (DAFs), 150, 153
Myrdal, G., 72

Nadler, E., 119*n*5
National Association of Social Workers,
  83*n*6
National Center for Charitable Statistics,
  81
National Committee for Responsive
  Philanthropy (NCRP), 140, 156, 158,
  171*n*14
National Lottery Charities Board, 253
National Science Foundation, 141
NCRP (National Committee for Respon-
  sive Philanthropy), 140, 156, 158,
  171*n*14
Nelson, D., 3
Netherlands, foundations in, **8,** 194,
  204, 212, 245
New York. charitable trust laws, 63,
  75–76
New York City, 76, 143–44
New York Community Trust, 154
New York Public Library, 63
New York Society for the Suppression of
  the Vice, 85*n*20
New York Times, 6
New York University, 86*n*26
NGOs (non-governmental organiza-
  tions), 196

Nielsen, W., 3
9/11/01, 143–44
non-governmental organizations
(NGOs), 196
nonprofits: accountability, 43; cost-effectiveness, 34–35; in Europe, 9,
196; grant seeking as priority, 190;
history of, 64, 82*n*3; independence of,
103; industrial foundations as, 237,
238; legal forms for, 9–10; legitimacy
of, 52–53; and legitimacy of founda-tions, 79–82, 111–12; and mandated
payout changes, 109; performance,
242–45; public goods provision, 40;
revenues, 27–28, 125; role in U.K.,
255, 256; role in U.S., 52; surveys of,
105; tax-exempt status, 6; types of,
52
normative legitimacy, 19, 113, 236,
240–42
normative questions, 5–6
norms, 22
North Carolina, foundations in, 76
Northern Baptist Education Society,
84*n*15
Northern Ireland Voluntary Trust
(NIVT), 258
Norway, industrial foundations in, 245
Novo-Nordisk, 248

Ogden, W., 83*n*12
Oklahoma, foundations in, 77, 78
Olasky, M., 85*n*21
Oldham Little Church Fund, 76
open houses, 105–6
Open Society, 35, 38
operas, 52, 280
operating foundations: complementary
role, 198; definition of, 196; in
Europe, 195–96; in Germany, 228; in
U.S., 10
orchestras, 52
Ostrower, F., 119*n*7, 159, 168
Oticon Foundation, 237–38

Packard Foundation, 30
Partners Hungary Foundation, 199
paternalism, 138–39
path dependency, 178
Patman hearings, 80

patronage, 226
payout rates, 4, 12, 81, 108–9
Peabody College, 86*n*26
Peabody Education Fund, 63, 71,
83*n*11
peer review, 44, 103–4, 110, 112
Pepperdine Foundation, 77
performance, of industrial foundations,
242–45
Peterson Commission, 81
Pew Foundation, 28, 60, 78
Phelps-Stokes Fund, 85*n*18
philanthropic foundations. *See* founda-tions, private
philanthropy: cultural issues, 223; Rock-efeller on, 29; social and policy
change, 202; as U.S. core value, 22
pluralism, 24, 204–5, **208,** 209, 276–77
Poland, role of foundations in, 202
political science, 185
political theory, of corporate gover-nance, 240–42
pooling, of bequests, 164
population ecology theory, 160
Porter, M., 119*n*7
Portuguese Centre for Foundations,
212
Portuguese foundations, 205, 212,
227
positive discrimination, 24
poverty relief, 31–32, 201
power, 101, 110
pragmatic legitimacy, 242–45, 249
Presbyterians, 76, 77, 84*n*15
Princeton University, 64, 86*n*26
private foundations. *See* foundations,
private
private label gift funds, 153
procedural accountability, 43–44
procedural legitimacy, 19, 112
professionals and professionalism, 43,
81, 105–7, 111, 134
profitability, of industrial foundations,
238, 244
progressive taxation, 130, 136
Protestant churches, 64, 76–78, 179
public affairs, **127, 128**
publications, 73–75, 158
public charities, 150–51. *See also* com-munity foundations

public good(s), 40–41, 100, 130, 256
public health, 35, 141
public information, 158–59
public libraries, 35, 63, 86n24
public policy: community foundations'
response to cuts in, 169; in Europe,
202–4, **208,** 213; funders' awareness
of and response to, 163–65; and
legitimacy, 111; shift in (1980s), 37
public schools, 141
public support test, 151

railroad property, 84n13
Randolph-Macon College, 86n25
Raymond Rich and Associates, 73–74,
83n6
Reagan administration, 37
recreation, 200
Red Cross, 68
redistribution: data limitations and
needs, 124, 125–26, 145, 147; definition of, 22; in Europe, 200–202, **208;**
evidence of, 33; as explanation for
government support of foundations,
33–34; by foundations, 132–40,
144–45, 200–202; by government,
129–31, 144; by individual donors,
131–32; and regulation, 140–44;
research considerations, 123, 145–48;
by sector, 126–29, 141; in short term
vs. long term, 135–37, 141; tax policy,
130; vertical vs. horizontal, 278–79
Reece Committee, 42
Reformation, 179
regional distribution, 58–62, 75–79
regulation: current issues, 108–10;
impact of, 89n43; payout rates, 81; for
redistribution, 140–44; by states, 75;
in U.S. vs. Europe, 11–12
religion, and culture, 223
religious causes and organizations: in
Europe, 273–74; foundation grants,
127, 128, 129; foundations supporting, 60, 63, 76–78; in Germany, 224,
225; higher education, 64, 71, 77,
84n14; individual donations, 129;
nonprofit status in U.S., 52
requests for proposals (RFPs), 166
resource dependency theory, 160, 164,
168

return on equity, **243, 245**
revolutions, 277
RFPs (requests for proposals), 166
Rhodes Scholarship, 87n29
Rice University, 67
Ridings, D., 153
risk-taking propensity, and innovation,
205, 207
Robert Bosch, 245, 248
Robert Wood Johnson Foundation, 36,
129
Robin Hood Foundation, 135–36
Rockefeller, J., 28–29, 64, 65, 68, 76
Rockefeller Foundation: causes sup-
ported by, 58, 77; establishment, 66;
European programs, 184; Foundation
Center support, 75; Green Revolu-
tion, 29–30; NY headquarters, 76;
public health campaign, 35; research
contributions, 72–73; on top twenty-
five list, 28; Walsh Commission findings, 68–69
Roe, M., 240–41
Roelofs, J., 202
Roman Catholic Church, 64, 77, 78,
179, 275
Roosevelt, T., 68
Rosenberg Foundation, 59
Rosenwald Fund, 66
rule of law, 231
Russell Sage Foundation: achievements, 87n32; annual reports,
87n31; disclaimer, 72; establishment
of, 66–67; Olasky's criticisms of,
85n21; publications about foundations, 73–75

Salamon, L., 139, 194
Samuel Roberts Noble Foundation, 59
Sanitation Commission, 84n18
SAP, 243
Saraceno, P., 186
Savigny, C. von, 179
Scaife Foundation, 16
Schaar, J., 19
Schwertmann, P., 232
scientific advancement, 278–79
scientific research: in Europe vs. U.S.,
180; in Germany, 222–23, 226,
227–28; government programs, 141;
grants for, 126, **127, 128**

secularization, 50, 273
self-assessments, 157
self-dealing prohibitions, 12
self-evaluation, 43–44
self-legitimization, 112–13
self-owning institutions, 238
Senate, 83*n*5
Senate Finance Committee, 6, 108
September 11, 2001, 143–44
Sewanee, 64
shareholders, of industrial foundations, 239–40
Siebert Lutheran Fund, 77
Simon Foundation, 60
Sixteenth Amendment, 64
social change, 35–39, 187–90, 202–4, **208,** 253
social democratic model, of welfare state, 211
socialism, 275
social mobility, 136
social problems, 17, 28–29
social roles, 21–24, 31–33
Social Science Research Council, 185
social sciences, **127, 128,** 185–87
social service organizations, non-profit status of, 52. *See also* human services
Sombart, W., 275
Soros, G., 35, 138
Soros Foundation, 203
The South, 84*n*16
Southern Education Board, 71
Spain: anticlericalism in, 275; foundations in, **8,** 212, 276
Spreafico, A., 186
Staedel Foundation, 224–25
staff, 159
Standard Oil Company, 68
standards: accrediting system, 110; certification, 156. *See also* accountability
Stanford University, 65, 67, 86*n*26
Stansfield, J., 71
state regulation, 75
Statuto Albertino, 181–82
Stefan Batory Foundation, 202
Stevens Institute, 70
Stiftung Preussischer Kulturbesitz, 227
Story, J., 82*n*3

strategic grant making, 29, 112–13, 190
Student Loan Fund, 76, 84*n*15
substantive accountability, 42, 43
substantive legitimacy, 113
substitution role, of European foundations, 199–200, **208,** 209
supplementary relationship, to government, 114–15
Supreme Court, 64
Surdna Foundation, 66
surveys, of grant recipients, 105
Sutton, F., 29
SVIMEZ (Association for the Development of Southern Italy), 185
Swarthmore, 86*n*26
Sweden: industrial foundations in, 245; innovation of foundations, 205, 206; IRIS corporation, 198; number of foundations in, **8**; role of foundations in, 210, 211
Swedenborg Foundation, 63
Switzerland: industrial foundations in, 245; number of foundations in, **8**; role of foundations, 200, 201, 204; types of foundations, 194

taxation: of community foundations, 151; estate taxes, 100, 111, 136; income tax, 7, 64, 67, 79; of industrial foundations, 246; investment income, 100; redistributive effects, 130
tax deductions: as donor motivation, 100, 111; individual charitable tax deduction, 28, 100, 131–32, 151; scientific achievement as justification for, 278–79
tax-exempt status, 6, 111
Tax Reform Act (TRA) (1969), 10, 12, 56, 80, 88*n*33, 151
Teachers' Insurance and Annuity Association, 70
technologies of influence, 71–72
terrorism, 16
Texas foundations, 59, 60, 76, 77–78
Thatcher, M., 37, 255
think tanks, 137, 140
Thomsen, S., 246, 247
Tilden, S., 63, 84*n*12
tradition, preservation of, 200, **208**

transparency, 43, 53, 105, 211–12
trust, 112, 261, 267, 281
trusts, 9, 170*n*6
Tulane University, 86*n*25, 26
Turgot, J., 51, 82*n*2, 180, 218, 275
Turner, T., 138
turnover, in funded agencies, 167
Twentieth Century Fund, 72, 73–74,
    83*n*6

umbrella organizations, 81, 142
uncertainty, and innovation, 205–6
United Kingdom, foundations in:
    history of, 179–80; innovation of,
    206; legislation, 276; legitimacy of,
    253–57; number of, **8,** 253; role of,
    200, 202–3, 210, 253–54; Welcome
    Foundation, 245–46, 249. *See also*
    community foundations, in United
    Kingdom
United Way (UW), 159, 160, 163, 164,
    172*n*22
universities, generally. *See* higher
    education
University of Chicago, 64, 86*n*26
University of Iowa, 86*n*26
University of Pennsylvania, 67, 86*n*26
University of Rochester, 86*n*26
University of Wisconsin Alumni Foun-
    dation, 59
Urban Institute, 81
U.S. Census, **61, 62**

Vanderbilt University, 71, 86*n*25, 26
Van Kleeck, M., 72, 85*n*21
vertical redistribution, 278
Virginia, foundations in, 77
Visions and Roles of Foundations in Europe
    (Nuno), 214*n*3

Volkswagen Stiftung, 222
voter registration, 16
voting rights, 102
Wallenberg Foundation, 206
Walsh Commission, 42, 68–69
waqf, 177, 178

Warren Foundation, 78
Washington University, 86*n*25,
    26
wealthiest Americans, 85*n*19
Weaver, W., 278, 281
Weber, M., 19
Web sites, 159
Weingart Foundation, 60
Welcome Foundation, 245–46,
    249
welfare programs, 130–31. *See also*
    human services
welfare state: criticism about founda-
    tions' role in, 51; in Europe, 184, 210,
    211, 218, 274–75
Weston, J., 263, 265
White, W., 22
White-Williams Foundation, 63
Wilder Foundation, 59
William Demant, 237–38, 243
Winston-Salem Foundation, 59
Wisconsin, foundations in, 77, 78
Woodruff Foundation, 59
Wooster, M., 119*n*4
World War I, 49
Wuthnow, R., 177

Yale University, 25*n*2, 64, 65, 67, 86*n*26

Z. Smith Reynolds Foundation, 59
Zeiss Foundation, 221, 245, 248
Zunz, O., 188